JOHNSONVILLE

Union Supply Operations on the Tennessee River
and the Battle of Johnsonville, November 4–5, 1864

Jerry T. Wooten

For Denise –

Best Wishes

Jerry T. Wooten, Ph.D.

Nov. 5, 2022

SB

Savas Beatie
California

Library of Congress Control Number: 2019949307

First Edition, First Printing

ISBN-13: 978-1-61121-477-2 (hardcover)
ISBN-13: 978-1-61121-478-9 (ebook)

SB

Savas Beatie
989 Governor Drive, Suite 102
El Dorado Hills, CA 95762

916-941-6896
www.savasbeatie.com
sales@savasbeatie.com

Savas Beatie titles are available at special discounts for bulk purchases in the United States by corporations, institutions, and other organizations. For more details, please contact Savas Beatie, P.O. Box 4527, El Dorado Hills, CA 95762, or you may e-mail us at sales@savasbeatie.com, or visit our website at www.savasbeatie.com for additional information.

Proudly printed in the United States of America

For Mother and Father

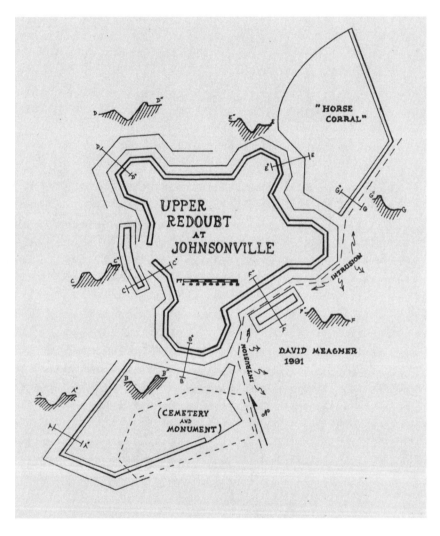

Footprint drawing of Redoubt No. 2 (Upper Redoubt), Johnsonville, Tennessee, 1992.
Courtesy of David J. Meagher

Table of Contents

Table of Contents (continued)

List of Maps

Photos and illustrations have been distributed throughout the book
for the convenience of the reader.

Acknowledgments

I could not have written the story of Johnsonville without the editorial guidance of Dr. Carroll Van West, whose abilities as a wordsmith are unparalleled. I am also indebted to the wonderful staff at the Tennessee State Library and Archives who assisted me with my research, including: Dr. Wayne Moore, Trent Hanner, Darla Brock, Myers Brown, Megan Spainhour, Dr. Tom Kanon, Dr. Kevin Cason, and others too numerous to list. Additionally, many outstanding professionals at the National Archives, Library of Congress, Tennessee State Museum, Duke University, Kansas Historical Society, William L. Clements Library at the University of Michigan, Wisconsin Historical Society, Wisconsin Veterans Museum, Columbus City Library-Ohio, New York City Library, and Middle Tennessee State University, provided invaluable assistance.

Many excellent historians and friends gave generously of their time, advice, and expertise. I owe a tremendous thanks to Dr. Joe Baily, Steven Bartlett, Judith Byrd, Dr. Peter Cash, A. Wilson Greene, Thomas Cartwright, and Dr. Wayne Moore for copy editing and proofreading my work. Additionally, I thank Joseph Brent, David Currey, Reed Dreaden, Ken Ingram, and Don McFall for their historical knowledge and photographic contributions. I am particularly grateful to artist David Meagher for his extraordinary historical knowledge and artistic contributions of battle maps and original drawings.

A huge thank you also to the great folks at my publishing company, Savas Beatie, and especially Theodore P. Savas for taking the time to deeply read and critique my final submission; Sarah Keeney, Lisa Murphy, and Sarah Closson for their marketing skills; and Lee Merideth for shepherding this through production.

Other colleagues and friends who helped me and supported my efforts in writing this book include: Dr. Joey Gray, Dr. Brenden Martin, Dr. Robert Hunt, Al Hethcoat, Meriam Tummons, Fred Prouty, David Fraley, Bud Alley, Dr. Curt Fields, Debbie Shaw, and Dan Pomeroy. I would also like to particularly thank the park staff and Friends of Johnsonville State Historic Park for their continued support and encouragement.

When Warren Atwood appeared one day at Johnsonville State Historic Park, our encounter changed the course of this book. I quickly learned his Civil War ancestor was Cpl. Lorenzo D. Atwood of the 43rd Wisconsin Infantry, and that he was stationed at Johnsonville during the November 4-5, 1864 battle. The young corporal wrote a series of letters to his wife, Cordelia, that provide rich details about the inner workings of the supply depot that exist no where else. I owe an enormous debt of gratitude to Warren C. Atwood II, his sister Robin R. Atwood, and their late father, Leon W. Atwood, for their generous and important contribution of their ancestor's letters. I hope they are pleased with the final product.

Finally, I offer my sincerest love and gratitude to my family, William, Frances, and Billy Wooten. My embedded passion for history was channeled through their love and encouragement.

Foreword

Too often the Civil War in Tennessee is defined in popular memory by its major national battlefield parks, such as those memorializing Shiloh, Chattanooga, Fort Donelson, and Stones River. In the 21st century, historians have been asking different questions and following rarely studied lines of inquiry about Tennessee's Civil War experiences.

These more recent roads of inquiry include the study of the long Federal army occupation, the impact of slaves becoming contraband laborers, whether Unionist supporters were to be found across the entire state, and not just East Tennessee, and much more. What links occupation, emancipation, and free black community building? Why have we mostly underplayed or ignored—other than the battles of Fort Donelson and Memphis—the dominance of the Federal navy on the inland rivers? How significant was control of the inland river system dividing East and Middle Tennessee in the development of strategy and tactics in the state?

Johnsonville: Union Supply Operations on the Tennessee River and the Battle of Johnsonville, November 4-5, 1864, by Dr. Jerry Wooten takes important steps toward answering these significant questions. Of the more than three dozen designated nationally significant battles in Tennessee, Johnsonville's importance was recognized by only a handful of specialists. Now, with Wooten's comprehensive treatment of Johnsonville as a military base, battleground, and launching ground for emancipation, its transformative story will gain a new and larger audience.

And "transformative" is the best word to describe the Johnsonville Civil War story. First, the 1864 battle along the Tennessee River at Johnsonville has long needed a comprehensive historical treatment. Past accounts in Tennessee history ranked the battle as a smashing Confederate victory for renowned Confederate Maj. Gen. Nathan Bedford Forrest. More regional and national accounts of the war in the Western Theater merely footnoted the battle or ignored it completely. But as Dr. Wooten makes clear, the battle was a considerable victory by seasoned Confederate troops against a Federal naval base—and the loss of gunboats, transports, and tons of supplies shocked the collective Union army leadership.

Next, Wooten explores how Federal commanders used both rivers and rails to supply its advancing armies. By underscoring the significance of logistics—the moving of supplies and men—in the chaotic operations of the Western Theater, Wooten helps to transform understanding of how the war was fought in Tennessee. Wooten cogently explains why Johnsonville was such a key target for a Confederate command desperate to slow the Federal advance southward.

Digging deep into the primary sources of official records, soldier letters, diaries, and period newspapers, Wooten also brings to the forefront what military bases like Johnsonville meant to both the occupiers and the occupied. These bases transformed the landscapes and the peoples of the region. The Tennessee Valley would never again be the same, for suddenly what had been a minor river port became connected by railroad to the capital city of Nashville.

The transformation of land and lives along the rails of the military railroad was especially significant for African Americans, once enslaved and now working as contrabands of war. They not only built a new transportation system, but a new life as emancipated men and women. Dr. Wooten is at his best in discussing the role of United States Colored Troops stationed at Johnsonville during the last months of the conflict.

Here is the story of Johnsonville that was always documented in the primary sources, but ignored by generations of historians until now. Thankfully, the author looks beyond the battle into the story of how emancipated slaves became citizens and permanent residents. Within the Johnsonville park today is the A.M.E. cemetery, an invaluable cultural resource that documents this early emancipation community in Tennessee.

Johnsonville: Union Supply Operations on the Tennessee River and the Battle of Johnsonville, November 4-5, 1864, never loses sight of the author's larger mission: to explain the totality of war, occupation, and emancipation in the larger narrative of what the Civil War meant then, and to Americans today.

What happened at Johnsonville mattered then as it does today, and this study ably tells that important story with passion and insight.

Carroll Van West, Ph.D.
Tennessee State Historian

Preface

THE contribution of Johnsonville to Union operations in the Civil War's Western Theater has never been fully assessed. This important supply depot comprised almost every subject associated with military operations: black and white soldiers, sailors, naval vessels, cavalry, military engineers, field and naval artillery, U.S. Quartermaster's Department personnel, officers, civilian laborers, Army and Navy administrators, politicians, horses and mules, trains, towns, forts, food, and burials.

The task of illustrating Johnsonville's significance during the Civil War is challenging. Johnsonville evolved from a convoluted mix of ideas that included elements of geography, agriculture, engineering, emancipation, supply, and combat. More than a year and a half after the occupation of Nashville in February 1862, the Union Army still lacked a defined plan for defeating the Confederacy. Even by mid-1863, the Union forces now operating throughout Middle and West Tennessee and northern Alabama had no solid plan for how to adequately supply its forces in the field. The war had moved rapidly into the Deep South, and the lack of railroads and depots severely hampered the Union effort to supply its troops. Johnsonville was built to solve this challenge. Simply put, it was a quick fix for a critical need.

Past scholarship on Johnsonville has addressed three recurring themes. First, was the Confederate's West Tennessee raid of October and November

Second, was the Union naval vessels captured and occupied by Confederate cavalrymen. Third, was the role of Major General Nathan Bedford Forrest and his troops in one of the last Confederate tactical victories in the Western Theater at the Battle of Johnsonville.

Most of what we know about Johnsonville has come down to us from the Confederate perspective, which is unusual since it was an important Union depot and town. Nearly all other elements of its history and operation have been ignored. My desire to learn about what else happened at Johnsonville challenged me to write this book.

I wanted to tell the complete story from as many angles as possible: Why was it built? Who built it? Who defended it? What daily activities were carried on inside the supply depot, and how did its existence affect Union operations elsewhere? I also wanted to explore the military aspects of what took place on both sides of the Tennessee River before, during, and immediately after the Battle of Johnsonville on November 4-5, 1864. My goal was to examine both Union and Confederate perspectives and establish an unbiased conclusion based on primary sources.

Johnsonville's legacy remains. In 1969, the state of Tennessee purchased 400 acres of the historic town site and Civil War-era supply depot. Two years later, the Tennessee established the Johnsonville State Historic Area. The park included two original Civil War earthen forts and a mile-long line of Union-built rifle pits. In 1977, a museum opened to the public beside one of the park's main earthworks known then (and now) as Fort Johnson (Lower Redoubt, or Redoubt No 1).

However, the museum's exhibits focused mainly on Confederate history and excluded practically anything about the Union supply depot and the role played by United States Colored Troops and other Federal soldiers and personnel in Johnsonville's contribution to the ultimate Union victory. The civilian and military story about the building of the Nashville and Northwestern Railroad was absent, as was information on the construction of the supply depot and earthen fortifications by the Union army, the black and white infantry and artillery regiments that defended Johnsonville, the Union gunners' tough resistance during the battle (as attested to by Forrest himself), and why the town of Johnsonville was built by the Union Army and still exists today as New Johnsonville. None of this was seen or heard by visitors. Instead, from 1971 to 2011, Johnsonville State Historic Area was used largely as a recreational experience rather than an educational one.

In addition to Johnsonville's Civil War story, park visitors can also view building foundations from the original town site that was only partially submerged by the Tennessee Valley Authority in 1944. Today, these foundations and Civil War earthworks connect park visitors to life at Johnsonville during and after the Civil War. Additionally, other cultural elements include white cemeteries and an African-American cemetery (a vivid reminder of segregation), a railroad turntable, and many historical roadbeds. In 2012, a new park visitor center and museum opened at Johnsonville State Historic Park with updated exhibits that focus on the complete story of Johnsonville during the war.

My intention in writing this book was threefold. First, I wanted to provide a full and fair treatment of the Johnsonville story using primary sources from both civilian and military personnel. To accomplish this, I needed to discover fresh information about the Union supply efforts, rather than just another tidbit of information about the battle itself. I focused on the "why" and was determined to expose the multitude of peripheral elements that made Johnsonville so interesting and relevant.

Why, for example, did the earliest Humphreys County settlers choose to live there ? Why was the Nashville and Northwestern Railroad so important, even before the war? Why was the construction of a depot seventy-eight miles from the Union's central Tennessee base in Nashville such a critically important decision? The civilians in all this fascinated me, including the African-Americans, politicians, and the employees of the Quartermaster's Department. How did they, together with the officers, sailors, and common soldiers make Johnsonville what it became—an extraordinary operation desperately needed to help win the war for the Union?

My second goal was to deliver a detailed and balanced account of the campaign's battles. The story has almost always been told within the tight confines of a magazine article, or within a few pages of a book. It demanded and deserved more. I accomplished this by referencing accounts from the participants, including personnel who served in the U.S. Army (including United States Colored Troops), Quartermaster's Department, and Navy, as well as Confederate accounts including some previously unpublished.

Finally, I wrote this book because Johnsonville during the Civil War is a remarkable story that had never received the full treatment it so rightfully deserves. I hope I have done it justice.

Hopefully, I have succeeded and Johnsonville's importance and overall significance within the vast scholarship of the American Civil War will finally takes its rightful place.

Introduction

LORENZO Dow Atwood was born in Bethel, Vermont on July 28, 1825, and lived there until 1848-49, when he moved to Hopkinton, New York. There, he met and married Cordelia Phelps on January 1, 1850. He was 24 and she was 19. The couple had two children, daughter Leona (1851) and son Arthur (1854).

In the early 1860s, Lorenzo moved his family west from New York to Fayette, Wisconsin, as did many other families from Hopkinton. The earth there was rich and fertile and he made his living as a small farmer. Their lives were peaceful, if not that prosperous, but the country was being torn apart by the Civil War.

Lorenzo was in his mid-30s and had resisted the call to arms for several years. Like many others who eventually answered President Abraham Lincoln's call to fight, Lorenzo believed it was his patriotic duty to serve and help put down the rebellion. After kissing his wife and kids goodbye, he traveled to Camp Washburn in Milwaukee and on August 29, 1864, signed up as a private in what would be Company E, 43rd Wisconsin Infantry. Because of his age and ability to read and write, he was elevated to corporal almost immediately. What he did not know was that he would never see his beloved wife Cordelia and daughter Leona again.

The new Wisconsin outfit was a late-war regiment, a unit mustered into service during the last year of the war. After a month of basic training the

Lorenzo D. Atwood and his
son Arthur, ca. 1860.
Warren, Robin, and Leon Atwood.

men of the 43rd boarded trains with other Wisconsin soldiers and headed south to war-ravaged Tennessee. They arrived in Nashville for a quick stay in early October, and then Atwood and his regimental companions boarded a military train and traveled seventy-eight miles west to the Tennessee River. These troops had yet to "see the elephant," that is, engage in combat. Heading west, it may have seemed to many of them that they never would.

After a day-long journey through dense wilderness routinely traversed by Confederate guerrillas, the 700 fresh recruits arrived at their destination on October 15 around 10:00 p.m. Once off the train, they were ordered inside "a large building built for a machine shop on the banks of the Tenn. River," where they spent the night. The following evening, Cpl. Atwood finally found an opportunity to write a letter to Cordelia. "This is a new place, probably not on the map," he explained,

> [T]here is some 6, thousand soldiers at this post now. . .the Reb. Forrest is about 100 miles south of this place it is the terminus of the railroad that we came on from Nashville, a thousand rumors as to what we shall do are afloat in camp but nothing certain some think that our Reg. will stay here till spring, but we may be ordered to move in 24 hours. I am geting used to it.[1]

---

1 Corporal Lorenzo D. Atwood, 43rd Wisconsin Volunteer Infantry Regiment, to Cordelia Atwood, October 16, 1864, Johnsonville, Tennessee. Special thanks to Warren and Robin Atwood for permission to use their ancestor's letters and for providing personal information about Lorenzo for inclusion in this study.

The "terminus of the railroad" Atwood described was Johnsonville, a relatively new post named that May after Tennessee's military governor, Andrew Johnson.

Johnsonville was a ninety-acre supply depot built on the eastern edge of the Tennessee River in Humphreys County for receiving and shipping military supplies to Union forces operating in Tennessee and other southern states. Johnsonville was an extension of the larger Nashville Depot, the central base for Union supply operations in Tennessee.

As the war progressed into the Deep South in the spring of 1864, it became harder to supply the large Northern war machine with the food and tons of military supplies required to win the war. The construction of Johnsonville on the Tennessee River was designed to help achieve this war aim, which allowed officials to direct an enormous flow of supplies to front-line troops in Tennessee and Georgia. By that fall, Johnsonville had become central to the Federal train of logistical support for the armies of Maj. Gen. William T. Sherman in Georgia and Maj. Gen. George H. Thomas in Nashville. All of this changed on November 4, 1864, forever altering the lives of Cpl. Atwood, thousands of other soldiers, sailors, and civilians, and the course of the Civil War in Tennessee.

This is the story of Johnsonville.

CHAPTER 1

Before the Soldiers Came

T HE story of Johnsonville began decades before civil war divided the nation in 1861. Johnsonville was established in a region named after a tributary that flows year-round through a valley of meadows and forests called Trace Creek. The Trace Creek region is thought to be one of Tennessee's oldest inhabited areas, both by Native Americans and white settlers. The area is located in Middle Tennessee's northwestern angle of the Highland Rim, a geological anomaly resembling an oval fish bowl 600 feet above sea level (also called the Nashville Basin). As Trace Creek meanders west through Humphreys County, it gradually widens and terminates at the Tennessee River 500 yards north of where Johnsonville was established in 1863.[1]

How Trace Creek got its name is a mystery. Prior to 1800, Trace Creek was known as Brevard's Creek, after Captain Alexander Brevard of Lincoln County, North Carolina, the first Revolutionary War land grant recipient in the Trace Creek region. Brevard hired Martin Armstrong and Henry Rutherford to survey land adjoining the creek in 1785. The 3,849 acres they examined included the area north of Little Dry Creek and south of Trace Creek bordered on the west by the Tennessee River.[2]

---

1 John Finger, *Tennessee Frontiers: Three Regions in Transition* (Bloomington, 2001), 3; Jill Knight Garrett, *The History of Humphreys County, Tennessee* (Columbia, 1963), 3-6.

2 Registrar's Office of Humphreys County (hereafter ROHC), *Deed Book A: 1810-1816*, 74, 111-112; Humphreys County Land Grant Book, A-1 (Revolutionary), Grant #260,

John Baptista Ashe, 1780. *Library of Congress*

Lieutenant Colonel Jonathan Baptista Ashe, another Revolutionary War land grant recipient, also owned land in the Trace Creek region. His 4,457 acres were just south of Brevard's tract, where Trace Creek flowed into the Tennessee River. Almost eighty years later, in 1863, Ashe's tract south of Trace Creek would become the town and military supply depot at Johnsonville.[3]

By the time white settlers began entering the Trace Creek region, the name "Brevard's Creek" had passed from usage. Records suggest that Moses and Nancy Box were the first settlers to establish a permanent homestead in the region. According to land deeds, Box and his wife moved west from the Laurens District of South Carolina and settled there in March 1800. John and Hannah McAdoo from Guilford County, North Carolina, both just nineteen years old, followed the Box's two years later in 1802. Together, the two families established temporary camps before building permanent log houses somewhere along Trace Creek near the Tennessee River. Box and McAdoo provided the foundation for later widespread settlement. Over the next three decades the Trace Creek region became one of the most populated areas near the Tennessee River in Middle Tennessee.[4]

warrant #761, microfilm, TSLA, Nashville, TN, 131; Lyman Draper to Henry Rutherford, 1844, Lyman Copeland Draper Manuscript Collection, Wisconsin Historical Society (Madison), 29, microfilm, 55-66, hereafter cited as Draper Manuscripts; Jonathan K.T. Smith, *The Wyly Saga* (Memphis, 1981), 19; ROHC, *Deed Book A*, 111-12.

3 ROHC, *Deed Book E*, 111.

4 Worth S. Ray, *Tennessee Cousins: A History of Tennessee People* (Austin, 1950), 370; Wayne Moore, "Farm Communities and Economic Growth in the Lower Tennessee Valley: Humphreys County, Tennessee, 1785-1980," Ph.D. Dissertation, University of Rochester, 1990, 78; Garrett, *The History of Humphreys County, Tennessee*, 11-12, 16-19.

Knott's Landing

There is evidence that settlers established a small landing at the confluence of Trace Creek and the Tennessee River before the creation of Humphreys County in 1809. This primitive docking point, called Knott's Landing, was the first of its type established in the county. It is unknown how Knott's Landing received its name, but there is strong evidence it was named after the Knotts of Bedford County, Tennessee, descendants of James Knott from Virginia. Although the Knott genealogical record shows no evidence of business activity in Humphreys County, the Knotts' business interests were known to include timber "found along water courses" near the Tennessee River.

The fact that they harvested timber along "water courses," is important in understanding why John Knott and his cousin, James Knott, sought permits from the Bedford County court to "build a dam across Duck River," which in turn may explain the existence of Knott's Landing. For instance, John Knott noted that his search for timber exceeded the boundaries of Bedford County for "fertile soil upon river banks and rich hill sides." Therefore, it is likely the Knotts established a Tennessee River landing near Trace Creek where hickory, sycamore, and ash trees were abundant—all the materials necessary for profiting from a thriving inland river timber trade. No known records indicate what year Knott's Landing ceased to exist, but it is believed the landing continued servicing commercial riverboat operations well into the nineteenth century.[5]

Reynoldsburg

Humphreys County, named after Tennessee Superior Court Judge Parry W. Humphreys, encompassed 532 square miles, making it one of Middle Tennessee's largest. The population rapidly expanded as more settlers moved into the Trace Creek region. By 1810, families who had settled there had constructed a blockhouse, a type of protective wooden fort that could be secured from the inside to provide a safe environment from Indian attacks.

---

5 Garrett, *The History of Humphreys County, Tennessee*, 11; Willie Mae Caldwell, *The Genealogy of the Knott Family 1617-1989* (Published by the Author for Knott's Berry Farm, 1989), 75-77.

The primitive fortification was on a high knob two miles north of Trace Creek and about four hundred yards from the bank of the Tennessee River.[6]

Because of rapid growth, the Tennessee General Assembly made provisions in 1811 to establish a permanent county seat somewhere along the Tennessee. Eventually, the legislature designated a fifty-acre tract for a new town site on the east bank of the river across from Cypress Creek and two miles above Trace Creek. They named the town Reynoldsburg, in honor of James B. Reynolds, a genial Irishman and member of the United States Congress from Tennessee.[7]

Reynoldsburg's geography provided many advantages for development, especially for a ferry operation because sediment had washed out of the creeks and formed a shoal in the middle of the river, narrowing the river at Reynoldsburg and created large shallows that could be easily forded. This elongated shoal, later named Reynoldsburg Island, would come into play during the Civil War as Union naval vessels navigated the Tennessee River.[8]

In 1813, a fine two-story 30-feet square brick courthouse constructed in the center of the town became Reynoldsburg's main public building. Designed in the Federal style with bricks fired in a kiln that stood just north of the building, the courthouse boasted five rooms, three upstairs and two downstairs, and two large fireplaces, one each in the lower rooms. After Union forces occupied Middle Tennessee in 1862, the Reynoldsburg courthouse became a headquarters for Union officers until the end of the Civil War and remained Tennessee's oldest public courthouse until it was razed in 1929. Reynoldsburg's close proximity to other Middle Tennessee river towns, such as Clarksville, Port Royal, and Palmyra, made it a preferred destination along the post road from Ohio, Indiana, and Kentucky, and to the state of Mississippi, the Alabama Territory and New Orleans, a

6 Jonathan K.T. Smith, "Old Reynoldsburgh" (Unpublished essay, no date), 3; Garrett, *The History of Humphreys County, Tennessee*, 11-12.

7 Westin Goodspeed, et. al., *History of Tennessee: From Earliest Time to the Present: Together with an Historical and Biographical Sketch of Montgomery, Robertson, Humphreys, Stewart, Dickson, Cheatham, and Houston Counties* (Nashville, 1886), 871-72; Smith, "Old Reynoldsburgh," 3; Jerome D. Spence and David L. Spence, *A History of Hickman County, Tennessee* (Nashville, 1900), 91.

8 Moore, "Farm Communities," 91; Jonathan K.T. Smith., *An Historical Survey of the Road System of Benton County, Tennessee* (Memphis, 1976), 10-11.

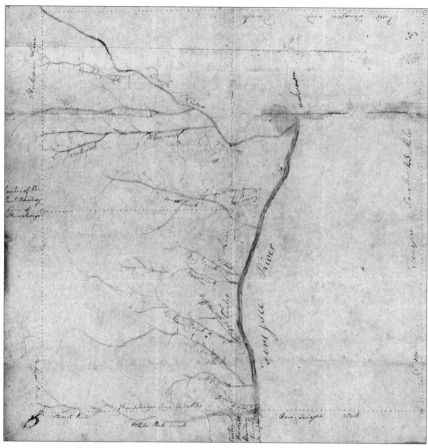

Map of Humphreys County, Tennessee, 1812. *Tennessee State Library & Archives*

transportation route popularized after the signing of the Treaty of Fort Jackson in 1814.[9]

At the base of the town along the river's edge, Brevard employed his attorney, Samuel Polk, to establish what was described as a "publick ferry." This natural river crossing was the endpoint for persons wanting to cross the

9 Smith, "Old Reynoldsburgh," 3; Goodspeed, *History of Tennessee: Sketch of Montgomery, Robertson, Humphreys, Stewart, Dickson, Cheatham, and Houston Counties*, 875; Smith, *The Wyly Saga*, 20; Scrap Book of John F. Shannon, clipping about Old Reynoldsburg by J. Ben Fuqua in Jill Knight Garrett Collection, manuscripts, TSLA, hereafter cited as Fuqua; Garrett, *The History of Humphreys County, Tennessee*, 17; Fuqua, "The Town of Cumberland," in the *Nashville Whig and Tennessee Advertiser*, March 20, 1819.

Courthouse, Reynoldsburg, Tennessee,
ca. 1929. *Tennessee State Library & Archives*

Tennessee into the Western District. Today, the Western District is better known as West Tennessee, the state's "last frontier."[10]

The Western District included all of the land between the Tennessee River and the Mississippi River, some 10,700 square miles of fertile Chickasaw tribal territory. In 1820, this western Chickasaw land, which included the western portion of the state of Kentucky (about one-tenth of the state), was officially ceded to the young United States. All transportation routes from Nashville, which included established roads and horse paths on the eastern side of the Tennessee River, specifically Glover's Trace and a branch of the Natchez Trace, converged at Reynoldsburg.[11]

Reynoldsburg gained popularity as a active center of commerce for Tennessee's western travelers, and soon two stage lines were organized to run tri-weekly along the 240-mile trek between Nashville and Memphis. One line ran from Columbia to Somerville, Tennessee, and crossed the Tennessee River at Savannah. A second stage line, running from Charlotte to Jackson, Tennessee, traversed the edge of Trace Creek and crossed at Reynoldsburg. After stages made it over the Tennessee River at Reynoldsburg, the stage road continued on, rounding the foot of Pilot Knob (which is in today's Benton County), before veering off to the northwest toward Paris. For fifteen years, from 1821 to 1836, this route known as the

10 ROHC, *Deed Book A*, pp. 122-126; Moore, "Farm Communities," 93; Smith, *The Wyly Saga*, 20; Finger, *Tennessee Frontiers: Three Regions in Transition*, 240-41.

11 Finger, *Tennessee Frontiers: Three Regions in Transition*, 248; Moore, "Farm Communities," 96; Garrett, *The History of Humphreys County, Tennessee*, 11.

Paris-Reynoldsburg Road, became familiar to nearly every traveler heading into the Western District.[12]

A branch of the second stage road included part of the Charlotte-Jackson route called the Reynoldsburg-Huntingdon Road. Like the Paris-Reynoldsburg Road, this route began opposite Reynoldsburg and ran directly west to Hollow Rock, Huntingdon, and eventually into Jackson. These stage roads became so muddy during the winter and early spring that only horse-drawn two-wheeled carts could be used to haul mail and carry passengers. A passenger traveling from Nashville to Reynoldsburg paid $5.50. The fare for taking the coach the entire way from Nashville to Memphis, a three or four-day trip depending on the weather, was $17.00.[13]

On December 24, 1816, Washington's *Daily National Intelligencer* reported that the U.S. House of Representatives spent time that day discussing a bill about the opening of a United States Road through Reynoldsburg. After much debate regarding the costs associated with construction of a national road, Congress finally determined to open such a route from states in the north "to Reynoldsburg and from there to points south." This highway, or rather, stage road, led fifty miles south from the town of Cumberland (near Clarksville, Tennessee) to Reynoldsburg. From there, the highway continued "thence to the Chickasaw Old Towns, a fine road opened by the United States, intersecting the road leading from Nashville to Natchez."[14]

The addition of the new northern stage road increased business on the ferry crossing at Reynoldsburg because travelers arrived destined for the Chickasaw lands in West Tennessee. Prior to the construction of railroads,

12 G. H. Slaughter, *Stage Coaches and Railroads or The Past and the Present of Transportation Facilities From Nashville, through Tennessee, Kentucky, and Surrounding Territory* (Nashville, 1894), 13; Eastin Morris, eds. Robert M. McBride and Owen Meredith, *Tennessee Gazetteer 1834 and Matthew Rhea's Map of the State of Tennessee 1832* (Nashville, 1971), 266; Smith, *An Historical Survey of the Road System of Benton County, Tennessee*, 25. In November 1864, Maj. Gen. Nathan Bedford Forrest's Confederate troops used a branch of the Paris-Reynoldsburg Road, a community road that ran through Beaver Dam Valley along its eastern ridge, to attack the Union supply depot at Johnsonville.

13 Smith, *An Historical Survey of the Road System of Benton County, Tennessee*, 22; Slaughter, *Stage Coaches and Railroads*, 13-14.

14 Slaughter, *Stage Coaches and Railroads*, 13-14; Ursula Smith Beach, *Along the Warioto or a History of Montgomery County, Tennessee* (Nashville, 1964), 76-77.

anyone traveling from Nashville would either take stage coaches overland or steamboats down the Cumberland River and then up the Tennessee River to reach destinations like Chattanooga. Reynoldsburg soon became the most popular crossing point on the Tennessee River west of Nashville and the arriving travelers transformed it from a sleepy frontier town into a thriving center of commerce. Sixteen different stage lines eventually departed in all directions from Nashville. Of these, the two most popular and heavily traveled intersected at Reynoldsburg.[15]

In 1828, Reynoldsburg was considered as a potential location for Tennessee's new state capital. It lost by only five votes to Murfreesboro, before it was ultimately decided that Nashville would become the state's new seat of government. By the end of the 1820s, Reynoldsburg was a well-established and thriving town with a population of 108 citizens and forty buildings that included a "courthouse, jail, twenty-eight dwelling houses, two taverns, three stores, and a blacksmith, saddler, cabinetmaker, shoemaker, and tanner."[16]

The Reynoldsburg courthouse became the meeting site for the western branch of Tennessee's Supreme Court from 1827 to 1835. When in session, court members stayed at homes of residents or at a "two-story log hotel built of poplar logs which stood right across from the courthouse and a log jail." The Tennessee Supreme Court's tenure at Reynoldsburg proved short-lived, and in 1835 it moved to Centerville, then on to Murfreesboro, and eventually to its permanent location in Nashville.[17]

That same year, the citizens of Waverly, a rapidly growing town nine miles to the east and dissected by Trace Creek, petitioned county residents and the General Assembly to designate their town as the county seat because Reynoldsburg's population was declining. The General Assembly approved the petition and officially moved the county seat to Waverly in 1836. Despite its early promise, Reynoldsburg never grew to become a major town of importance. By 1840, it had fallen into sharp decline primarily because of

---

15 Beach, *Along the Warioto or a History of Montgomery County, Tennesse*, 18; Moore, "Farm Communities," 97-99.

16 Williams, *Beginnings*, 221; Morris, *Tennessee Gazetteer*, 242.

17 Smith, *The Wyly Saga*, 20; Garrett, *The History of Humphreys County, Tennessee*, 21-28; Goodspeed, *History of Tennessee: Sketch of Montgomery, Robertson, Humphreys, Stewart, Dickson, Cheatham, and Houston Counties*, 888-890.

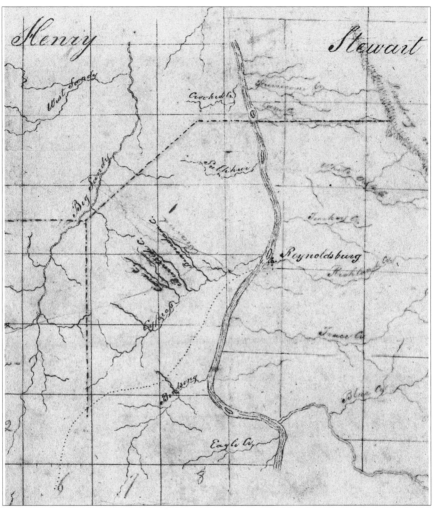

Map of Humphreys County, Tennessee, 1832. *Tennessee State Library & Archives*

annual winter and spring flooding along the Tennessee River and competition from nearby Waverly.[18]

18 *The River Counties Quarterly*, vol. 4, No. 3 (July 1975): 191; Garrett, *The History of Humphreys County, Tennessee*, 22-25.

Lucas Landing

Humphreys County's richest businessman, Thomas K. Wyly, owned 4,509 acres on both sides of the river, including the site of Reynoldsburg. In 1847, he bought the Knott's Landing property from Alexander Brevard's son, John, and renamed it Wyly's Landing. After Thomas's death in 1857, his son James, who served as the estate's administrator, divided his late father's land holdings between he and his sister, Blake "Babe" Wyly Lucas.

The next year, Thomas Wyly's widow, Hester, who now lived in the abandoned Reynoldsburg courthouse, allowed her children to sell the rest of the riverfront property on the east side of the Tennessee. Before they did, however, James awarded Blake's husband, John G. Lucas, 1,077 prime acres along the Tennessee River near the mouth of Trace Creek. This property included the site that would become Johnsonville during the Civil War.[19]

In 1859, just two years before the start of the war, John Lucas renamed the place Lucas Landing. As the primary riverboat landing in the Trace Creek region, Lucas Landing gained notoriety among other mooring locations in the region such as Cuba Landing (also in Humphreys County), Paris Landing (Henry County), and Pickwick Landing (Hardin County), all of which prospered from a bustling steamboat industry.[20]

Lucas built a large home near the waterfront in 1859, a strategic position that provided convenient access to assist merchants day and night. With the help of slaves, he operated an enormously profitable river landing while cultivating the rich farmland along the Tennessee River. With its substantial wharf, Lucas Landing soon drew the attention of surveyors and engineers who identified it as a potential military shipping and receiving point. The future of Lucas Landing showed more promise now than ever before.[21]

---

19 Smith, *The Wyly Saga*, 21, 26; ROHC, *Deed Book E*, 324; ROHC, *Deed Book O*, 173. In 1840, John G. Lucas married into the Wyly family taking Thomas Wyly's daughter, Babe, as his wife. John was the younger brother of Hugh Ross Lucas, a member of the Tennessee General Assembly in the 1850s who would serve in the Civil War as a Confederate captain in the 11th Tennessee Infantry Regiment, which recruited heavily from Humphreys County.

20 Goodspeed, *History of Tennessee: Biographical Sketch of Montgomery, Robertson, Humphreys, Stewart, Dickson, Cheatham, and Houston Counties*, 890.

21 Smith, *The Wyly Saga*, 26; Byron and Barbara Sistler, eds., *1860 Census-Tennessee*, vol. 3 (Nashville, 1982), 335.

CHAPTER 2

Andrew Johnson's Quandary

On April 12, 1861, Brig. Gen. Pierre G. T. Beauregard, the commander of the defenses of Charleston, South Carolina, ordered his men to open fire on the masonry fort sitting out in the harbor. The one-sided bombardment of Fort Sumter, followed by its surrender on April 14, marked the beginning of the Civil War. Northerners and Southerners alike thought the war would resolve a great "national question" much like the Europeans had experienced during the 1848 revolutions. Most Americans thought the rebellion would be over by fall.

Tennessee remained divided on the issue of secession when open hostilities began. Middle and West Tennessee held strong Confederate sympathies, while most East Tennesseans supported remaining in the Union. Seven states (South Carolina, Mississippi, Florida, Alabama, Georgia, Louisiana, and Texas) had already seceded. Virginia, Arkansas, and North Carolina followed them out of the Union. After much debate, Tennessee confirmed by formal referendum on June 8 that it, too, would join the new Confederacy. It was the last state to do so.[1]

---

1 Andre Fleche, *The Revolution of 1861: The American Civil War in the Age of Nationalist Conflict* (Chapel Hill, 2012), 2; James M. McPherson, *Ordeal by Fire: The Civil War and Reconstruction* (New York, 1982), 264; Belle B. Sideman and Lillian Friedman, eds., *Europe Looks at the Civil War* (New York, 1960), 117-18; Larry H. Whitaker, "Civil War," in Carroll Van West, ed., *The Tennessee Encyclopedia of History and Culture* (Nashville, 1998), 168.

The Confederates fought for the right to secede and create a new nation that would allow slavery. President Abraham Lincoln's administration, however, refused to recognize the right of secession and sent Union armies into the field to maintain a unified nation. America's standing army was small when the war began, so most of the men who rallied to their respective colors were wholly inexperienced in military matters. Pressed by Lincoln, Maj. Gen. Irwin McDowell moved south with his green army into north-central Virginia and met an equally unprepared Southern army on the plains of Manassas under Beauregard, the hero of Fort Sumter. After some preliminary fighting, the war's first large-scale engagement unfolded at Bull Run on July 21, 1861. It was a decisive Union defeat and sent the Union soldiers fleeing back toward Washington, D.C. America had never witnessed such bloodshed, with nearly 900 men killed and another 2,500 wounded in a single afternoon. McDowell lost his command, the Confederates found it impossible to capitalize on their victory and end the war, and President Lincoln, perhaps for the first time, fully understood that the war would not end quickly.[2]

The Union's first major field victory would not come for another seven months until Fort Henry on the Tennessee River fell on February 6. Fort Donelson on the Cumberland River fell ten days later. Some 13,000 of the 21,000 Donelson Confederate defenders became prisoners when an obscure Union brigadier general named Ulysses S. Grant demanded the garrison unconditionally surrender. News of the twin Union victories, which followed months of Union setbacks, flooded the pages of newspapers across the country. The capitulation of the forts opened river arteries leading into the deep South and exposed significant weaknesses in the Confederate defensive perimeter strategy espoused by Confederate President Jefferson Davis and implemented by Gen. Albert S. Johnston, the commander in the Western Theater. The decision to spread his troops across some 300 miles of Kentucky to protect Nashville from Federal incursions was in ruins.[3]

---

2 Peter Kolchin, *American Slavery 1619-1877* (New York, 1993), 201; Ira Berlin, *Many Thousands Gone: The First Two Centuries of Slavery in North America* (Cambridge, 1998), 360-361.

3 Benjamin F. Cooling, *Forts Henry and Donelson: Keys to the Confederate Heartland* (Knoxville, 1987), xi-xiv; Kendall D. Gott, *Where the South Lost the War: An Analysis of the Fort Henry-Donelson Campaign, February 1862* (Mechanicsburg, 2003), 263; *The War of the Rebellion: A Compilation of the Official Records of the Union and Confederate*

The "Great Panic"

When the startling news of Fort Donelson's surrender reached Nashville, a "Great Panic" ensued, recounted one citizen, who recalled "men and women were to be seen running to and fro in every portion of the city, and large numbers were hastening with their valuables to the several railroad depots, or escaping in private conveyance to some place of fancied security in the country."[4]

Newspaper accounts detailed reports of Nashville's chaotic state. "A perfect panic reigned throughout the whole city," confirmed the Washington *Daily National Intelligencer*. "The streets," continued the paper,

> were thronged with people wild with excitement. Leading rebels were making speeches from store goods boxes and from the street corners, to the excited populace, stating that the Federals were upon them, the city was defenseless, and appealing to every man who had a species of firearms to rally to the defense of the place.[5]

In 1862, Nashville was the second largest city in the state behind the Mississippi River city of Memphis, with a population that included 29,000 native-born whites, 2,000 European immigrants, 1,000 free blacks, and about 5,000 slaves. This major shipping point for riverboat traffic also developed into an important manufacturing and railroad distribution point for goods flowing north and south. A contingent of Confederates remained in the city following the fall of Fort Donelson, primarily rearguard troops from Gen. Johnston's dispersed command. Hundreds more from a variety of states who had escaped from Donelson milled about in disorder and only added to the chaos.[6]

Armies, 128 vols. (Washington, DC: Government Printing Office, 1880-1901), Series 1, vol. 7, 136-144, 148-152, 170-182, hereinafter cited as *OR*. All references are to Series 1 unless otherwise noted.

4 John M. McKee, *The Great Panic: Being Incidents Connected with Two Weeks of the War in Tennessee* (Nashville, 1862), 8-9.

5 *Daily National Intelligencer* (Washington, D.C.), February 27, 1862.

6 Walter Durham, *Nashville: The Occupied City, 1862-1863* (Knoxville, 1985, 2008), 3; *Nashville City and Business Directory for 1860-61* (Nashville, 1860), 25; *OR* 7, 428.

With his defensive shell broken, Johnston began moving his army south from Bowling Green after the fall of Fort Henry to a temporary base in Murfreesboro, Tennessee, thirty miles south of Nashville. Brig. Gen. John B. Floyd, who had disgracefully escaped from Fort Donelson rather than suffer the fate of his men, was put in command at Nashville. The city's mayor, Richard B. Cheatham, together with its police force, had failed to control the unruly citizens, who had taken over the quartermaster's depot and commissary stores and burned several buildings. Floyd successfully contained the bedlam by ordering Lt. Col. Nathan Bedford Forrest to take action against the rioters. Forrest, a cavalry commander who had refused to surrender at Donelson and escaped with about 700 Rebels, subdued the unruliness by ordering his mounted troops to charge into the crowd of "straggling soldiers and citizens of all grades." Once the threat was put down, Forrest reported that "wagons could be placed for loading and resumed shipments south to the Army."[7]

Forrest's troops labored day and night to save what supplies they could and ship them off to safety. Once the evacuation was complete, explained the cavalry commander, "Nearly one thousand wagon loads of ammunition, clothing, bales of osnaburgs, artillery and food stores," had been saved. "If the quartermaster and commissary had remained at their post and worked diligently with the means at their command," he hastened to add, "the government stores might have all been saved between the time of the fall of Fort Donelson and the arrival of the enemy at Nashville."[8]

Grant's troops, meanwhile, spent the two days following the surrender at Fort Donelson consolidating captured munitions, weapons, and food. Thousands of Rebel prisoners lined the shore of the Cumberland River waiting for steamboats to carry them to Northern prisons. On February 19, Grant's bluecoats crossed the Cumberland south of Dover and marched east toward Clarksville. Aside from a few brief skirmishes with Confederate partisans, Grant's infantry advanced overland with little difficulty while

---

7 McKee, *The Great Panic*, 11-12; Durham, *Nashville: The Occupied City*, 31-33; Gott, *Where the South Lost the War*, 266.

8 *Indianapolis Daily Journal*, May 7, 1862; Durham, *Nashville: The Occupied City*, 31-33; Eddy W. Davison and Daniel Foxx, *Nathan Bedford Forrest: In Search of the Enigma* (Gretna, 2007), 60-61; *OR* 7, 428-432.

Flag Officer Andrew H. Foote's naval flotilla plied the river in a coordinated effort to reach Clarksville the next day.[9]

Grant remained in Clarksville with Foote while his infantry continued advancing toward Nashville. At the same time, Maj. Gen. Don Carlos Buell's Army of the Ohio moved south toward Nashville from Bowling Green, Kentucky. Buell, a West Pointer who was considered by his peers to be "soft" on war, considered it acceptable to allow Southerners to retain property. He believed doing so would "persuade the majority to return to the Union."[10]

On Saturday, February 22, Buell telegraphed Foote in Clarksville: "I am marching on Nashville. Your gunboats should move forward instantly. I believe they will meet no serious opposition." As Buell would soon discover, Southerners at Nashville were not in the mood to welcome the arriving bluecoats. Mrs. Louisa Brown Pearl, a Nashville resident whose husband was serving in the Confederate Army, described the scene in the city prior to the Union Army's arrival. "The rain," she began, "poured in torrents all night & till since dinner, and I have not felt worse anytime than today." Louisa continued:

> Gov. Harris, Gen. Johnston & others are in town & we fear a return of the Army—Harris has issued a proclamation calling out 30,000 of the militia & everybody says he will need an armed force to get them, for nobody will go at his call—the contemptible man—He has lost the few friends that he had, by his cowardly behaviour and flight. The lower part of the town is overflown & many people must leave their houses—Poor Nashville seems doomed.[11]

On February 23, advance elements of Buell's 3rd Division under Brig. Gen. Ormsby M. Mitchel arrived at Edgefield just across the Cumberland River from Nashville. The following day, Mayor Cheatham, who had twice crossed the river in a rowboat because the retreating Confederates had burned both bridges leading to Edgefield, unofficially surrendered his city to

9 Stephen D. Engle, *Struggle for the Heartland: The Campaigns from Fort Henry to Corinth* (Lincoln, 2001), 90-91; *OR* 7, 644-45.

10 Cooling, *Forts Henry and Donelson*, 227-28; Robert Hunt, *The Good Men Who Won the War: Army of the Cumberland Veterans and Emancipation Memory* (Tuscaloosa, 2010), 11-12.

11 *OR* 7, 653; Mrs. Louisa Brown Pearl, Diary, February 22, 1862, TSLA, Nashville, TN.

Col. John Kennett of Mitchel's 3rd Division. That same afternoon, Brig. Gen. William "Bull" Nelson, with his 4th Division, marched into Edgefield. Once he was informed that Cheatham had informally surrender to Col. Kennett, Nelson and a few members of his staff crossed the river, walked to the top of Cedar Hill (upon which the Capitol building sat), and raised "Old Glory" once again over the Tennessee state capitol.[12]

The next morning, February 25, Mayor Cheatham returned to Edgefield to formally surrender Nashville to Gen. Buell as the commanding officer of the occupying Union forces. Mitchel's division crossed the river from Edgefield on an abandoned transport. Led by the 6th Ohio Infantry's regimental band, Mitchel's men disembarked from the boats and marched straight up Broadway Street to Church Street and halted at Nashville's courthouse square.

"At last we have seen the bluecoats—Indeed we can see nothing else," penned a distressed Louisa Pearl. "About ten thousand landed this morning from eleven gunboats—The public square is filled with them." The Nashville civilian watched as "a large body of them marched up Church St. this morning with a fine band of music playing Dixie—they present a striking contrast to our troops as regards dress & arms—I am told they are all mostly Irish & Dutch & seem well disciplined."[13]

A Military Governor

In just three weeks, from mid-February to early March 1862, Union forces had gained control of most of Middle Tennessee. President Lincoln understood that he would need to act quickly to forestall any congressional interference if he wanted to maintain and execute authority over Nashville, the first captured Confederate capital. On March 3, he appointed staunch Unionist and United States Senator Andrew Johnson to the new position of Military Governor of Tennessee. Johnson was the only senator from a seceded state who had remained loyal to the Union. Even though Lincoln had already experimented with a civilian military governor in North

---

12 Lee, *The L&N Railroad in the Civil War*, 34-36; Durham, *Nashville: The Occupied City*, 31-35.

13 Bobby L. Lovett, *The African-American History of Nashville, Tennessee, 1780-1930* (Fayetteville, 1999), 49; Pearl Diary, February 25, 1862, TSLA.

Andrew Johnson, ca. 1860.
Library of Congress

Carolina, the state was returned to military control. The same day of Lincoln's announcement, Secretary of War Edwin M. Stanton informed Johnson of his new important appointment, which carried with it the rank of brigadier general.[14]

As Lincoln anticipated, Johnson's appointment met with immediate opposition. The most damning condemnation came from the "fighting" generals, especially the commander of the Army of the Potomac, Maj. Gen. George B. McClellan. Two months earlier on January 6, McClellan had written to Buell that "Bowling Green and Nashville are of secondary importance. Interesting as Nashville may be to the Louisville interests, it strikes me that its possession is of very secondary importance to East Tennessee, West North Carolina, South Carolina, North Georgia, and Alabama." Now, with Nashville in Union hands, McClellan's opinion changed. The city, he insisted, was of such importance that the military, not one of Lincoln's political appointees, should manage its occupation. Tennessee's old-line Whig party, which despised Johnson, also lined up in opposition to his appointment. The state's Democrats hated Johnson for his stance against secession, and prior to the

14 Paul H. Bergeron, "Andrew Johnson," in *The Tennessee Encyclopedia of History and Culture, ed. Carroll Van West* (Nashville, 1998), 482; Paul H. Bergeron, Stephen V. Ash and Jeanette Keith, *Tennesseans and Their History* (Knoxville, 1999), 151-54; Gregory P. Downs, *After Appomattox: Military Occupation and the Ends of War* (Cambridge, 2015), 65; Earl J. Hess, *The Civil War in the West: Victory and Defeat from the Appalachians to the Mississippi* (Chapel Hill, 2012), 22; Bergeron, Ash, and Keith, *Tennesseans and Their History*, 147-149; Leroy P. Graf and Ralph W. Haskins, eds., *The Papers of Andrew Johnson*, vol. 5 (Knoxville, 1979), xl-xliii.

Civil War, supporters of Southern Democratic presidential candidate John C. Breckinridge had burned Johnson's effigy in the streets of Nashville.[15]

Lincoln ignored them all. The president believed Johnson shared his vision of restoring the South and possessed "the kind of Southern loyalism that Northerners hoped would undermine the Confederate war effort." Lincoln could also depend on Johnson to help restore Nashville to its prewar condition and reintegrate Tennessee into the Union. Nashville's pro-Confederates were infuriated that Johnson had been given presidential authority to take whatever steps he deemed necessary to put down the Southern rebellion in the state. As far as the senator and now brigadier general was concerned, Middle Tennessee's white citizenry had been tricked into secession by ill-informed and villainous men. Whatever his course, Johnson's immense task would test every reserve of patience and judgment he possessed.[16]

Johnson looked to Nashville's Unionists to help foster loyalism and restore the civil government in Middle Tennessee "after purging the body politic of the truly disloyal." The region was not lacking for them. When Maggie Lindsley, a faithful Nashville Unionist, heard about the surrender of Fort Donelson, she recalled that she "ran screaming over the house, knocking down chairs and tables, clapping my hands, and shouting for the 'Union' until the children were terrified." Next, recorded Maggie, she "rushed to the parlor and thundered 'Yankee Doodle' on the piano in such a manner that I had never done before . . . the Governor and Legislature left the very day Donelson surrendered. May they never return!"[17]

In order to keep Confederate sympathizers at bay, Federal officers ordered the jailing of Nashville citizens who refused to comply with

---

15 *OR* 7, 531; David H. Donald, *Lincoln* (London, 1995), 334-35; Bergeron, Ash and Keith, *Tennesseans and Their History*, 147-149.

16 Hess, *The Civil War in the West*, 42; Graf and Haskins, *The Papers of Andrew Johnson*, vol. 5, xlii.

17 Stephen V. Ash, *Middle Tennessee Society Transformed 1860-1870* (Baton Rouge, 1988), 97; Ormsby M. Mitchel to Andrew Johnson, March 30, 1862, in Graf and Haskins in, eds., *Papers of Andrew Johnson*, vol. 5, 177, 257, and Secretary of War Edwin Stanton to Andrew Johnson, March 3, 1862, in Graf and Haskins, eds., *The Papers of Andrew Johnson*, vol. 5, 257, 177; Peter Maslowski, *Treason Must Be Made Odious: Military Occupation and Wartime Reconstruction in Nashville, Tennessee, 1862-65* (New York, 1978), 6-7, 19-20; Durham, *Nashville: The Occupied City*, 57-59.

Nashville and Chattanooga Railroad Depot, Nashville, Tennessee, 1864. *Library of Congress*

Johnson's orders. As this resistance continued, Johnson, who earlier had restricted Union soldiers from harming or looting Nashville's civilians, lifted those restrictions on private property and ordered troops to seize any supplies they needed. Each time Confederate guerillas attacked Nashville, Johnson ordered Union troops to "retaliate by looting or burning nearby homes or by holding local residents hostage until the guerillas desisted."[18]

Destination: Tennessee River

President Lincoln told his military leaders that as long as the rebellion continued, troops of the United States government would be well-supplied, and he made it his personal responsibility to ensure the military had the best and most up-to-date equipment. Shortly after the occupation of Nashville, procedures for supplying the invading Union army in Tennessee were

18 Bergeron, Ash, and Keith, *Tennesseans and Their History*, 150-153.

enacted. Since Nashville was an important railroad terminus for shipping military supplies to several directions, Johnson ordered the construction of warehouses and loading platforms to make shipping and receiving military supplies by rail faster and more efficient. Using mostly impressed former slaves as a labor force, Johnson ordered the construction of a vast railroad yard and supply depot just below the state capitol along McLemore Street (between today's Church and Cedar Streets). As the war progressed, rail cars, supply boats, and barges hauled critical military supplies from Nashville to Union forces operating in campaigns across the South.[19]

While Andrew Johnson continued his strict military rule over Nashville and across Middle Tennessee, Albert S. Johnston reorganized his divided Confederate army at Corinth, Mississippi, a major rail hub just below the Tennessee border. Confederate authorities reinforced Johnston's command, which he renamed the Army of Mississippi, and urged him to take offensive action. U. S. Grant, meanwhile, moved his Army of the Tennessee up the Tennessee River and set up his headquarters at Savannah while his troops moved farther upriver to Pittsburg Landing. Maj. Gen. Henry Halleck, the overall commander of the Union Department of the Mississippi, ordered Gen. Buell to march his Army of the Ohio southwest out of Nashville to join Grant. The stationary Grant made for a tempting target, especially before Buell could reinforce him. Determined to rout Grant while the opportunity existed, Johnson led his army north and launched a surprise attack at Shiloh on the morning of April 6. Early successes across the line eventually turned to bloody stalemate by day's end. Johnston, who had been killed earlier that day, was replaced by Beauregard, but the opportunity for victory had slipped through Southern fingers. One of Grant's divisions joined him during the night, as did Buell's army. Union counterattacks on April 7 drove the Confederate army back to Corinth and ended the bloody battle. Total casualties approached 24,000, dwarfing the losses of Bull Run and Forts Henry and Donelson. Union wounded poured into Nashville. The presence of sick and dying soldiers, amputations, and death on a scale never before witnessed brought an end to much of the city's civilian unruliness. The horrific scenes carried the reality of war straight into their homes.[20]

19 Lovett, *The African-American History of Nashville, Tennessee*, 49.

20 Drew Gilpin Faust, *This Republic of Suffering: Death in the Civil War* (Cambridge, 2007), xii-xviii.

The Union occupation of Nashville opened the Cumberland River for the delivery of supplies and wounded men. Pilots steered packet boats from Cincinnati, Louisville, and St. Louis into Nashville's wharf laden with everything the Army needed. The arrival of a summer drought dropped the river's water level. By August, it was so low river traffic stopped for two weeks. Many of the boats traversing the river were deep draft vessels, and it was simply too dangerous to ply the river or dock at the city's steep main wharf. The river level was such a concern that Governor Johnson and Union commanders worried whether Nashville could be maintained as a base of operations.[21]

If Union forces had to abandon Nashville as a supply distribution point, where could a more reliable base of supply be established? Moreover, if Nashville was no longer used as a reliable supply base, how would the railroads, which entered the city from three directions, be kept operational and out of Confederate hands? Finally, if the Army abandoned use of the Cumberland River at Nashville as a supply artery, what existing western railroad would be used to connect Nashville with the Tennessee River, and who would build it? Able-bodied soldiers were needed at the front. These critical logistical decisions lay in the hands of Andrew Johnson.

The inability of Confederate forces to seriously threaten Nashville, coupled with the rise of the rivers, helped stabilize the situation. By the following summer (June 1863), the Union high command in Nashville had redirected much of its military resources and supplies by rail southeast to Murfreesboro to assist Maj. Gen. William S. Rosecrans' Army of the Cumberland in its advance toward Chattanooga. Rosecrans' army, which had been spread out between Nashville and Murfreesboro for six months after the Battle of Stones River (December 31, 1862-January 2, 1863), was at the end of what was described as a "massive and tenuous supply line." During his Middle Tennessee (or Tullahoma) Campaign (June 24 to July 3, 1863), Rosecrans planned a carefully executed strategy to gain control of a series of gaps south of Murfreesboro through the Highland Rim, rugged high terrain encircling the Nashville basin. Gen. Braxton Bragg's Confederate Army of Tennessee opposed him. After ten days of contested frontal and

---

21 Durham, *Reluctant Partners: Nashville and the Union, July 1, 1863 to June 30, 1865* (Nashville, 1987), 15-18. The river level had to reach 22 feet before river commerce and normal transportation could resume.

Major General William S. Rosecrans, 1862
Library of Congress

flanking maneuvers, Rosecrans succeeded in pushing Bragg's forces completely out of Middle Tennessee without having to fight a major battle. While Rosecrans dealt with Bragg, Governor Johnson and various military officials in Nashville determined that a new railroad needed to be built to connect the city with a supply base somewhere farther to the west at a location along the deeper Tennessee River.[22]

In August 1863, Johnson assigned military engineers the task of designing plans for a railroad extending seventy-eight miles to the Tennessee River. He wanted the railroad to be fully operational by the following spring—a very short window in which to finish such a large task. Military engineers were in high demand, and were needed on site each day to oversee the complex railroad construction project, which included a number of water-crossing trestles. The engineers estimated it would take a year to finish even with crews working around the clock.[23]

In a bid to solve the labor crisis, Rosecrans proposed using the 1st and 2nd regiments of United States Colored Troops (USCT) to do the work. Prior to Johnson's appointment as military governor and overseer of the project, the *Nashville Dispatch*, in August 1863, reported that "five thousand Negroes would be impressed" to work on the railroad. The use of black labor to build the rail link between Nashville and the Tennessee River had more impact on Johnsonville's existence than any other factor during the war.[24]

---

22 Hunt, *The Good Men Who Won the War*, xiii, 14. Rosecrans' Tullahoma Campaign, one of the most brilliant and significant of the war, was overshadowed by the simultaneous Vicksburg Campaign in Mississippi and Gettysburg Campaign in Pennsylvania.

23 *OR* 30, Series 3, 67.

24 *Nashville Dispatch*, August 23, 1863.

CHAPTER 3

Johnsonville's Lifeline:
The Nashville & Northwestern Railroad

O N January 22, 1852, nine years before the beginning of the war, the Tennessee General Assembly chartered the Nashville and Northwestern Railroad for the "purpose of establishing communication by railroad between Nashville and the Mississippi River, beginning at Nashville and terminating on the Mississippi River in Obion County." The residents of Martin in Weakley County had lauded the idea of an east-west railroad for some time. Prior to the charter, private funds had been raised to connect Martin with the Hickman and Obion Railroad, which consisted of only fourteen miles of finished track between Union City, Tennessee, and Hickman, Kentucky.[1]

The following month, the Tennessee General Assembly required the railroad companies of the Tennessee Central, Memphis and Nashville, and the Nashville and Northwestern, to "construct their tracks respectively with the same gauge as the Nashville and Chattanooga railroad." The state granted all three companies the right to pass their "locomotives and train of cars" to the depot of the Central Trunk Railroad Company, Nashville's primary trunk line. To accomplish this, the new railroad would have to build a bridge across the Tennessee River between the mouth of Duck River and

---

1 *ACTS OF TENNESSEE, 1853-1854*, 82; E.H. Marshall, *History of Obion County* (Union City, 1970), 159; Westin Goodspeed, et, al., *History of Tennessee: With Sketches of Gibson, Obion, Weakley, Dyer, and Lake Counties* (Nashville, 1887), 834-835.

White Oak Island in Humphreys County to reach the high ground on the western bank.[2]

To ensure the completion of the bridge, the legislature appointed a Board of Commissioners with representatives from the counties involved to oversee the task. Each commissioner received stock at a cost of $100 a share in the Central Trunk Railroad Company. Under Tennessee's General Improvement Laws of 1851-52, the state retained a lien as a security measure to finance the Nashville and Northwestern Railroad, and bonds were issued to raise $4.56 million to pay for the construction.[3]

By December 1854, Nashville's citizens had raised $270,000 to start the construction of the Nashville and Northwestern Railroad. Around the same time, the legislature authorized the Hickman and Obion Railroad Company to extend its rail lines to Dresden in Weakley County and connect to the Nashville and Northwestern Railroad "at such point as may be convenient" in either Weakley or Obion counties.[4]

In 1855, the Hickman and Obion Railroad connected to the western side of the Nashville and Northwestern Railroad (west of the Tennessee River) at Dresden to intersect with the Mobile and Ohio Railroad. However, the winter of 1855-56 was so cold that construction stopped until March 1856. That same month, the Kentucky General Assembly adopted a charter for the Nashville and Northwestern Railroad for its connection from Nashville to Hickman, Kentucky. For the remainder of the year, the Nashville and Northwestern Railroad Company continued work on its existing tracks from Union City to Martin and then to Dresden.[5]

By 1857, the Nashville and Northwestern Railroad had joined the critical junction of the Memphis and Ohio Railroad at McKenzie,

---

2 *ACTS OF TENNESSEE, 1851-52*, 528, 531.

3 *ACTS OF TENNESSEE, 1851-52*, 532; Edward W. Hines, *Corporate History of the Louisville & Nashville Railroad Company and Roads in its System* (Louisville, 1905), 321; *Legislative History of the Louisville & Nashville R.R. Co. and Roads in its System* (1898), 19.

4 John Wooldridge, Ed., *History of Nashville, Tenn* (Nashville, 1890), 330.

5 *ACTS OF TENNESSEE, 1853-54*, 702-703; *Report of the Committee of the City Council of Nashville, Upon the Affairs of the Nashville and Northwestern Railroad Company* (Nashville, 1859), 11; *The Annual Report of the President and Directors of the Louisville and Nashville Railroad Company: Commencing on the First Monday in October 1856, and Ending October 1857* (Louisville, 1857), 8-9; *ACTS OF KENTUCKY, 1855-56*, 80.

Tennessee.[6] From the center of Nashville, near the original depot site of the Central Trunk Railroad, the Nashville and Northwestern Railroad Company built 28 miles of finished rail to the town of Kingston Springs, Tennessee. Beginning at the Tennessee River heading east, an additional six miles of track was laid just south of Reynoldsburg. Since its beginning in 1852, the Nashville and Northwestern Railroad Company planned to build a draw bridge across the Tennessee River that did not obstruct "the free navigation of said river." However, funding issues delayed the bridge, which would not be built for another fifteen years.[7]

That September, Col. Vernon K. Stevenson, President of the Nashville and Chattanooga Railroad Company, submitted a report to Robert G. Payne, the State Railroad Commissioner of Tennessee, about the conditions of the Nashville and Northwestern Railroad. Stevenson reported to the Nashville City Council that $2.9 million was needed to finish all 170 miles of track. This included grading, cross-ties, iron of the u-pattern (rails), spikes, gravel, depots, locomotives, passenger and railcars, box and freight cars, repair cars, switches, eight miles of side track, labor, engineering, and contingencies.

Five months later, in February 1858, the Tennessee House of Representatives used the expiration of the railroad's original charter of January 1, 1858, to force concessions from the railroad to send its route through the center of Huntingdon in Carroll County. The charter was extended, but the representatives also negotiated to keep the original route to Hickman, Kentucky. Problems with funding the Nashville and Northwestern Railroad remained, and by 1860, on the eve of war, little of the route had been completed.[8]

---

6 Addie Lou Brooks, "The Building of the Trunk Line Railroads in West Tennessee, 1852-1861," *Tennessee Old and New, 1796-1946*, II (Memphis, 1942), 208-209.

7 *The Annual Report of the President and Directors of the Louisville and Nashville Railroad Company: Commencing on the First Monday in October 1856, and Ending October 1857* (Louisville, 1857), 8-9; *ACTS OF TENNESSEE, 1853-1854*, 703; Richard E Prince, *Nashville, Chattanooga & St. Louis Railway–History and Steam Locomotives* (Bloomington, 1968), 21.

8 Stevenson made the report to the State Railroad Commissioner because at that time there was "no Superintendent or Chief Engineer on this road." As mentioned in the: *Report of the Committee of the City Council of Nashville, Upon the Affairs of the Nashville and Northwestern Railroad Company,* 1859; R.G. Payne, *Report to the General Assembly on the Condition of the Railroads in Tennessee* (Nashville, 1857), 15-19. *Report of the Committee of the City Council of Nashville, Upon the Affairs of the Nashville and*

A Military Railroad

When Tennessee voted to leave the Union in June 1861, just fifty-one miles of the Nashville and Northwestern Railroad, less than one-third of the route, was complete between McKenzie, Tennessee, and Hickman, Kentucky. On the eastern side of the Tennessee River, twenty-eight miles of track had been finished between Nashville and Kingston Springs, and only six miles from the Tennessee River eastward.[9]

Tennessee's railroad network played a major role in Western Theater operations during the Civil War. The overall good condition of Tennessee's railroads and their ability to deliver troops and supplies in essentially every direction was used to advantage by the Confederacy early in the war, and thereafter by Union forces.[10]

Five of the six primary Tennessee railroads ran from north to south: the Mobile and Ohio Railroad in West Tennessee; the Nashville and Chattanooga Railroad and the Louisville and Nashville Railroad in Middle Tennessee; and the East Tennessee and Virginia Railroad and the Georgia Railroad in East Tennessee. The only east-west line of significance at that time was the Memphis and Charleston Railroad. The Nashville and Northwestern Railroad was nowhere near completion, so war planners gave it little consideration.[11]

As the war spread into Middle Tennessee in 1862-63, Federal officials were anxious to finish the Nashville and Northwestern line to provide an east-west transportation outlet to Nashville and to supplement the north-south links of the Louisville and Nashville and the Nashville and Chattanooga rail lines. The construction of the Nashville and Northwestern

---

Northwestern Railroad Company, 10: Payne, 23-26; *Nashville Union and American*, February 16, 1858.

9 Brooks, "The Building of the Trunk Line Railroads in West Tennessee, 1852-1861," 204-211.

10 Hess, *The Civil War in the West*, 208-212.

11 Edward A. Johnson, "Railroads," in *The Tennessee Encyclopedia of History and Culture*, Van West, ed., 769-72; Bonnie Gamble, *"Nashville and Chattanooga Railroad,"* in *The Tennessee Encyclopedia of History and Culture*, Van West, ed., 767-68; Russell Wigginton, "Louisville and Nashville Railroad," in *The Tennessee Encyclopedia of History and Culture,* Van West, ed., 765-66.

Brigadier General Alvan C. Gillem, ca. 1864
Library of Congress

Railroad remained essential to Nashville's importance as a major Federal base of operations and eventually became the solution to the Union's most critical logistical problem in the Western Theater: a failure of supply.[12]

On August 18, 1863, Governor Johnson wrote to Gen. Rosecrans, whose Army of the Cumberland was camped at Stevenson, Alabama, that work must commence on the Nashville and Northwestern Railroad. "The force necessary is a guard. Its construction need not be large," insisted Johnson. "The labor and money necessary can be readily obtained." The Tennessee governor wrote to Lincoln to request support for the railroad project. Shortly afterward, Johnson received a telegram from Lt. Col. Charles Goddard, assistant adjutant general for the Department of the Cumberland, informing him that Secretary of War Stanton had issued orders to Rosecrans to "authorize and direct the construction of the Northwestern Railroad as soon as possible."[13]

The next day Maj. Frank Bond, Rosecrans' aide-de-camp, informed Brig. Gen. Alvan C. Gillem, the commander of the troops along the Nashville and Northwestern Railroad, that Rosecrans needed him to assemble "all the negroes you can and notify him, and he will have them organized and mustered into service and put to work on the Northwestern road." On August 27, Rosecrans (who was senior in rank) assigned Governor Johnson, with support from Gillem, full oversight of the construction of the Nashville and Northwestern Railroad.[14]

12 Jesse C. Burt, "Sherman's Logistics and Andrew Johnson," *Tennessee Historical Quarterly* 15 (1956): 198.

13 *OR* 30, pt. 3, 67, 74.

14 Ibid, 80, 184-85.

Recently liberated African Americans living in the surrounding Tennessee counties of Giles, Maury, and Montgomery (as well as Logan and Todd counties in southern Kentucky), were rounded-up by Union troops and transported to Nashville, where they were organized into railroad labor detachments. Additionally, to make up for black labor shortages, Johnson ordered a variety of Union officers to organize and contribute all available white soldiers to assist in the line's construction. Col. Henry R. Mizner of the 14th Michigan cooperated in the effort, and wrote Johnson as much from Columbia, Tennessee. "Col Cypert (U.S. 2nd Tennessee Mounted Infantry) left this morning with nearly two hundred men," he began. "I sent advance guard to protect him to Franklin. I shall earnestly cooperate in furnishing Negroes for North western Road unless directed by Genl Comdg to do otherwise. I have suggested to officers here recruiting for Negro Regiments that they Return to Nashville & Report to Maj. Stearns."[15]

On September 7, after three years of inactivity, construction resumed along the Nashville and Northwestern Railroad. Despite the military sharing the railroad, Johnson committed the federal government to finishing the remaining fifty miles of track west from Kingston Springs to the Tennessee River. Rosecrans instructed Johnson to "employ a competent engineer, and other officers, agents, and workmen necessary to complete said line of railroad without delay." Johnson complied, replying that "Colonel Innes, Military Supt. of Rail-roads, will detail the requisite number of engineers, and furnish rolling stock to carry on the work." Col. William P. Innes, commander of the U. S. Military Railroad Department in Tennessee, informed Johnson that he "had a considerable force of soldiers and civilian laborers employed on the road." Construction continued under Innes' able leadership with the 1st Missouri Engineers working alongside military personnel and impressed laborers. However, later that month when the war intensified around Chattanooga and in North Georgia during and after the Chickamauga Campaign, the demands on Innes and the requirement for more railroad laborers slowed progress. Johnson concluded that additional

---

15 Maslowski, *Treason Must Be Made Odious*, 100; Henry R. Mizner to Andrew Johnson, September 3, 1863, in Graf and Haskins, *The Papers of Andrew Johnson*, vol. 6, 353. George L. Stearns was designated recruiting commissioner of colored troops by Secretary of War, Edwin Stanton in June 1863.

Colonel William P. Innes, ca. 1863
Library of Congress

black civilian laborers were needed to meet requirements, and ordered additional free blacks impressed for the project.[16]

On September 27, 1863, an advertisement in the *Nashville Daily Union* requested "one thousand men, white or black," and assured loyal slave owners that they would be paid "three hundred dollars for each of their slaves committed to the building of the North western road." The impressed laborers performed backbreaking work swinging pick-axes and using shovels, buckets, sleds, and wheelbarrows to move tons of earth and ballast in an effort to raise and level the height of the railroad bed. Explosives blasted "cuts" into the earth so track could be evenly laid. Work continued apace, sometimes twenty-four hours at a stretch.[17]

Protecting the Railroad

As the building of the railroad progressed west toward the Tennessee River, the enlistment of black soldiers had a significant impact on its completion. Soldiers in the 12th and 13th USCT had already started construction at Lucas Landing, the railroad's terminus on the Tennessee River. In addition to this work, the soldiers labored alongside Quartermaster's Department employees constructing buildings, corrals, and loading platforms for the new supply depot.[18]

---

16 *OR* 5, pt. 1, 943; Graf and Haskins, *The Papers of Andrew Johnson*, vol. 6, 343; *OR* 30, pt. 3, 184-85.

17 *Nashville Daily Union*, September 27, 1863.

18 Lovett, "The Negro in Tennessee, 1861-1866," 288-291.

Railroad Cut #29, Nashville and Northwestern Railroad, White Bluff,
Tennessee, ca. 1865. *Tennessee State Library & Archives*

Together with the 40th and 100th USCT, the 12th and 13th regiments
toiled alongside impressed black civilian laborers setting railroad ties,
moving heavy iron rails into place, and hammering spikes to hold it all
together. Many of the troops camped at or near fortifications at McEwen and
Waverly, Tennessee, and at Camp Mussey (today's Tennessee City in
Dickson County).[19]

Security details guarded the Nashville and Northwestern Railroad round
the clock to safeguard the track between Kingston Springs and the
Tennessee River. To ensure a successful project, Union officials also needed
to find enough troops to guard against any potential Confederate thrusts. The
task fell to Maj. Gen. Gordon Granger, who assigned guard details at various
points along the railroad, including the 12th, 13th, 40th, and 100th USCT,
the 8th Iowa Cavalry, and various other cavalry regiments.[20]

19 Ibid; *Supplement to the Official Records of the Union and Confederate Armies*, Janet
Hewitt, ed., 100 vols. (Wilmington, NC, 1994), vol. 77, 469-70, hereafter *OR Supplement*.

20 *OR* Supplement, 77, 471. From November 1863 to June 1864, the 12th and 13th USCT
guarded a variety of railroad sections described in various reports simply as "C-3, 26 ½, 38
and 53."

On October 12, Governor Johnson penned a letter to Rosecrans expressing his satisfaction with the progress along the Nashville and Northwestern Railroad and the assistance of the USCT as laborers and guards. "We are getting along very well with the North Western Rail Road, especially so, when we consider all that has transpired since its commencement," wrote the pleased governor. "We have started this morning a full Regiment of Negroes, armed and equipped to the North Western Rail Road, to work and fight. As they passed through the town [Nashville], they looked and behaved well. The work is going on."[21]

Three weeks later on November 3, Maj. Gen. George H. Thomas's adjutant sent a telegram to Brig. Gen. Gillem, who was in Chattanooga with the 1st USCT, about the need to guard the railroad:

> The First Regt. Colored Troops, from Elk River, will be ordered to report to you for duty on the Northwestern Railroad. A regiment of cavalry 1,100 strong [8th Iowa Cavalry], now marching from Louisville, will also be sent to you for guard duty. The general commanding wishes you to assist the colonel of this regiment in disciplining his regiment and perfecting it in drill. All the troops on the Northwestern Railroad are under your command while engaged on that work, and the general expects you to control them and enforce discipline.[22]

The railroad remained under constant threat of attack throughout Johnsonville's existence. Confederate guerillas regularly threatened and killed Union soldiers along the line and often did so with impunity. On August 30, 1864, guerillas under the command of the notorious guerilla "Chief Petty John," attacked Company G, 13th USCT, which "lost one man killed and one sergeant wounded severely." While stationed at Waverly,

21 Graf and Haskins, *The Papers of Andrew Johnson*, vol. 6, 418. Graf and Haskins footnote: "Circumstantial evidence indicates that this was the 13th [2nd] U.S. Colored Infantry. On October 7, at Nashville, Stearns had "six full companies of the 2nd U.S. Col. vol. of one hundred men each of a Lt. Col. and a commissioned officer to each company. If I receive the order for them to move in the morning they will be ready in the following morning." Twelve days later Lt. Col. Theodore Trauernicht reported the 13th encamped on the Northwestern Railroad thirty miles from Nashville. Stearns to William P. Innes, October 7, 1863, Johnson Paper. LC; *OR* 30, pt. 4, 482.

22 *OR* 31, pt. 3, 28. It should be noted that the "First Regt. Colored Troops" Gillem referred to included men in the 12th, 40th, 100 and 101st USCT infantry regiments. This should not be confused with the 1st and 2nd regiments of the U.S. Colored Heavy Artillery regiments who were mustered in and operated around Memphis, TN.

Tennessee, two days later on September 1, an officer in Company H, 13th USCT, reported, "while out, had a skirmish with guerillas and lost two men killed and one wounded. Lieutenant Ekstrand was wounded while riding along the road by guerillas."[23]

Confederate partisans under Alexander Duval McNairy routinely attacked points along the Nashville and Northwestern Railroad. In October 1864, while a group of "track repairers" worked along railroad Section 36, McNairy's men sabotaged rails by removing spikes along this section. To their surprise, the first train that came along chugged right past without incident. The next day, three supply trains rolled over the sabotaged section, but this time they were "heavily fired into by McNary's gang [with] a shower of bullets." The train escaped, but three guardsmen were killed, as was a boy, "who was [a] cook and brakeman, found dead on the bunk where he happened to be lying."[24]

The raids continued almost daily along the Nashville and Northwestern Railroad and usually resulted in some form of destruction. Tracks were torn up, trestles and cars burned, and support buildings set afire. The quick mounted assaults often killed railroad guards, especially men in the 12th and 13th USCT, who guarded Sections 49 through 78, which started near Camp Mussey and ended at Johnsonville.

Railroad Materials

The intense work along the Nashville and Northwestern Railroad required the constant search for and acquisition of construction materials. Fighting for military contracts was a highly competitive and potentially

---

23 Hunt, *The Good Men Who Won the War*, 15; *OR Supplement 77*, 470-71, 477, 482, 495-496.

24 *OR* 39, pt. 1, 877. Confederate partisan Alexander Duval McNairy originally served as a lieutenant in Company B, 20th Tennessee Infantry. He commanded a company of independent scouts known as the 'Swannee Rifles' and fought at Fishing Creek and Shiloh; they later organized a battalion of partisan cavalry, which operated behind Union lines in Tennessee. They operated between the Cumberland and Tennessee Rivers in Tennessee during 1862 and 1865. McNairy terrorized the Federals. His gang specialized in harassing railroad workers. On Oct 18, 1864, track workers were captured by McNairy and his men between Smeedville and White Bluff. Three days later the bushwhackers burned the dwellings and worker huts on the railroad. Myers E. Brown, *Tennessee's Confederates* (Charleston, 2011), 65; *OR* 39, pt. 1, 877.

lucrative business for civilian contractors. Captain Simon Perkins, Jr., assigned to the Nashville depot, was one of many assistant quartermasters responsible for administering thousands of requisitions for these materials. The requisitions themselves reveal the complexity of the work involved, and potential dangers. Timber suppliers G. M. Anderson and William B. Ewing competed for a military contract, which the latter apparently won. An August 1863 memorandum, which registered a payment to Ewing, included this language:

> Not to cut such timber as will be needed for Rail Timber, but such as will be selected from places designated by said Ewing paying for the same at One Dollar per board, payable when Five Hundred Cords shall be cut. Timber to be measured in Gov't Wood Yard. Mr. Anderson agrees his Hands shall commit no depredations on said place.[25]

Different types of wood were required for different projects. Many requisitions were for "Rail Timber" needed to make railroad ties and construct trestles. Thirteen trestles were built between Kingston Springs and Johnsonville. The longest on the Nashville and Northwestern line was one-half mile east of McEwen in Humphreys County.

On October 24, 1863, for example, a procurement officer at the Nashville Depot issued a "Wood Contract" for the Nashville and Northwestern Railroad to W. G. Harding. The timber contract provided Harding "four dollars per Cord for One thousand cords of wood to be cut and delivered where corded near the North Western Rail Road by the first day of January 1864 for supply of United States Troops Stationed at this Depot. Wood to be delivered within Seven & half miles of this city."[26]

The awarding of military lumber contracts was so competitive that on occasion they became deadly. According to the *Louisville Daily Journal*, "a most atrocious murder was committed on the Northwestern railroad, 45

25 Memorandum from the Assistant Quartermasters Office, August 26, 1863, in the *Papers of Simon Perkins, Jr., Assistant Quartermaster, Nashville Depot*, microfilm accession # 1527, Box 2, Folder 1, TSLA, Nashville, TN.

26 Wood Contract by A.Q.M. Simon Perkins for W.G. Harding, October 24, 1863, *Papers of Simon Perkins, Jr., Assistant Quartermaster, Nashville Depot*, Microfilm Accession # 1527, Box 2, Folder 11, TSLA, Nashville, TN. This was not the William Giles Harding of Nashville's famed Belle Meade Plantation.

Nashville and Northwestern Railroad Trestle outside of
McEwen, Tennessee, ca. 1864. *Tennessee State Library & Archives*

miles from that city [Nashville]." The story recalled how an "old gentleman, about 60 years of age, a former resident of Nashville, an owner of blooded horses, and a man of considerable wealth, and his wife were found in their own house bearing the marks of a bloody crime." Grisly details described the scene:

> The old gentleman was found lying upon his face, a large stab in the back, and, a large number of stabs visible upon his chest, and his throat was gashed in three places. The body of the woman—apparently a woman of 30 years of age—was found lying across the bed, her throat cut from ear to ear, and two large gashes upon her forehead. A large butcher knife, covered with blood, was found lying near her head.

Evidence later revealed that the murdered man and his wife were likely victims associated with a government lumber contract that had been awarded to them over another local competitor.[27]

---

27 *Louisville Daily Journal,* August 30, 1864.

Brigadier General Daniel C. McCallum, ca. 1864 *Library of Congress*

Regardless of how difficult the work was, Maj. Gen. U. S. Grant, who would soon be promoted to command all the Union armies, was not satisfied that the railroad was moving along as fast as it should be. Unhappy with Innes' management, in February 1864 Grant assigned Brig. Gen. Daniel C. McCallum responsibility for completing the Nashville and Northwestern Railroad to the Tennessee River. McCallum, an immigrant from Scotland who had served in the Eastern Theater as a director of Northern railroads, was now under Gen. Sherman handling railroad operations between Nashville and Chattanooga. McCallum's effective oversight of the Nashville and Northwestern Railroad project provided the strict discipline and leadership required to fulfill the army's accelerated need for supplying its troops in the field.[28]

The depot at Johnsonville officially opened on May 19, 1864, and accessed by the completed Nashville and Northwestern Railroad. Unfinished sections of track remained, however, and laborers continued to "dress up the embankments and clean out the cuts." By August 9 the U.S. Army assumed operation of the railroad and it officially became a military railroad.[29]

After a year of backbreaking construction, regular guerilla attacks against labor details and the line itself, and cost overruns, the Nashville and Northwestern Military Railroad was completed on September 1, 1864. By

28 Thomas Weber, *The Northern Railroads in the Civil War, 1861-1865* (Bloomington, 1952), 135-37.

29 *OR* 5, Series 3, 943-45; Dain L. Schult, *Nashville, Chattanooga, and St. Louis: A History of "The Dixie Line"* (Lynchburg, 2001), 30.

the time construction ended, 14,500 men had participated in building and protecting its fifty miles of track and trestles from Nashville to the Tennessee River, including 7,300 impressed black laborers, 6,500 USCT, white soldiers and cavalrymen, and some 700 engineers. This little-known accomplishment remains as one of the greatest engineering feats of the Civil War. The original Nashville and Northwestern Railroad bed is still being used today.

CHAPTER 4

Effecting Emancipation in Tennessee

BLACK Americans made significant contributions to the building of the Nashville and Northwestern Railroad and at Johnsonville. The Civil War offered opportunities for free and enslaved blacks to fight for freedom and their own sense of American nationalism. Early in the war, abolitionists argued that slaves were under the protection of international laws of war, which included the proclamation by the United States of an Atlantic blockade and the treatment and imprisonment of Confederate captives as prisoners of war. Federal officials could emancipate slaves as "the confiscation of enemy property," a "belligerent right recognized by international law."[1]

During the summer of 1862, with the support of abolitionist Frederick Douglass and U. S. Senator Charles Sumner, Congress approved two laws that paved the way toward ending slavery and enlisting blacks into military service. The first included the Second Confiscation Act, which addressed property confiscation and freed slaves of people who were loyal to the Confederacy, and provided Congress alone, without the president, the power to "emancipate rebel owned slaves within Union lines in the seceded states." The second law was the Militia Act, which approved the recruitment of persons of "African descent in any military or naval service for which they may be found competent." This amended law overturned the Militia Act of

---

1 James M. McPherson, *Ordeal by Fire: The Civil War and Reconstruction* (New York, 1982), 267.

July 17, 1792, which restricted military service to "every free able-bodied white male citizen."[2]

Every branch of the service needed more men to fill the ranks. The Army had excluded blacks from serving in the military since the War of 1812. The total number of free black men in the Northern states (of all ages), numbered about 200,000. Few free blacks resided in Southern states, but almost four million slaves lived there. As a rule, Lincoln's military leaders did not want to use black combat soldiers, but they had a grave need for more labor battalions to free up white soldiers for combat. The 1862 Militia Act had allowed for the recruitment of men of "African-descent," but restricted them from participating in combat in favor of using them to garrison "forts, positions, stations, and other places."[3]

On July 22, shortly after the Militia Act went into effect, President Lincoln shared with his cabinet his intention to issue a proclamation emancipating slaves in those areas of the country in rebellion. He understood that, politically speaking, he needed to do so from a position of strength and needed a decisive military victory before he could publically announce a proclamation to end slavery. When Gen. McClellan beat back Gen. Robert E. Lee's Army of Northern Virginia from Maryland that September, the strategic victory that cleared the state of Rebels gave Lincoln enough political capital to move ahead with his plan. A preliminary announcement was made on September 22. The longer the war continued, he believed, the greater the chance that slavery would in fact end. On December 1, Lincoln told Congress, "in giving Freedom to the slave, we assure freedom to the free. We must disenthrall ourselves, and then we shall save our country."[4]

The Emancipation Proclamation took effect on January 1, 1863. The revolutionary announcement freed slaves in all parts of the Confederacy not yet under federal control: "All persons held as slaves within any State or

---

2 Ibid, 226-227; Silvana R. Siddali, *From Property to Person: Slavery and the Confiscation Acts, 1861-1862* (Baton Rouge, 2005), 32-42, 182-189; Gary Gallagher, *The Union War* (Cambridge, 2011), 90; Oakes, 360-61; Elizabeth D. Leonard, *Men of Color to Arms! Black Soldiers, Indian Wars, and the Quest for Equality* (New York, 2010), 7-8.

3 Leonard, *Men of Color to Arms!*, 8; James M. McPherson, *Battle Cry of Freedom: The Civil War Era* (New York, 1988), 564.

4 Roy P. Basler, ed., *The Collected Works of Abraham Lincoln* (CWL), 9 Volumes, vol. 5 (New Brunswick, 1953-55), 537. Lincoln used his war powers to issue the proclamation, so by definition it excluded the Union states (areas not in rebellion).

designated part of a State, the people whereof shall then be in rebellion against the United States, shall be then, thenceforward, and forever free." In one fell swoop Lincoln had changed the country's war aim from keeping the Union together to a campaign to free the slaves. The proclamation said nothing about free blacks, North or South. Lincoln had thus far had shown little interest in the idea of enlisting blacks into military service, but that changed after the signing of the proclamation. Days later, Lincoln promoted Daniel Ullman, a New York officer who had approached the president about arming blacks, from colonel to brigadier general and ordered him to go to Louisiana and "organize a brigade of blacks whether found within or beyond the New Orleans area."[5]

The ground work for this social experiment had already started in Louisiana. After Union forces under Maj. Gen. Benjamin F. Butler seized New Orleans on May 1, 1862, Brig. Gen. John W. Phelps, an ardent abolitionist and one of Butler's key subordinates, took steps to organize blacks into soldiers. When Butler learned what he was doing, he informed Phelps that only"the president could authorize the arming of blacks." When Ullman arrived in Louisiana, he created a successful system for black recruitment, which was soon authorized nationwide for a new program called the Bureau of Colored Troops.[6]

The Emancipation Proclamation drew immediate condemnation from Confederate officials in Richmond, Virginia, who called it a "Yankee trick." Their concern was understandable. Lincoln had shrewdly positioned the document as a war measure against the Confederacy. Even though the president and the military had the right to seize enemy resources, such as slaves, the Constitution did not protect slaves that were not owned by the enemy. Changing the war aim to freeing the slaves made it nearly impossible for European powers to recognize the Confederacy because countries like England and France had already outlawed slavery. Supporting the Confederacy would have been the same as supporting slavery. Anger at the proclamation was not confined to the South. Sizable numbers of Northern

5 Dudley T. Cornish, *The Sable Arm: Negro Troops in the Union Army, 1861-1865* (New York, 1956), 100-101; Howard C. Westwood, "Lincoln's Position on Black Enlistments," in *Black Troops, White Commanders, and Freedmen During the Civil War*, ed. Howard C. Westwood (Carbondale, 1992), 9.

6 Westwood, "Lincoln's Position on Black Enlistments," 6-7; Leonard, *Men of Color to Arms!*, 6-7.

civilians and soldiers alike were unhappy with the sudden change in direction. Many argued that fighting to preserve the country was one thing, but fighting to free the black man was something altogether different and was not why they had enlisted to fight or had sent their sons off to war.[7]

The Contrabands of War

The Emancipation Proclamation also impacted communities and societal norms. All across the South, slaves slipped away from farms and plantations in a bid for freedom. As Union troops filtered into Tennessee communities, thousands of black men, women, and children flocked into their lines. During the four years of the Civil War, more than 500,000 of the three-and-a-half million slaves living in the Confederacy gained their freedom in this manner. The flood of runaways was so acute that Gen. Grant created a policy addressing freed blacks who sought such aid and protection. Although he felt compassion for the enslaved blacks, he also considered former slaves as part of the process of military occupation. Essentially, Grant believed that wherever Union armies marched, slavery disintegrated.[8]

In November 1862, Grant appointed John Eaton, Jr., a chaplain in the 27th Ohio Infantry, to take charge of the thousands of Tennessee "contrabands," a term used to describe a new status for former slaves who affiliated with their Northern liberators. As part of his appointment, Eaton was bestowed with the title General Superintendent of Freedmen for the Department of the Tennessee, an area that included West Tennessee, eastern Arkansas, northwestern Mississippi, and northern Louisiana.[9]

Eaton wasted little time establishing a contraband camp at Grand Junction, the first of its kind in Tennessee. Inside the camp, Eaton introduced sanitation policies, fed and clothed thousands of displaced men, women, and children, provided food and medical care, and helped place able-bodied men

---

7 McPherson, *Ordeal by Fire*, 298; Gallagher, *The Union War*, 80.

8 "No More Auction Block for Me," in James M. McPherson *Marching Toward Freedom: The Negro in the Civil War, 1861-1865* (New York, 1965), 33. Marse Bob is a nickname for "Master Bob." The term "Master" is a reference to slave master, or rather, the owner of the slave(s); Hess, *The Civil War in the West*, 73.

9 McPherson, *The Negro's Civil War*, 122; Benjamin Quarles, *The Negro in the Civil War* (Boston, 1953), 97.

to work on government projects. Grant wrote to his sister about the plight of the former slaves: "I don't know what is to become of these poor people in the end, but its weakening the enemy to take them from them."[10]

Two years later in June 1864, Robert W. Barnard, colonel of the 101st USCT regiment in Tennessee, was assigned to assist Chaplain Eaton as administrator of the contraband camps at Fort Donelson and Hendersonville, Tennessee. Fully committed to seeing emancipation realized in Tennessee, Barnard provided himself with the grand title Superintendent of Freedmen for the Department of the Cumberland. Contraband camps sprang up mainly in Middle and West Tennessee during the war. There is evidence they existed in Chattanooga and in Knoxville late in the conflict, but East Tennessee had a much smaller slave population than did the rest of the state.[11]

Eaton and Barnard strived to make their contraband camps as self-sufficient as possible. For example, Eaton secured equipment, such as spinning wheels and looms for women to weave their own clothing. One such camp located in Clarksville, Tennessee, even produced shoes. During the winter of 1862-63, Eaton put thousands of recently liberated Tennessee blacks to work on projects that helped further military goals. His efforts in establishing contraband camps led to the organization of work parties that supported Union military forces. Contrabands were frequently assigned such tasks as picking cotton on abandoned plantations, and, as the War Department suggested to Grant, put to work in the U. S. Quartermaster's Department as teamsters, cooks, laborers for field fortifications, roads, and railroads.[12]

In Nashville from 1862 to 1864, there were so many fugitive slaves seeking military protection that they became an annoyance to army officers as well as Governor Johnson. During the first three months of Nashville's

10 Cheri LaFlamme Szcodronski, "From Contraband to Freedmen: General Grant, Chaplain Eaton, and Grand Junction, Tennessee," in *Tennessee Historical Quarterly* 72, No. 2 (Summer 2013): 106-27; McPherson, *The Negro's Civil War*, 122-124; Grant to Sister, August 19, 1862, in *The Papers of Ulysses S. Grant*, 28 Volumes, vol. 5, ed. John Y. Simon (Carbondale, 1967), 311.

11 Cimprich, *Slavery's End in Tennessee*, 51-52; Bobby L. Lovett, "Contraband Camps (1864-1866)," in *The Tennessee Encyclopedia of History and Culture*, ed. Carroll Van West (Nashville, 1998), 203-04.

12 Quarles, *The Negro in the Civil War*, 46, 97; *Cincinnati Gazette*, March 24, 1862.

occupation in 1862, for example, the problem forced Gen. Buell to issue orders forbidding the admittance of any more "contraband" inside the army's defensive lines.[13]

Larger population centers that had been occupied by the Federal army, such as Nashville and later Memphis, offered contrabands their greatest chance for safety and employment. Refugee camps appeared around every town in which an army made camp. Contraband families usually moved into abandoned homes and outbuildings, or, though rarely available to them and only when they could afford it, rented rooms. In Memphis, Maj. Gen. Stephen Hurlbut reported that 2,000 refugees were "not supported by the government, were crowded into all vacant sheds and houses, living by begging or vice. I see nothing before them," he added, "but disease and death."[14]

A majority of Union officers did not agree with Johnson's war aim of following President Lincoln's call for abolition in Tennessee. At times, even Johnson did not fully agree with Lincoln's policy of emancipation. During the summer of 1862, the Federal government issued orders prohibiting the return of runaway slaves to their masters, a common occurrence in Nashville. For example, Maj. Gen. Lovell Harrison Rousseau, an opponent of Lincoln's emancipation policies, was just one of many of Lincoln's generals who thoroughly disliked the idea of emancipation. Rousseau reported, "negroes leave their homes and stroll over the country uncontrolled. Hundreds of them are now supported by the government who neither work or are able to work."[15]

After Lincoln issued the Emancipation Proclamation on New Year's Day 1863, Johnson strove to exempt Tennessee, though he did support the proclamation as a war aim through his faithful support of the president. Even after Stanton's War Department sanctioned the enlistment of blacks, there were still many regions in the Union-occupied South that detested the enlistment of blacks. In truth, a majority of Union officers shared the same opinion as Maj. Gen. William T. Sherman's brother, Senator John Sherman,

---

13 *Nashville Dispatch*, June 14, 1862.

14 *OR* 24, pt. 3, 149.

15 Hunt, *The Good Men Who Won the War*, 17.

who argued that black enlistees should be used only as "laborers and railroad guards."[16]

Black Soldiers

Black men in every Northern state had been attempting to offer their services as soldiers since the first day of the war, most for the same practical motives that urged whites to join up. Like most people in the South, many Northerners remembered the horrors wrought by Nat Turner's uprising in 1831 and feared that putting guns in the hands of blacks would trigger the organization of armed mobs and result in murdered whites.[17]

When Lincoln became president on March 4, 1861, he told Congress that he had "no purpose, directly or indirectly, to interfere with slavery in the States where it exists." Initially, Lincoln believed that the North was fighting the war for the restoration of a slaveholding Union, or "the maintenance of the Union," a war aim that the majority of Northerners ranked above the abolition of slavery. Lincoln's methods early in the war to "restore the Union quickly and with minimal disruption to its racial traditions and institutions," or in other words, to fight a "soft war," presented many obstacles to the enlistment of black soldiers.[18]

The Emancipation Proclamation, however, signaled Lincoln's abandonment of his original "soft war" approach when it came to handling the Confederacy. After January 1, 1863, the recruitment of blacks into the military quickly doubled. "The colored population is the great available, and yet unavailable, force for restoring the Union." Lincoln wrote Johnson on March 26, 1863. "The bare sight of fifty thousand armed, and drilled black soldiers on the banks of the Mississippi, would end the rebellion at once," insisted the president. "And who doubts that we can present that sight, if we

16 Mark W. Summers, *The Ordeal of the Reunion: A New History of Reconstruction* (Chapel Hill, 2014), 22; Anne Bailey, "The USCT in the Confederate Heartland, 1864," in *Black Soldiers in Blue: African American Troops in the Civil War Era*, ed. John David Smith (Chapel Hill, 2002), 227.

17 Leonard, *Men of Color to Arms!*, 5.

18 *Saturday Review*, September 14, 1861, in Ephraim D. Adams, *Great Britain and the American Civil War*, 2 vols., I (New York: Green and Company, 1925), 181; Basler, *CWL*, vol. V, 263; Gallagher, *The Union War*, 34; Leonard, 5-6, 8.

Sergeant George Singleton, 17th U.S.C.T., Company C., ca. 1863.
Tennessee State Library & Archives

but take hold in earnest? If you have been thinking of it, please do not dismiss the thought."[19] There is no evidence Johnson replied to the president. Despite Johnson's inaction, Lincoln's letter provides a clear look into what he was thinking at the time regarding the enlistment of black troops.

On September 19, 1863, Maj. George L. Stearns, who Secretary Stanton had designated Tennessee's Commissioner for the Organization of United States Colored Troops, wrote to the war secretary about his concerns regarding their pay. The blacks, Stearns explained, "are anxious to enter the Army as soon as they can be treated fairly and paid promptly, but many have been employed for months without pay, some few I am told for twelve months and they distrust the officers who have thus neglected their duties." This distrust infuriated Governor Johnson who, in an earlier letter to Secretary Stanton, had already made clear his complete dissatisfaction with Maj. Stearns' organization of Nashville's black workers. As Governor Johnson put it,

> Maj Stearns proposes to organize and place them in Camp where they in fact remain idle this will to a very great extent impede the progress of the works & diminish the number of hands employed. I must be frank in stating my opinion that

---

19 Basler, *CWL*, vol. VI, 149-50; Cornish, *The Sable Arm*, 94-95; *OR* 3, Series 3, 103.

Maj Stearns mission with his notions will give us no aid in organization Negro Reg'ts in Tennessee.[20]

Stearns ultimately recruited six regiments of United States Colored Troops in Tennessee. His attempt at providing bounties for black recruits, however, strained his relationship with Secretary Stanton, and his outspoken objections to impressment made him unpopular with his fellow field officers. Because of a general lack of support from his superiors, Stearns resigned from the army on March 30, 1864. A year later, the Boston native returned to his hometown and established a radical Republican newspaper called the *Right Way*.[21]

Black soldiers were rarely if every popular with the white rank and file men. In 1863, for example, a private in the 19th Indiana, part of the famed Iron Brigade, threatened, "if emancipation is to be the policy of this war . . . I do not care how quick the country goes to pot." The majority of white soldiers preferred that black troops serve in support roles such as laborers on railroads and garrisoning rear areas like Johnsonville. However, white soldiers and officers viewed their enlistment pragmatically. They understood that blacks entering the ranks weakened the overall Confederate war effort.[22]

Black troops regularly experienced bias, especially when it came to pay issues. As set forth by Congress, paymasters were required to pay black troops "$10 per month from which $3 was automatically deducted for clothing, resulting in a net pay of $7." In contrast, white soldiers received $13 per month from which no clothing allowance was drawn. Congress eventually granted equal pay in June 1864 and made the action retroactive. Black soldiers finally received the same rations and supplies and comparable

20 Major George L. Stearns to Hon. Edwin M. Stanton, 19 September, 1863, in Ira Berlin, Joseph P. Reidy, and Leslie S. Rowland, eds., *Freedom: A Documentary History of Emancipation 1861-1867, Selected from the Holdings of the National Archives of the United States, Series II, The Black Military Experience* (Cambridge, 1982), 173-74

21 Cornish, *The Sable Arm*, 94-95; Berlin, Reidy, Rowland, *Freedom*, 120, 172; Graf and Haskins, *The Papers of Andrew Johnson*, vol. 6, 354.

22 James M. McPherson, *For Cause and Comrades: Why Men Fought in the Civil War* (New York, 1997), 120; Cornish, *The Sable Arm*, 95.

medical care. Prejudice still prevailed, however, and black soldiers were almost always paid last.[23]

Impressed Laborers

The military government in Tennessee dealt with its labor shortage by seizing and forcibly inducting men into service. The impressment of Tennessee's black men into the Union war effort spanned three significant periods. The first occurred in August 1862, when Gen. Buell requested 1,000 slaves "for hands to work" on a variety of military buildings and at the wharf in Nashville. A second period of impressment occurred in October 1862, when Governor Johnson in Nashville ordered the impressment of local blacks to work on fortifications around the city, which required enormous amounts of labor. Union forces voluntarily took in or impressed against their will hundreds and perhaps thousands of blacks to be used as laborers.[24]

The final period of impressment, and probably the most important as it relates to Johnsonville, occurred in August and September of 1863, when Union authorities impressed 2,500 blacks to help build the Nashville and Northwestern Railroad. This action had been urged earlier that year by Secretary of War Stanton, who had directed Governor Johnson in a letter to "take in charge all abandoned slaves or colored persons who have been held in bondage and provide for their useful employment and subsistence in such a manner as may be best adapted to their necessities and the circumstances."[25]

Using Stanton's directive to his advantage, Johnson began ordering the impressment of free blacks in Nashville. Moreover, he now had a lawful order to use his position to "round-up" free blacks statewide to assist with work on military projects, such as the railroad being built from Nashville

---

23 Elsie Freeman, Wynell Burroughs Schamel, and Jean West "The Fight for Equal Rights: A Recruiting Poster for Black Soldiers in the Civil War." *Social Education* 56, 2 (February 1992): 118-120; Mark M. Boatner III, *The Civil War Dictionary* (New York, 1959), 624.

24 Maslowski, *Treason Must Be Made Odious*, 100; Stephen V. Ash, "Civil War, Black Freedom, and Social Change in the Upper South: Middle Tennessee, 1860-1870," Ph.D. Dissertation, University of Tennessee at Knoxville, 1983, 335.

25 Stephen V. Ash, "Civil War, Black Freedom, and Social Change in the Upper South: Middle Tennessee, 1860-1870," 335.

Impressed laborers working on the
Nashville and Chattanooga Railroad
near Murfreesboro, Tennessee, ca. 1863.
Library of Congress

west to the Tennessee River. In
the first eighteen months of the
Union occupation of Nashville,
blacks were mistreated and
impressed into labor details,
where they were provided food,
clothing, and housing in
exchange for back-breaking labor.[26]

Blacks impressed into working on Union war projects were rarely paid.
When laborers complained to white officers about not receiving pay, they
were often verbally and physically beaten, abused, and deprived of food.
This treatment led to high levels of desertion, especially among those along
the Nashville and Northwestern Railroad. From August 1863 to September
1864, 7,300 impressed black laborers worked on the Nashville and
Northwestern Railroad.[27]

In August 1863, the *Nashville Daily Press* advertised for loyal slave
owners to "join the labor force," and suggested that the longer they held out,
the less likely it was they would get paid. Black railroad workers forcibly
agreed to be paid ten dollars a month. An example of how impressed laborers
were paid, or supposed to be paid, was illustrated by James E. Yeatman in
1864. Yeatman, a representative of the Western Sanitary Commission who
visited Eaton's Department of Tennessee in Memphis, described a particular
discriminatory act regarding pay for blacks:

> I saw a number of colored men pressed into service (not military), to labor at a rate
> of $10 a month. Besides the fact that men are thus pressed into service, thousands

26 John Cimprich, *Slavery's End in Tennessee, 1861-1865* (Tuscaloosa, 1985), 46.

27 Bobby Lovett, "The Negro in Tennessee, 1861-1866: A Socio-Military History of the
Civil War Era," Ph.D. Dissertation, The University of Arkansas, 1978, 33-34;
Correspondence of General Alvan Gillem, Adjutant General, Department of the
Cumberland, *Telegraph Book*, Vol. 40 and *Letter Book*, Vol. 41, RG 21, microfilm, TSLA.

have been employed for weeks and months who have never received anything but promises to pay, thus he was promised freedom, but how is it with him? He is seized in the street and ordered to go and help unload a steamboat, for which he will be paid, or sent to work in the trenches, or to labor for some Quartermaster, or to chop wood for the Government. He labors for months, and at last is only paid with promises. Under such treatment he feels that he has exchanged one master for many masters.[28]

Johnson's endorsement of using blacks to build the Nashville and Northwestern Railroad created an immediate outcry from abolitionists. His plan, they argued, demonstrated that under his military governorship, which had been created by President Lincoln, the Army endorsed the use of free blacks for labor purposes. Imposing slave labor upon free civilians, they continued, was no different than re-enslaving them.[29]

Union officers routinely ordered infantry and cavalry detachments to visit predominantly black communities and force free men into service against their will. In 1863, for example, Union cavalry rounded up former slaves in Ashland City, Tennessee, and made them walk more than twenty miles to Nashville, where they were organized into labor detachments to work on the Nashville and Northwestern Railroad. The majority of black men used as laborers to build the line were from Middle Tennessee and southern Kentucky counties between the ages of 12 and 66.[30]

Some blacks, like Nathan Anderson, Jr., a blacksmith from Centerville, Tennessee, were impressed strictly for their skills. Others, such as Benjamin Pitts, eventually found their way into the military ranks of the USCT. Pitts mustered into the 40th USCT, one of the newly organized colored regiments that labored on and guarded the Nashville and Northwestern Railroad. Black men were better off in a uniform than in shackles, but their primary role

---

28 *Nashville Daily Press*, August 25, 1863; Maslowski, *Treason Must Be Made Odious*, 100; James E. Yeatman, "A Report on the Condition of the Freedmen of the Mississippi (St. Louis, 1864)," in *The Negro's Civil War: How American Negroes Felt and Acted During the War for the Union*, ed. James M. McPherson (New York, 1965), 123-25.

29 Ibid; *OR* 5, Series 3, 944-49.

30 *Telegraph book*, Adjutant General Alvan Gillem to Captain M.S. Moore, September 28, 1863, Nashville, Tennessee, in the correspondence of Alvan Gillem, RG 21, TSLA, Nashville, TN; Roster of Negroes impressed for work on the Northwestern Railroad, 1863, USCT Archives, TSLA, Nashville, TN.

remained relieving white soldiers from menial and laborious duties so they could serve at the front in combat roles.

Prior to becoming soldiers, a majority of the men who later enlisted in the 12th USCT had been impressed as contraband laborers in August and September 1862 and forced to build Nashville's Fort Negley and other surrounding fortifications. Many of these men remained in government service as impressed laborers until August 12, 1863, at which time they enlisted as volunteers in the United States Army at Nashville. After their recruitment, blacks from the 12th, 13th, 40th, 100th, and 101st USCT regiments were used as military labor details, and, in some instances, were ordered to work side-by-side with impressed civilian laborers along the Nashville and Northwestern line.[31]

While skilled carpenters built trestles over rivers or soggy terrain, black laborers raised the railroad bed, set railroad ties, and pounded rail spikes for 50 miles across often nearly impassable terrain and completed the line in just one year. The contributions of African Americans had an enormous impact on the history of Johnsonville and the completion of the Nashville and Northwestern Railroad.

31 *OR* 77, Supplement, Records of Events, 482-83.

CHAPTER 5

Living and Working in Johnsonville

Constructing the Supply Depot

CIVILIAN laborers from Nashville and surrounding communities arrived at the depot on September 1, 1863. Soldiers toiled alongside the civilians constructing buildings, loading platforms, corrals, and every other structure necessary for operating a supply depot. Except for impressed black laborers, most of the civilian workers hailed from the surrounding region and sympathized with the Confederacy. Many had relatives fighting for the South.[1]

As more civilians and soldiers arrived at the Tennessee River depot, they were put to work using axes and cross-cut saws to open a ninety-acre patch of forest in a circular pattern around Lucas Landing. Once the trees were chopped down and their limbs removed, buck sawyers cut them into logs. Soldiers used the logs to build administration buildings, barracks, and camp shelters in the bottomland south of Trace Creek about three-quarters of a mile from the Tennessee River.[2]

The local geography made it necessary to construct the depot's buildings at river level to allow trains to enter and load at normal elevation. This, however, made them vulnerable to flooding, and the Tennessee River

1 Garrett, *The History of Humphreys County, Tennessee*, 49-50, 53-56, 60.

2 Atwood, October 19, 1864. Buck sawyers were loggers responsible for cutting felled trees into logs to be purposed into lumber. During the Civil War, many of these men had extensive tree cutting experience and were used in army pioneer companies.

Johnsonville, Tennessee, 1864. This rare photo shows supply depot buildings, service road, and a stack of railroad ties and rails. *Library of Congress*

was more than happy to expose that vulnerability. Heavy rains and unpredictable flooding occasionally raised the water level of the river until it covered the inside of the depot, which in turn spawned hordes of mosquitoes (even more than usual) during the warmer months. When the army arrived and removed trees, advanced erosion posed a problem inside the ninety-acre depot.

Johnsonville's swampy terrain created problems for wagons, cannons, limbers and caissons, as well as horses, mules, and the men themselves. Mud posed constant challenges. Two major corrals filled with livestock and horse dung generated clouds of flies, which, combined with smoke from cook fires and steam engines, created an unappealing atmosphere.

A slim handful of individuals, including a newspaper reporter, a young corporal, and an assistant inspector general for the Army, left three firsthand accounts of what Johnsonville and the surrounding area looked like in the spring and fall of 1864 and midwinter 1865, each from a different perspective. The first, a newspaperman writing for the *Nashville Dispatch*, visited the hilly and forested region in May of 1864 and described the view across the Tennessee River from the supply depot. "On the opposite side is a dense forest, extending as far as the eye can reach; the water is smooth as glass, and all nature is hushed," he waxed rather poetically. "At this point, the river is 903 feet wide at low-water mark, and there is at least four feet of water at all seasons of the year."[3]

Five months later in October 1864, Cpl. Lorenzo D. Atwood, of the 43rd Wisconsin provided a fuller description of the area surrounding the depot from inside the facility. Fortunately, it included some of its defenses. "The country as a whole," he began,

> is far as the eye can reach from the eminence on which we are stationed is an unbroken forest with the exception of some 100 acres around Johnsonville which is partially cleared through, the most of it is just as it was slashed, the timber is very thick and heavy. Many trees being from 4 to 6 feet through, this timber has been fallen every which way to form a barrier against the Rebel Cavelry.[4]

Finally, Lt. Col. William Sinclair, an assistant inspector general for the Union army, examined the Federal base in the last January of the war. "Johnsonville," he began, "is located on the right bank of the Tennessee River. There is a range of hills coming down to within 100 yards of the river bank, the railroad running some distance along the base of these hills before reaching the river." Sinclair continued:

> The country north of the railroad, in the direction of Reynoldsburg, is flat, the timber has been cut off hills and flats for more than a mile out from the depot on the river bank. The river at this point is about 400 yards wide, and the course straight. The ground on the left bank of the river is flat and heavily wooded, no timber having been cut down on that bank.[5]

These rare glimpses into the interior of Johnsonville and the terrain surrounding it paint the challenges Union forces wrestled in overcoming or used to their advantage. It was not the most desirable post.

Governor Johnson oversaw the completion of the Nashville and Northwestern Railroad and supply depot. The Quartermaster's Department,

---

3 *Nashville Dispatch*, May 21, 1864.

4 Atwood, October 19, 1864.

5 *OR* 39, pt. 1, 861.

U.S. Quartermaster General
Montgomery C. Meigs, 1864.
Library of Congress

however, operated under the command of Quartermaster General Montgomery C. Meigs, an 1836 graduate of West Point, staunch Unionist, and a major general. Meigs carried the enormous responsibility of overseeing all Union supply operations, including those conducted at Johnsonville.

The chief quartermaster assigned to oversee the massive Nashville Depot was Col. James Lowry Donaldson, a personal friend and West Point classmate of Meigs. The Nashville Depot became Johnsonville's primary administrative base and employed more than 3,000 men who worked day and night receiving supplies from trains and riverboats. Every shipment received and distributed at Nashville occurred under Donaldson's careful oversight. In September 1864, Donaldson received a promotion to brevet brigadier general and before the end of the war, to brevet major general. He was one of only a thin handful of quartermaster officers to achieve such a rank during the Civil War.[6]

Donaldson arranged for a variety of assistant quartermasters to move west to the Tennessee River and run operations at Johnsonville. The first assistant quartermaster so assigned was Capt. Charles A. Reynolds in May 1864. Serving under him were acting assistant quartermasters Henry Howland, Joseph D. Stubbs, and James E. Montandon. In August, Reynolds received a reassignment to a different post in Alabama and Capt. Henry Howland was elevated to replace him. That fall, the escalation of Federal

---

6 "General Montgomery Cunningham Meigs," *Scientific American*, January 30, 1892, 71; David W. Miller, *Second Only to Grant: Quartermaster General Montgomery C. Meigs* (Shippensburg, 2001), 183-88; Wainwright papers, microfilm accession number 1652, Box 1, Folder 1, TSLA, 5; *New York Tribune*, October 1, 1864, 1; *OR* 5, Series 3, 948.

Colonel James L. Donaldson, Chief
Quartermaster of the Nashville Depot, U.S.
Quartermaster's Department, ca. 1863.
William L. Clements Library, University of Michigan

operations into northern Georgia increased, and the mammoth obligation
of ensuring that the supplies received
at Johnsonville were delivered on
schedule to the front fell upon
Howland's shoulders.[7]

Johnsonville's Photographer

Aside from larger Union-occupied supply operations like those at
Nashville and City Point, Virginia, photographic evidence of outlying
supply depots is almost non-existent. Johnsonville offers the rare exception.

In 1864, photographer Jacob Frank Coonley traveled on the Nashville
and Northwestern Railroad making images of trestles and military buildings
while en route to Johnsonville. It is unknown when Coonley arrived there,
but the images were produced onsite, so he likely created them in
mid-November 1864. It is also uncertain how many photographs he made at
Johnsonville. Five images known to exist are in the Civil War photograph
collection at the Library of Congress. Coonley's images are important
because they capture the raw appearance of the Johnsonville depot and
include one of the only images of United States Colored Troops in the
Western Theater wearing military overcoats.

The man responsible for documenting this tiny slice of the conflict
trained as a sign and ornamental painter in New York before the war. The
economic Panic of 1857 changed his plans, and Coonley turned to a more
lucrative art form of the period: daguerreotype photography. When the Civil
War began, Coonley left New York to work at the gallery of photographer

7 *OR* 30, pt. 3, 310-11.

Captain Henry Howland, Assistant
Quartermaster at Johnsonville,
Tennessee. ca. 1862.
Tennessee State Library & Archives

Matthew Brady in Washington, D.C. Together with his mentor, George Barnard, Coonley traveled with various Union commands photographing camp scenes and field portraits.

In 1864, he contracted with the United States Quartermaster's Department to photograph railroads. "I was informed that a contract had been awarded me by the Quartermaster-General for photographic work along the lines of the railroads in possession of and used by the War Department, extending from Nashville to Chattanooga, Knoxville, Johnsonville, Tenn.; Atlanta, Ga., and Decatur and Huntsville, Ala.," he recorded in his memoirs. Coonley continued:

> On arriving at Nashville the military authorities had a box-car equipped for my work, and this, with an engine, was placed at my disposal with authority to go over the territory. The work had many interruptions, owing to the destruction of bridges or being chased by cavalry or similar charges.[8]

Coonley's panoramic photographs of the interior of the supply depot capture many elements that are important in understanding its clear-cut landscape, pools of standing water and muddy roads, and, importantly, railroad locations, corrals, loading platforms, and buildings.

8 Bob Zeller, *The Blue and Gray in Black and White: A History of Civil War Photography* (Westport, 2005), 159-60; "Pages From A Veteran's Notebook", a short autobiography by J. F. Coonley. *Wilson's Photographic Magazine*, Vol. 44, 105-107; Gary W. Ewer, ed., *The Daguerreotype: An Archive of Source Texts, Graphics, and Ephemera*, http://www.daguerreotypearchive.org.

Photographer Jacob F. Coonley, ca. 1862. *Gift of Larry J. West, National Portrait Gallery, Smithsonian Institution*

Saw Mill No. 1

There is no evidence to indicate which building was constructed first, but the depot's immediate need for board lumber makes it likely it was the large saw mill (Saw Mill No. 1) south of the central rail line about 100 yards southeast of the river. The Quartermaster's Department oversaw the construction and operation of all the saw mills along the Nashville and Northwestern line.[9]

Saw Mill No. 1 was a board-roofed, open-air shed with seven enclosed frame offices and support buildings. It was approximately 150 feet long and 40 feet wide, and its machinery faced southwest. The manner in which it was positioned was important because it provided sawyers with the most daylight possible to operate the mill's machinery. Coonley's photograph of the lower depot's southern view (below) identifies Saw Mill No. 1 in the middle of the depot and what appear to be offices or support buildings on its eastern end. The machinery inside was steam-powered and belt-driven. Enhancing the photograph reveals a worker standing under the roof of the saw mill posed as if to receive a recently sawn board about to come through the saw blade. The steam engines used to turn the saw's belt were powered by burning cut lumber, wood shavings, bark, and sawdust—abundant recyclable on-site fuel sources.

Saw Mill No.1 proved instrumental to Johnsonville's quick success. Sawyers immediately brought down the largest trees in the immediate

9 *OR* 5, Series 3, 948-49.

Johnsonville, Tennessee, 1864. Southern view of depot buildings with Saw Mill No. 1 (middle), south railroad spur, and Fort Johnson (Redoubt No. 1) on the top of the hill in the middle of the image. The Tennessee River was off to the right. *Library of Congress*

vicinity inside the depot to produce massive amounts of milled wood. Between January and November 1864, for example, the mill produced 488,000 board feet of lumber. When the depot officially began operations in May 1864, Johnsonville boasted some 180 wooden buildings including many log huts. The mill produced all of the lumber used to construct every building in the complex, including soldiers barracks and huts, houses and out-buildings for civilian workers and officers, administrative buildings, sheds, warehouses, corrals, blockhouses, cannon and train platforms, and loading ramps. Perhaps most importantly of all, the mill churned out the 107,000 railroad ties (also called crossties) used in laying track for the Nashville and Northwestern Military Railroad.[10]

In addition to Saw Mill No. 1, other mills were established at strategic points along the 78-mile length of the railroad running east to Nashville.

10 Ibid, 947-48.

These mills were numbered sequentially, beginning with Saw Mill No. 1 at Johnsonville and ending at Nashville. The precise locations and number of these mills, however, remain unknown. A former Quartermaster's Department clerk named Eleazer A. Greenleaf mentioned another mill, Saw Mill No. 2, in a letter to Vice President Andrew Johnson in early 1865: "I was a clerk in the Q.M. Dept and stationed at Saw Mill No. 2 about a mile below the Village on the River bank." The only description of the mill, which is vague at best, is found in the *Official Records*, and mentions a "saw mill and a house for carpenters" being destroyed and rebuilt, but thereafter, offers no other mention of either Saw Mill No.1 or Saw Mill No. 2.[11]

Saw Mill No. 1 and many of the abandoned buildings at Johnsonville were still standing after the war when the site was purchased by former Union brevet major Junius M. Palmer, Jr. In 1866, he established the Palmer Lumber Company and immediately won a contract from the federal government to "furnish plank for 8 U.S. National Cemeteries." Despite its auspicious beginning, the Palmer Lumber Company proved short-lived. In February 1867, large numbers of Confederate sympathizers residing in the Trace Creek region found Palmer's business with the United States "exceedingly offensive" and burned Saw Mill No.1, including all of its machinery and many of the other buildings, to the ground.[12]

The Freight Transfer Warehouses

A combination of animals and military supplies of every variety, from mules, hogs, and horses to hardtack, blankets, uniforms, ammunition, whiskey, lumber, barrels of food, and crates of medical supplies, were delivered primarily by steamboats to Johnsonville. Trains steamed into the depot pulling empty box cars and cattle cars and approached the Tennessee River along "an embankment seventeen feet high above the surface of the ground." In order to readily accommodate these long supply trains,

---

11 Eleazer A. Greenleaf to Andrew Johnson, January 13, 1865, in Graf and Haskins, *The Papers of Andrew Johnson*, vol. 7, 400; The mill's description is from an original photograph taken by Jacob Coonley in November 1864; *OR* 5, 947-48; *Nashville Daily Union*, May 18, 1865. The number associated with the saw mill in Nashville is unknown. No numbers associated with any of the mills outside of Johnsonville have been located.

12 *Nashville Daily Press and Times*, February 21, 1867, 2.

Captain Junius M. Palmer, Jr., ca. 1865.
Library of Congress

engineers oversaw the construction of two large freight warehouses and associated platforms—the two largest of the 180 buildings erected at Johnsonville. They were erected along the riverbank on both sides of the center rail line to make the transfer of freight from steamboats to rail cars not only possible, but as smooth and easy as circumstances would allow. Considering the enormous amounts of board lumber needed to build their warehouses, the proximity of Saw Mill No. 1 helped speed the construction. The freight transfer warehouses stored all of the military supplies delivered to Johnsonville by river, and were designed so the arriving steamboats could be unloaded, the cargo stockpiled at the base of the wharf, and then transferred into the awaiting buildings.

The freight transfer warehouse located north of the central railroad bed, called the "lower warehouse" or Warehouse No. 1, was "600 feet long by 30 feet-wide, and hastily knocked up so as to bring it into immediate use." Warehouse No. 1 had a "levee in front graded off to the water's edge with a slope of 9 degrees or about 16 feet rise and 100 feet horizontal."

Two hundred yards south of Saw Mill No. 1 sat the "upper warehouse" or Warehouse No. 2—the largest building ever erected at Johnsonville. This massive second warehouse boasted a double roof and dimensions "600 feet long and 90 feet wide." The floor stood less than three feet above the river's high-water mark, with a levee in front "graded to a slope of 14 degrees designed to lay railroad tracks from low-water mark" to the floor of the warehouse.[13]

13 *OR* 5, Series 3, 944.

Johnsonville, Tennessee, 1864. Freight Transfer Warehouse No. 2. *Library of Congress*

Constructing Johnsonville's wharf required extensive grading with about "30,000 cubic feet of earth that had to be removed." By November 1864, only a portion of it had been paved "in a covering of broken stone." Once steamboats docked there (usually towing barges full of supplies), workers unloaded freight and stockpiled it along the river bank. Once the boats and barges were emptied, the freight was transferred onto waiting wheeled carts on tracks. Workers hoisted the freight up the steep and mainly dirt wharf to the warehouse floors by using a large pulley and a 500-foot cable running through the center of the building below the floors powered by a steam engine. When the carts reached the warehouse floors, workers transferred the freight into boxcars on the opposite side.[14]

"There was 12 steam boats and 3 gunboats at the wharf when I was there besides some 15 flatboats," explained Cpl. Atwood in a letter to his wife that described both warehouses and their contents. The Wisconsin soldier continued:

> The store house is 40 rods long and 100 feet wide with a double roof on one side of the centre track of the Rail road and on the other side 40 rods long by 50 feet wide; these buildings are full of Army supplies and the ground between the wharf and store house is piled six feet deep with sacks of oats and bails of hay. There is five

14 Ibid.

heavy loaded trains run from here to Nashville daily and yet there is a number of boats waiting to unload.[15]

Despite their mammoth size and importance, Johnsonville's freight transfer warehouses lasted only a short time. The Confederate attack on Johnsonville on November 4, 1864, burned Warehouse No. 1 to the ground with its contents. Warehouse No. 2 escaped being burned but could not be fully used again until April 1865. In the early 1870s, Warehouse No. 2 was taken apart and its materials used to reconstruct non-military buildings in the expanding civilian town of Johnsonville.[16]

The Turntable

Trains entering Johnsonville from Nashville rolled on another one-half mile along a single section of track before stopping 500 yards from the Tennessee River. It was there the empty cars were detached and the engine transferred from the main track onto a turntable.

Johnsonville's turntable was a round open-air wooden structure built atop a stone foundation. In the middle, a single section of railroad track called a "bridge," was supported by a pivoting iron post anchored to a stone foundation with wheels on either end. The wheels rolled along curved channeled rails positioned atop the stone wall that allowed the bridge to rotate 180 degrees. After the engine was serviced for any mechanical needs, it was rotated to face in the direction of Nashville. How Johnsonville's turntable was powered is unknown. Almost certainly the bridge was either turned using a steam engine and belt system, or by long poles pressed into iron pockets attached to the bridge and manually rotated.[17]

While this process was underway, a second engine (called a "switch engine" and permanently stationed at the depot) hauled the newly arrived

15 Atwood, October 27, 1864. A rod is a measurement of 5.5 yards or 16.5 feet. The 40 rods that Atwood described equals 220 yards. In other words, the upper freight transfer warehouse at Johnsonville was longer than two football fields.

16 *OR* 5, Series 3, 945-47.

17 "Turntables: A Short History and Theory of Operation," a video presentation by Bob Van Cleef to the North River Railway Club, Coventry, CT. Online source: www.northriverrailway.net.

Civil War railroad turntable with train engine, E. M. Stanton, 1864. *Library of Congress*

empty rail cars onto one of two spur lines, one curving to the north and the other to the south. As the last cars passed a junction at the end of each spur, a switchman transferred the cars onto a straight section of track running parallel to the warehouses on the depot side. The switch engine then backed the empty cars into position in front of the warehouses, where they could be loaded with military supplies that had recently arrived by boat. In front of the track paralleling the warehouses was a second section where extra boxcars could be loaded or unloaded until an engine became available to attach and deliver the loaded cars to another main locomotive ready to return to Nashville. When the cars were loaded, the switch engine pulled them forward along the parallel track until the last car cleared the intersection of the spur track.

Once this was finished, the switchman performed the same routine as before and switched the loaded cars—with the switch locomotive now moving them in reverse—onto the spur track. After the switch process occurred, this switch engine, in reverse, pushed the cars back up the track to the vicinity of the turntable, where, by this time, the primary locomotive had been serviced and turned around facing Nashville. As the cars were being attached to the main engine, the switch engine was being detached from its rear position. Once the head switchman cleared the loaded trains for departure, the fully loaded train exited the depot toward Nashville loaded with everything needed by the troops at the front.

The entire process, from arrival to departure, usually took twelve hours. The sequence of transferring supplies between Nashville and Johnsonville did not follow a set schedule to help prevent Confederate attacks on the valuable trains.[18]

Johnsonville: Complete

On Thursday, May 19, 1864, a large number of influential men, including Governor Johnson, assembled in Nashville at the depot of the Nashville and Northwestern Railroad at "6 o'clock for the purpose of celebrating the opening of that important route to the Tennessee River, a distance of seventy-eight miles." Once congratulations had been passed out, they boarded a special excursion train Johnson had arranged for their journey. "The road is an excellent one, and is well laid, the wheels gliding smoothly over it," extolled a reporter for the *Nashville Diplomat* accompanying the party on the ride to the Tennessee River. "There are numerous bridges of various dimensions," he continued,

> the trestle work of some being from fifty to eighty feet high; the Harpeth River is crossed five times, some of the bridges being very long, and all of them well guarded by troops, some white others black, infantry, cavalry, and artillery, and strong stockades and fortifications, the strongest, neatest, and best, we have ever seen.[19]

Johnson and the other officials hoped the new railroad would improve communications and transportation between the capital and points west. The Nashville and Northwestern Railroad was not only important for military purposes, but also as a means of trans-state commerce for Tennessee's citizens, who had begun lobbying for the railroad as far back as 1852.[20]

"It does great credit to the builders," reported the *Nashville Daily Times and True Union*, that "there is not a better made road in the county due to its remarkable smoothness and evenness of the new-laid portion of the track."

18 Ibid; *OR* 5, Series 3, 945-47, Hess, *The Civil War in the West*, 202-04, 217-20.

19 *Nashville Dispatch*, May 21, 1864.

20 Goodspeed, *History of Tennessee: With Sketches of Gibson, Obion, Weakley, Dyer, and Lake Counties*, 834-35.

The train steamed through Waverly, the seat of Humphreys County, which was described as being "cleaned out and Court House, Church, and nearly all the dwelling houses appropriated by Uncle Sam." Finally, after passing cannon salutes by the 1st Kansas Battery just outside Waverly, the ceremonial train entered the newly finished supply depot at the Tennessee River at noon.

The ceremonial train stopped near the end of the track at the Tennessee River, where the party disembarked, strolled along the riverbank, and talked amongst themselves. The men returned to the rail cars at 1:00 p.m, reported the paper, for

> an excellent cold collation spread in the spacious depot of sandwiches, cobblers, lemonades, cigars, ice-water and other patriotic refreshments, all lavishly distributed through the cars by the managers of the excursion. After full justice having been done to the edibles, wine flowed like water, and inspired all with good natured sentiments which they seemed anxious to proclaim to the assembled guests.[21]

John Smith, Nashville's mayor and one of Johnson's distinguished guests, lifted his glass and proposed a toast, calling upon all attendees "to fill up and drink a bumper to Andrew Johnson, who, amid storm and tempest, secession and disunion, has always been firm and consistent." Loud applause and upturned glasses followed, "after which the governor was called upon for a speech." Johnson delivered a speech to about 100 onlookers including citizens from the small town just outside the military depot, soldiers assigned to the post, and workers at the depot. He lauded his ideas about loyalty to the Union and the effects of emancipation:

> We have had slaves and bondmen among us, to-day the great idea of freedom is abroad, and this struggle which agitates the land is a contest of merit, of human right, and freedom. Let the people see facts as they are and no longer delude themselves with old prejudices. Let the blacks understand that they must assume responsibilities, and take that position which their merits or demerits may assign them. In the words of Mr. Lincoln: Let all have a fair start and an equal share in the race of life. As soon as you can, acknowledge the legality of emancipation. Unless you people show a desire to put down these guerrillas and restore the law no

---

21 *Nashville Dispatch*, May 21, 1864.

General can save you from ruin. Do your part and the soldiers will protect and sustain you.[22]

Johnson probably gave the speech standing on the rear stoop of the caboose. Accounts clearly suggest Johnson was aboard the train where "refreshments were lavishly distributed through the cars by the managers of the excursion." The fact that Mayor Clark suggested a toast to Johnson "at the table" implies that the party ate inside the railcar. Then, once dinner had been served and finished, Governor Johnson likely stepped out onto the caboose platform to address the crowd that had assembled around the excursion train.

A contemporary account by local writer Robert G. Wyatt appeared in the *Nashville Banner* about a colorful story on how the depot may have gained its name. According to Wyatt's account, Governor Johnson "stood on a pile of cross-ties and delivered a flowery dedicatory speech about the new town and depot. Then, following the speech, he dramatically broke a bottle of wine on the railroad track and named the place after himself." If the story is true, the newspapers of the time failed to pick up on it. It seems implausible that the naming of the new military depot and town by the governor himself, after breaking a bottle of wine over iron rails, would have slipped through the accounts of two onsite reporters. In all likelihood the story was probably passed down through the years as oral history and embellished a bit with each telling.[23]

It is unknown whether the name Johnsonville was first used on May 19, 1864, but the name spread after the train excursion and was being printed in newspapers and on military correspondence. On a piece of military correspondence dated July 20, 1864, for example, Assistant Quartermaster William A. Wainwright, who was assigned to the Nashville Depot, signed

---

22 *Nashville Dispatch*, May 21, 1864. A bumper is when a group of people hold their drinking glasses above their heads (usually filled with an alcoholic beverage), and after a toast is presented, the group, together at the same time, "bump" the glasses together for the purpose of creating a high-pitch, clanging noise. After the bumper, the drinks are then consumed.

23 Robert G. Wyatt, "Johnsonville Times: Johnsonville, Held by Federals, Destroyed in Battle," in *The Nashville Banner* (March, 1958), 1. The account cannot be verified and Wyatt's piece cites no primary source about the event.

equipment vouchers with the words, "purchased for immediate use at the Port of Johnsonville, Tenn."[24]

"On the 9th of May this Road [Nashville and Northwestern Railroad] was turned over to the Military for all Military and Governmental purposes," Johnson wrote in a letter to Secretary Stanton early that August. "A population has accumulated of over six thousand at Johnsonville since the connection was made with the Tennessee River. The importance of the North Western Rail Road is now being seen and felt and our Army could not be sustained without it."[25]

Johnson, clearly pleased that the supply depot at Lucas Landing was now active and serving the Union cause as he had anticipated it would, boasted about is capabilities:

> We are loading seven or eight boats and as many Barges for your place. Six hundred tons of R Road iron leave here tonight. From two to five Boats arrive daily now with large quantities of Commissary stores, Five thousand and twenty one packages this A.M. in from steamers. This is a mere beginning of what the construction of this road will open up to the Gov't and the Country, demonstrating the wisdom and propriety of improvement at this time.[26]

Despite the successful launch of the supply depot, the security concerns that plagued the building process also hampered the Nashville and Northwestern Railroad. The opening of the new railroad was not enough to guarantee smooth transportation. On August 16, Col. Donaldson, chief

---

24 Capt. William A. Wainwright to J.W. Wilson and Co., July 23, 1864, Nashville, Tennessee, in *The Papers of William Alonzo Wainwright, 1832-1904*, United States Assistant Quartermaster Records 1861-1870, Nashville, TN, Roll #36, ac. # 1652, TSLA, 5.

25 Graf and Haskins, *The Papers of Andrew Johnson*, vol. 7, 104-05. Graf and Haskins points out that th figure of 6,000 "appears to be an exaggeration." In Goodspeed's *History of Tennessee: From Earliest Time to the Present: Together with an Historical and Biographical Sketch of Montgomery, Robertson, Humphreys, Stewart, Dickson, Cheatham, and Houston Counties Humphreys County*, it was mentioned that at the time of Johnsonville's supply depot and the Nashville and Northwestern Railroad in May 1864, the town "had upward of 1,000 population, not including the soldiers." In all, the town's population, combined with the military personnel at Johnsonville, equaled around 3,500 individuals. Only after the arrival of Federal reinforcements on November 5, 1864, would Johnsonville experience its largest population during the Civil War, as well as for the remainder of its existence.

26 Johnson to Stanton, August 19, 1864, in *The Papers of Andrew Johnson*, vol. 7, 104-05.

quartermaster of the Nashville Depot, wrote Maj. Gen. Rousseau, "We have a large number of horses and cattle now at Johnsonville,"

> and it is exceedingly important that they should be brought here [Nashville]. Unless the Northwestern railroad is properly guarded we shall have terrible disaster and stoppage of supplies. A regiment of troops must at once be placed at important points on the road, and men sent to Johnsonville to drive cattle here. [27]

Union officials turned to the 12th, 13th, 40th, 100th, and 101st USCT regiments to do the job. Donaldson's plea for help also eventually gained the use of Cpl. Atwood's 43rd Wisconsin, which was assigned to garrison Johnsonville. The Badgers arrived at their new post in the middle of October 1864. According to Cpl. Atwood,

> Arrived here at 10 in the evening were marched into a large building built for a machine shop [the Upper Freight Transfer Warehouse] on the banks of the Tenn. river, we moved out early in the morning to where we are now, we have got our tents up and our dinners eaten, some of the men are out on picket duty on the rail road some are cleaning up the camp ground some are diging a trench for a privy. I have just been out with a squad of men after water about 1 ½ miles into the woods along the banks of the Tenn. [28]

An "Embryo City"

With the supply depot now in operation, some of the more prominent civilians living in the town of Johnsonville saw it and the railroad that served it as a viable means to a profitable end. In the late summer of 1864, W. H. Blankenship, H. H. Garner, Elijah G. Hurst, Thomas H. Mabry, John T. Street, and William W. Swain petitioned Governor Johnson to seek his help in getting their cotton, which was being grown in the fertile river bottom soil near where Trace Creek intersected with the Tennessee River, to Northern markets. On September 23, Hurst accompanied the petition in its journey to Johnson in Nashville with a formal letter. "The People of these Sections cannot dispose of their little crops of cotton," it began, "as a very large

---

27 *OR* 39, pt. 1, 464-65.

28 Ibid, 465; Atwood, October 16, 1864.

Johnsonville, Tennessee, 1864. Terminus of the Nashville and Northwestern Railroad, a loading platform, and the town of Johnsonville (in the distance). *Library of Congress*

Majority of them raise a less amt. than will Justify them in taking the rounds required to get their Small lots to Market." The letter continued:

> That there are many loyal Citizens and Union Soldiers families in these Sections nearly entirely destitute of Supplies and whose Sole dependence is the proceeds of their little crops of cotton. The Premises Considered we Respectfully ask that you give your influence to the proper authorities for a Supply Post at Johnsonville Tenn.

For the benefit of the Loyal People of those counties in that Portion of the State, as also for the benefit of Government in obtaining the cotton raised in this section. And your Petitioners as in duty bound will ever Pray & c.[29]

One description of the town of Johnsonville dates to May 1865. The author, identified only as "A Looker On," obviously did not intend to reveal his official identity. From this account, "A Looker On," reported: "I came to this embryo city in company with several gentlemen to attend the sale of lots. We found the ravages of war had made sad havoc in the sole row of houses. All the buildings of the town were burned except one, numbering more than one hundred." As the only account known to provide an actual number of buildings in the town of Johnsonville, this helps establish a more realistic accounting of the approximately 180 buildings constructed, including those at the military depot. Additionally, Cpl. Atwood wrote that Johnsonville was "A little one horse town in the woods about 6, months old."[30]

Bucked and Gagged: "The Johnsonville Controversy"

The increasing supply requests in early 1864 from Maj. Gen. William T. Sherman's armies in North Georgia put a heavy demand on Quartermaster's Department employees. For workers assigned to outlying supply posts like Johnsonville, the daily demand of administering these supply shipments was simply too much and before long weeks of backlogged requisitions stacked up. The workers were tired and overworked, and administrative chaos, especially with payroll, helped throw sand into the gears of the Quartermaster's Department.

The civilian workers hired by the U.S. Army to build the Nashville and Northwestern Railroad and Johnsonville were paid by the Quartermaster's Department in Nashville. After the completion of the supply depot in May 1864, the civilian employees received their pay directly from the Nashville Depot. This was but another reason to prevent the trains from being attacked: Some of them were extremely valuable even empty. "I have been at Nashville two days of the past week," recalled Lt. Walter Howland at

29 Petition from Elijah C. Hurst and Others, Johnsonville, TN, September 23, 1864, in *The Papers of Andrew Johnson*, vol. 7, 185.

30 *Nashville Daily Union*, May 18, 1865; Atwood, November 17, 1864.

Johnsonville, "leaving on Thursday, and returning Saturday bringing out with me some over twenty thousand dollars for the payment of employees here."[31]

Soldiers in the field were supposed to receive their pay every two months, but in many cases were fortunate if they received their pay at four-month intervals. In some instances soldiers went "six and eight months without pay," recalled one of them. During the summer of 1864, when Sherman was driving his armies deep into Georgia against Gen. Joseph E. Johnston's Confederate command, the demands for more of everything flooded the Quartermaster's Department and affected every civilian worker in Nashville. It didn't take long for their pay to also get delayed, sometimes months at a time.[32]

Corporal Atwood complained about the delay of military payroll at Johnsonville. "We muster for pay today," he wrote his wife, "and shall get two months pay within a few weeks, to muster for pay is to sign the pay roll. As soon as we get it 24 dollars will be sent from Maddision to you." When their pay finally arrived, many of Johnsonville's garrison troops had debts to settle. "Some of the boys in our company have spent all of their Town bounty that they received in advance (60) dollars and their 33 1/3 Government bounty," explained the Wisconsin corporal, "and are living on borrowed money, and as a natural consequence some of them are in the Hospital and the rest are puney and sickly. I started from Camp Washburn with 6.25 and have 4.75 now," he continued. "I have paid for mending my boot and washing cloths 40cts out of that."[33]

At times, the paymaster withheld wages from Irish civilians and black laborers employed at the depot. John O'Flanagan, one of the civilian

31 Walter Howland to Mother, September 23, 1864, Walter Howland Papers, Rubenstein Rare Book and Manuscript Library, Duke University, North Carolina (hereafter cited as Walter Howland or his brother, Henry Howland). It is unknown in what capacity Walter Howland served while stationed at Johnsonville during the fall months of 1864. Walter was the brother of Johnsonville's chief assistant quartermaster, Henry Howland. It is possible that he served as the depot's paymaster, considering that he wrote a letter to his mother about "bringing out with me some over twenty thousand dollars for the payment of employees here."

32 Fred Albert Shannon, *The Organization and Administration of the Union Army 1861-1865*, 2 vols. (Cleveland, 1928), 21-33, 55-61.

33 Atwood, October 31, 1864.

employees working in the Quartermaster's Department, moved to Tennessee to work at the Johnsonville depot. In July 1864, O'Flanagan questioned the truthfulness of newspaper advertisements submitted by the Quartermaster's Department in Massachusetts, New York, Pennsylvania, Wisconsin and elsewhere that had convinced him to take the job. One such advertisement, he recalled, claimed that "civilian employees were wanted for the department principally at Nashville, Chattanooga, and Johnsonville," and would be supplied transportation to their destinations, provided free rations, and would be paid good wages for work as wheelwrights, carpenters, teamsters, and laborers. O'Flanagan was enraged that he and other Irishmen had come all the way to Tennessee and had yet to be paid for work performed there.[34]

On August 3, 1864, O'Flanagan penned an angry letter to the editor of the *Nashville Daily Press* addressing the issue and a number of other ways he and his comrades were being mistreated by Quartermaster officers at Johnsonville. "Quartermaster Stubbs sent for me and a man named McCormick," he began, "when he in the most czar-like manner told us that after coming a thousand miles to work here, and after having worked nearly two months—that we 'must leave here' without time or voucher, for our work, or a cent in our pockets through a hostile country." The irate Irishman pressed on with his complaint:

> We have "left" Johnsonville, and after now having been in Nashville and, under no inconsiderable expense, we have no better prospects of being paid than at the date of the czar-like order to 'leave,' with the prospect of being forced, as those now with us, and others, have been forced to pay from 10 to 20 per cent of our wages *into the hands of speculators* to cash our vouchers. I can never believe that our Government intends such a wholesale raid as this upon our labors for the benefit of capitalists. To use a common and course expression 'there is a screw loose somewhere,' and a heavy one.[35]

It is likely that O'Flanagan and the other Irishmen were the victims of cheaper available labor. For instance, Col. James L. Donaldson, who oversaw the Nashville Depot, had instructed his officers to retain

---

34 *Nashville Dispatch*, January 31, August 23, 1864, 2; Durham, *Reluctant Partners*, 143-44.

35 *Nashville Daily Press*, August 3, 1864, 1.

Sketch of U.S. Sailor being "Bucked and Gagged," ca. 1850. *Library of Congress*

BUCKED AND GAGED.
TRICED UP.

contrabands, soldiers, and refugees in preference to Northern laborers (i.e., Irishmen) who were "the most costly of all and general reductions could better take care of itself." O'Flanagan's letter created a stir in the *Nashville Daily Press*, and for two weeks during that hot and consequential August the public debate came to be called "The Johnsonville Controversy."[36]

The "The Johnsonville Controversy" involved more than just pay for O'Flanagan and the Irish employees at the supply depot, for it soon escalated into a heated issue over race and the violation of "white" civil rights. The issue of "white" civil rights was apparent in O'Flanagan's original letter when he attested to an incident during his employment regarding the "arbitrary and barbarous treatment of some of us, in Johnsonville—white, loyal employees, from the North, bucked and gagged by negroes for absolutely nothing." In many cases, such as the one O' Flanagan described at Johnsonville, the accused was left to suffer this way for hours until freed.[37]

36 *OR* 52, pt.1, 684.

37 Ibid; In the 1860's, bucked and gagged was a form of military punishment. Bucked was when an individual was forced to sit on the ground bent forward with his hands bound together at his shins, his feet tied together at the ankles, and a long stick shoved over the arms and under the knees. Gagged involved having either a stick or rag placed in your mouth and tied behind your head. For more information on this and other Civil War punishments, see www.esquire.com/news-politics/news/a25915/punishment-and-torture-in-the-civil-war-111413/.

The "bucked and gagged" accusation by O' Flanagan spawned an outcry from Johnsonville's assistant quartermasters, and Governor Johnson ordered Col. Donaldson to investigate the incident. Eventually, a captain named Joseph D. Stubbs, Johnsonville's acting assistant quartermaster and the officer accused by O' Flanagan of having overseen the barbarous act, submitted an official response to the accusation to his superior, Capt. Charles A. Reynolds. "Since I have been here at this depot, there has been no employee bucked or gagged," he asserted. "The Provost Marshall at this place says that no employee has been bucked or gagged."[38]

Despite Stubbs' adamant statement refuting the accusation, Donaldson remained unconvinced and was troubled by discrepancies between Assistant Quartermaster Stubbs' official report and the sworn testimony of "Northern employees." Donaldson's unease with Capt. Stubbs' statement was the result of testimonies from various quartermaster employees at Johnsonville. One, a teamster named James Ford, swore under oath that he had, in fact, been bucked and gagged just as O' Flanagan had claimed. "On Sunday, July 24th, 1864, I was ordered to report on the levee to work at laboring work," testified Ford,

> before reporting, *the negro guards*, 13th U.S.C.I. put us in line, *in our own camp*, preparatory to working, when I asked 'how is it about green backs to-day,' as I had not had any money from the time I commenced the first day of May previous, when I was immediately ordered by an officer of said 13th U.S.C.I. to be *'bucked and gagged for five hours.'* I was immediately 'bucked and gagged' by the said negroes, and so held until released by the Brigade Wagon Master. All the above in Johnsonville, Tenn., whilst in government employ, as a teamster, under Captain J.D. Stubbs.[39] [Emphasis in the original]

George Sherwood, a 17-year-old Pennsylvanian employed at Johnsonville, provided additional testimony. According to Sherwood, an employee with the last name of King had been left "lying in the road in front of the guard house bucked and gagged and crying." On September 16, 1864, O' Flanagan submitted another letter, this time stating:

---

38 *Nashville Daily Press*, August 10, 1864, 1.

39 Ibid.

Negro soldiers humiliated and abused both white soldiers and civilians and that before the law creating Negro regiments could be passed, it was found necessary to plainly and explicitly provide that no negro could ever assume Command over white men, yet at Johnsonville, by placing Negroes in command of the guardhouse, a black sergeant daily commands alike all the white citizens and white soldiers temporarily immured for that most microscopic of peccadilloes, 'a military offence.'[40]

O'Flanagan's persistence and the various testimonies about "The Johnsonville Controversy" made an impression on Governor Johnson, but he concluded that, regardless of the accusations by O' Flanagan and other laborers at Johnsonville, he still supported the officers of the Quarter-master's Department. Johnson also stated that the "Controversy" had stained the reputation of the department in general, and especially Donaldson's reputation and leadership abilities in particular.

Eventually, after weeks of military inquiries into the "bucking and gagging" of white workers, and as a result of the testimony against him, a military tribunal court-martialed Capt. Stubbs. O' Flanagan responded, "I wish to know what earthly harm it can do the Government agents if they are only the victims of erroneous ideas, and if their intentions are right, to let their acts see the light so we can canvas them amongst us?"[41]

40 Graf and Haskins, *The Papers of Andrew Johnson*, vol. 7, 169-70.

41 William Given, Argument made by Col. William Given, 102nd O.V. in the Case of Capt. J. D. Stubbs, A.Q.M. before Court Martial in Nashville, Tennessee in *William Given Press Book and Job Office*, TSLA, Nashville, TN, 1864.

CHAPTER 6

Protecting Johnsonville:
Union Defense of the Supply Depot

DURING the height of Johnsonville's operation as a supply depot from May to November 1864, a garrison of both white and United States Colored Troops protected the logistics center. Johnsonville's garrison included artillerists, infantrymen (both foot and mounted), cavalrymen, and armed civilian laborers from the Quarter-master's Department in Nashville. The unique supply depot and railroad terminus also had two commanders, an army officer and a naval officer.[1]

Johnsonville's Commanders

Col. Charles R. Thompson of the 12th USCT commanded the U.S. Army forces, or "the troops," as one 1865 report put it, while Acting Volunteer Lt. Edward M. King served as the ranking officer for "the gun-boats." As correspondence between Thompson and King demonstrates, neither officer liked the other, and the records remain silent as to whether one served under the overall command of the other. Each made important command decisions that impacted operations at Johnsonville, and both

---

1 *OR Supplement*, vol. 77, 473, 477; *OR* 52, pt. 1, 655-59.

Colonel Charles R. Thompson,
Commander of the 12th U.S.C.T
Regiment, ca. 1862.
Dayton Metro Library, Dayton, Ohio

regularly communicated directly with the commander of the Department of the Cumberland, Maj. Gen. George H. Thomas in Nashville.[2]

Charles R. Thompson was born in 1840 in Bath, Maine, and was a resident of St. Louis, Missouri, by the age of nineteen. He was engaged in the mercantile trade there when the Civil War broke out in 1861. Thompson enlisted as a private in the Engineer Regiment of the West, Missouri Volunteers, and served under Brig. Gen. John C. Fremont. In March 1862, Thompson was promoted to 1st lieutenant and participated in the Battle of New Madrid, Missouri, and the Siege of Island No. 10, where, according to one writer, he assisted in building "the famous canal which led to the capture of the entire rebel force."[3]

That June, Thompson received an appointment as Post Quartermaster at Hamburg, Tennessee, and later as Ordnance Officer in the Army of the Mississippi under Maj. Gen. William S. Rosecrans. He was a young man on the rise, and Thompson's fellow officers in the Department of the Cumberland held him in high esteem. At the October 3-4, 1862, Battle of Corinth, Mississippi, Thompson served as Rosecrans' aide-de-camp and

---

2 *Official Records of the Union and Confederate Navies in the War of the Rebellion*, 30 Vols. (Government Printing Office, Washington, D.C., 1894-1927), vol. 26, Series I, 615, hereafter cited as *ORN*. All references are to Series 1 unless otherwise noted; *OR* 39, pt. 1, 861.

3 John Fitch, *Annals of the Army of the Cumberland: Comprising Biographies, Descriptions of Departments, Accounts of Expeditions, Skirmishes, and Battles* (Philadelphia, 1864), 53.

Major General George H. Thomas,
commander of the Army of the
Cumberland, 1864.

Library of Congress

turned in a fine performance. The army commander so revered Thompson that he awarded him with the "red ribbon of the Roll of Honor for his organization of the First Regiment of Colored Troops in the Department of the Cumberland, and for his meritorious services and gallantry as aide-de-camp to the general commanding at the battles of Corinth and Stone's River." Rosecrans also expressed his admiration "for the qualities which have raised Colonel Thompson from the position of private, in which he entered the service at the commencement of the rebellion, to his present rank, which has been attained solely by his own merit and attention to duty."[4]

In August 1863, Thompson was promoted to colonel and given command of the 12th USCT. His regiment was stationed at various locations in Tennessee and at practically every section along the Nashville and Northwestern Railroad from Kingston Springs westward to Johnsonville. Though Thompson's command performed primarily guard duty at these posts, the 12th USCT, along with the 13th and 100th USCT regiments, participated in their fair share of engagements with bands of marauding guerillas.[5]

It is unclear when Thompson arrived at Johnsonville, but various accounts point to reaching the depot in mid-October 1864. By that time Johnsonville was well-established with buildings, loading platforms, corrals, and barracks. How, exactly, he came to be there, and whether he was

4 Ibid., 54; *OR* 30, pt. 3, 298.

5 *OR Supplement*, vol. 77, 470-77.

at some point supposed to command the entire facility is something of a mystery. "I was in command of all troops on line of the N. and N. W. Rail Road, and went to Johnsonville when the place was threatened by [Gen. Nathan Bedford] Forrest early in October with about 600 Col'd Troops from the 12th, 13th and 100th U.S.C. and 43rd Wis.," Thompson confirmed in an affidavit later that year. "I was not ordered there but took my Head Quarters and all the men that could be spared from the defence of the Rail Road. My Quarters were about four hundred yards from the Levee in the beginning of the fight," he added, "when I moved on the hill."[6]

Thompson's statement makes it clear he was not ordered to move to Johnsonville to assume command. As he explained it, Thompson never received orders from Gen. Thomas, Governor Johnson, or any other superior officer assigning him to that effect. Instead, as colonel of the 12th USCT, he took it upon himself to move his command there to protect the vital logistics center. As one of the ranking officers present, Thompson established his headquarters at Johnsonville and awaited for new orders.

The 43rd Wisconsin's Cpl. Atwood provided a clue about this command confusion when he failed to mention anything about Col. Thompson being in charge of the post. Atwood and his Wisconsin regiment comrades arrived at Johnsonville in mid-October, and a short time later Atwood wrote home that "Colonel Cobb has received the command of this post and Lieu Paine has the com. of the Reg." The "Colonel Cobb" to whom he referred was Amasa Cobb, a seasoned veteran and former commander of the 5th Wisconsin Infantry in the Army of the Potomac. The Illinois native who had spent most of his life in Wisconsin was also a sitting member of Congress and had only just weeks earlier resumed his military career by taking command of the newly formed 43rd Wisconsin.[7]

The 43rd Wisconsin arrived at Johnsonville on October 15, and Atwood's reference to Cobb being in command was penned just four days later. Perhaps Cobb commanded at Johnsonville for a short period before

---

6 Affidavit account provided by Colonel Charles R. Thompson regarding the actions of the U.S. forces at Johnsonville, Tennessee, that resulted in the destruction of government property on November 4, 1864, for the Board of Survey at Nashville, Tennessee, in the Court Martial case of Acting Volunteer Lt. Commander, Edward M. King, December 29, 1864, *U.S. Navy Records 1864-65, Courts Martial*, RG 11-86, U.S. Navy Department Records, National Archives, Washington, D.C., page # not provided.

7 Atwood, October 19, 1864.

Colonel Amasa Cobb (center, seated) with staff officers of the 43rd Wisconsin Volunteer Infantry Regiment, Nashville, Tennessee, 1865. *Wisconsin Historical Society*

Thompson's arrival. It appears that Thompson became the overall commander simply because he got there and began making decisions before Col. Cobb and his 43rd Wisconsin arrived.

Cobb verified his subordination to Thompson's authority on November 4 when he reported, "I was ordered by Colonel Thompson to remain in the fort with my regiment. My orders from Colonel Thompson were to keep my men in the intrenchments." However it came to be, Col. Thompson was in command of the land forces at Johnsonville.[8]

Early that same November, Acting Volunteer Lieutenant Edward M. King was at "the town of Johnsonville, Tennessee as the senior naval officer present." King commanded the "USS *Key West* (Gunboat No. 32) in company with the USS *Tawah* (Gunboat No. 29) and the USS *Elfin* (Gunboat No. 52), all part of the United States Navy's Mississippi Squadron." Why he was sent to Johnsonville, or by whom, remains unclear. Very little is known about Johnsonville's ranking naval officer. King hailed from Massachusetts and enlisted in the U. S. Navy on October 31, 1863.

8 *OR* 39, pt. 1, 866.

Private Ralph Bushnell, 43rd
Wisconsin Volunteer Infantry
Regiment, 1864. *Courtesy of Mr. Don McFall
and Family*

Apparently, he shared dual-command responsibility with Thompson at Johnsonville, but there is no evidence to suggest that either officer understood his official capacity.[9]

Johnsonville's Defense Forces

Although Cpl. Atwood wrote home that Johnsonville's garrison included "nearly 4,000 men," the number of troops present prior to the arrival of reinforcements on November 5 was only about 2,200. No other site in Tennessee hosted such a convoluted array of U.S. Army and Navy forces assisted by armed civilian employees, all within a 90-acre perimeter whose duty it was to protect one of the country's most important military supply depots and railroads.[10]

It is difficult to calculate the exact number of troops stationed at Johnsonville prior to October 1864 because the place was a rotating door of troops present one week but ordered away the next to fill outposts at various

9 Jack B. Irion and David V. Beard, *Underwater Archaeological Assessment of Civil War Shipwrecks in Kentucky Lake, Benton and Humphries Counties, Tennessee. Study for Tennessee Dept. of Archaeology, Department of Environment and Conservation* (Nashville, 1993), 35, 39. There is very little biographical information on Edward King, other than a handful of thin references in the *Official Records*. It appears he was honorably discharged from the Navy on July 18, 1867. Acting Volunteer Lieutenant Edward M. King to Capt. Henry Howland, November 3, 1864, RG 94, Carded Records Relating to Civil War Staff Officers, National Archives, Washington, D.C; *ORN* 26, 607, 615.

10 Atwood, November 8, 1864; David W. Higgs, *Nathan Bedford Forrest and the Battle of Johnsonville* (Nashville, 1976), 59-62.

Unidentified Union Private, United States Colored Troops, ca. 1863.

Library of Congress

sections along the Nashville and Northwestern Railroad. Tabulating the forces there for October and November is much easier because when it became known that Nathan Bedford Forrest's Confederate cavalry had entered the region and the exact number of troops and where they were located was reported, various regiments or companies of regiments received orders to move to Johnsonville to defend it.

As a variety of Union officers stationed at Johnsonville in early November 1864 reported, the garrison included 700 men from the 43rd Wisconsin Infantry, various companies of the 12th,13th, and 100th USCT totaling 400 men, and another 800 armed Quartermaster's Department employees (300 civilians who had been working there since May 1864, and some 500 employees who arrived on November 3 from the Nashville Depot). Other troops included 20 men of the 11th Tennessee Mounted Infantry, and 100 men of the 2nd Tennessee Mounted Infantry (which was operating in the vicinity of Johnsonville, but who were not assigned to the post).[11]

11 The *Official Records* offers no evidence the 13th, 40th, 100th, and 101st USCT were present at Johnsonville after October 1864. Only two companies of the 12th USCT (Companies C and I) seem to have been at the supply depot during the battle of November

Unidentified Union Corporal, 2nd Tennessee Mounted Infantry Regiment.
Courtesy of Scott W. Gilmer

The artillery forces present at Johnsonville from September to November 1864 included six 10-pounder Parrott Rifles of the 1st Kansas Battery (80 men), two 12-pounder Napoleons of Battery A, 2nd U.S. Colored Light Artillery (40 men), two 12-pounder Napoleons belonging to a battery operated by the Quartermaster's Department from Nashville (about 30 men), and a pair of 20-pounder Parrott Rifles captured from the Confederates aboard the transport USS *Venus* "mounted on a hill north of the battery of 10-pdrs" (manned by 30 artillerists who were likely Quartermaster's Department employees).[12]

4-5, 1864. However, an after-action report by Lt. Col. William Sinclair, assistant inspector General, U.S. Army, on January 7, 1865, in *OR* 39, pt. 1, 861, claims that "detachments of the Twelfth, Thirteenth, and One hundredth U.S. Colored Infantry" were present at Johnsonville on November 4, 1864. Sinclair also mentioned in his report that Col. Thompson stated "the 400 colored troops were the only ones that were drilled." *OR* 39, pt. 1, 865. It is my conclusion that "the 400 colored troops" were "detachments" of the 12th, 13th, and 100th USCT regiments, and they were present at the post on November 4-5 and were engaged with the Confederates.

12 U.S. Navy Department, testimony of Acting 1st Assistant Engineer for the USS *Key West*, Peter Wagner, regarding the destruction of government property at Johnsonville, Tennessee, on November 4, 1864, for the Court of Inquiry at Mound City, Illinois, for the Court Martial case of Acting Volunteer Lt. Commander Edward M. King, May 15, 1865, *U.S. Navy Records 1864-65, Courts Martial*, RG 11-86, 75.

U.S. Navy and Quartermaster's Department

In addition to the land forces, Johnsonville had a thriving river front and served as a docking point for gunboats and privately owned transports leased to the U.S. Navy. The Quartermaster's Department operated the wharf, a macadamized surface (compacted layers of broken stone) at which riverine vessels regularly moored for unloading. Quartermaster employees ran wharf operations, and the Navy, garrison troops, and armed Quartermaster's Department civilian employees helped defend it.[13]

Johnsonville's riverfront was a hive of activity from dawn to dusk every day. Fifteen to as many as thirty boats and barges could be seen moored at the massive wharf at any given time. Sailors served primarily as deck hands, cooks, engineers, mechanics, and gunners aboard their assigned vessels, and assisted with the loading and unloading of supplies, and, at times, even helped haul them inside warehouses alongside employees.

When sailors were not performing the heavy manual labor associated with a busy supply depot, they were participating in gunnery drills or working on repairs and other associated naval matters. Most sailors on the gunboats at Johnsonville's wharf were not stationed there. Instead, they served as crew members aboard transports and other gunboats that frequently docked at the long wharf during their patrols of the 257 miles of the winding Tennessee River between Paducah, Kentucky, and Muscle Shoals, Alabama. In early November 1864, the U.S. Navy could count some 400 sailors and officers aboard the various gunboats and transports docked at the wharf.[14]

---

13 Affidavits from representatives of the states of Ohio, Tennessee, Kentucky, Illinois, and Iowa regarding the destruction of privately owned transports destroyed at Johnsonville, Tennessee, on November 4, 1864. Affidavits sworn and subscribed from January to February, 1865, at Nashville, Tennessee, *U.S. Navy Records 1864-65, Courts Martial*, RG 11-86, U.S. Navy Department, National Archives, Washington, D.C.; *OR* 52, pt.1, 659.

14 *Muscle Shoals Hearings, Before the Committee on Agriculture and Forestry, United States Senate, Sixty-Seventh Congress, Second Session* (Washington, 1922), 901; Charles Dana Gibson and E. Kay Gibson, *The Army's Navy Series, Volume II, Assault and Logistics: Union Army Coastal and River Operations 1861-1866* (Camden, 1995), 385; *ORN* 26, 589; Roscoe C. Martin, "The Tennessee Valley Authority: A Study of Federal Control," *Law and Contemporary Problems* 22 (Summer 1957): 351-377.

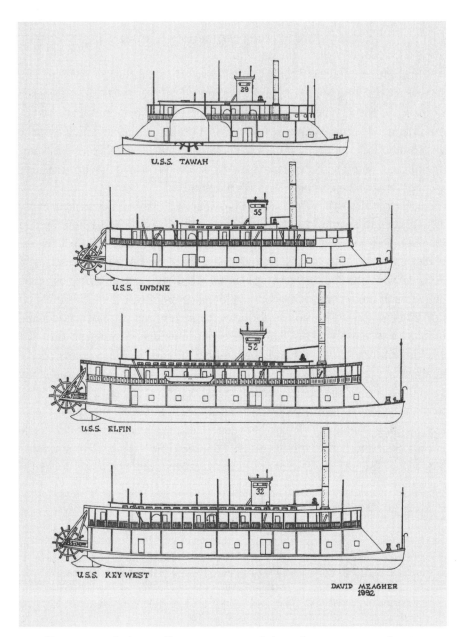

Profile Drawings of Johnsonville's U.S. Navy "Tinclad" Gunboats: U.S.S. *Tawah*, U.S.S. *Elfin*, U.S.S. *Undine*, and U.S.S. *Key West*, 1992. *Courtesy of David J. Meagher*

Johnsonville's gunboats, called "tinclads," were civilian packet boats converted to military use by adding guns and light armor to the front and sides. A gunboat's armor "was intended to deflect light arms fire and not much more, hence its name "tinclad" instead of the more heavily shielded "ironclads." Four gunboats regularly operated out of Johnsonville: USS *Tawah* (Gunboat No. 29), USS *Undine* (Gunboat No. 55), USS *Elfin* (Gunboat No. 52), and USS *Key West* (Gunboat No. 32). The latter was the flagship of Johnsonville's naval commander, Acting Volunteer Lt. Edward M. King. The gunboats at Johnsonville were all stern-wheels except for the side-wheeler USS *Tawah*.[15]

Drill and Quarters

Officers drilled infantry in the open areas of Trace Creek and along the Tennessee River on the clear-cut bank north of the supply depot's central area. Brothers Henry and Walter Howland shared quarters at the supply depot, along with other officers and enlisted men permanently assigned to Johnsonville. On September 23, 1864, Walter described a brief sojourn outside the depot and discovered just how dangerous it was there. "I went with two others some eight miles into the country to attend a meeting," he began,

> It was a little exciting too as a guerrilla band stopped there the night before and interrupted a meeting which was then going on. We are hearing reports constantly of guerrillas abroad and I suppose it is not quite safe to venture out. Rumors are again afloat of an anticipated attack from Forrest and the men are today out drilling.[16]

Captain McConnell of the 71st Ohio Infantry (who was also acting assistant-inspector general for the District of Tennessee), filed an informative report about the lack of military drill and training by infantry forces at Johnsonville. "None of the troops, except the men of the First

15 Stephen R. James, Jr., "Additional Archaeological Investigations of Two Battle of Johnsonville Troop Transports Site 40HS338, Tennessee River, Humphries County, Tennessee," Pan-American Consultants, Inc., Memphis, Tennessee (February 2011): 11; *ORN* 26, 605-18.

16 Walter Howland, September 23, 1864; *OR* 39, pt. 1, 865.

Original Sketch of Johnsonville's Interior by Corporal Lorenzo D. Atwood, 43rd Wisconsin Volunteer Infantry, October 19, 1864.
Courtesy of Warren, Robin, and Leon Atwood

Kansas Battery, had ever been under fire," he complained, and "the 400 colored troops were the only ones that were drilled." The infantry "were posted in rifle pits that had been dug on the flat just north of the railroad—the remainder of the troops were stationed in and around the fortifications."[17]

When not serving on picket duty or drilling the men did all the things soldiers have been doing for centuries: sleeping, resting, telling stories, writing letters, or playing games. They were housed in a variety of shelters, including 30x60 clapboard barracks with bunks along the walls and a stove at each end. The 43rd Wisconsin built small wooden huts with chimneys in anticipation of a long winter. Generally speaking, garrison troops had it easy, and certainly much easier than soldiers at the front. They went to sleep each night in roofed quarters and usually prepared their own meals or were served hot meals by regimental cooks. Cpl. Atwood seemed content with the posting and even wrote home that his friend "Jairus" was "a good bunk mate."

In one of his letters to his wife Cordelia, Atwood enclosed a remarkable sketch showing the perimeter of Johnsonville that included many interior details of the depot. The young corporal sketched the barracks in which he lived, how they were arranged like row houses, and even identified them by their company letter. (It is interesting to note that the sequence of company letters did not match military alphabetical sequence.) Atwood's sketch also identified specific postings, such as "No. 1 is a battery of 6, guns," and "No 2. Reg. of Cavelry." Another important detail found no where else was his semi-circular sketch identifying a "picket line five miles long."

17 *ORN* 26, 641.

Atwood's drawing is an extremely important contribution to Johnsonville's Civil War history because it identifies details, including the existence of eleven wooden barracks, the location of a second corral at the position of ("No.2 Reg. of Cavelry), and possibly the position of Redoubt No. 2 (described in the sketch as "No. 3, Company Battr'y of our Reg. on a high hill 100 rods.")[18]

Land Defenses at the Supply Depot

When a train from Nashville arrived at the entrance of the supply depot, a combination of USCT troops, various mounted infantry and cavalry, and men from the 43rd Wisconsin searched the cars for any unauthorized persons. Cpl. Atwood told his wife about how he served as "Corparel of the guard" that conducted some of these searches, and, on occasion, helped "keep out a picket guard in the edge of the woods."[19]

A wagon road sixteen feet wide ran along the left side of the railroad directly into the central area of the depot. The rutted dirt route accommodated regular trains of supply wagons, trotting cavalry, tramping infantry, civilians, and every individual who entered the supply depot who wasn't aboard a train.

No records or correspondence indicate whether the post had a formal entrance gate. Other similar posts and forts, including Fort Donelson in Dover, Tennessee, and Fortress Rosecrans in Murfreesboro, Tennessee, did have such designated entrances, which at least suggests that Johnsonville almost certainly did as well. An entry gate is in fact visible in one of Coonley's photographs of Fort Johnson Redoubt No. 1 (i.e., the lower redoubt), so it makes sense that something similar or even identical would have been constructed at the supply depot's main entrance—especially since there were nearly constant "reports constantly of guerrillas abroad." Soldiers stationed at Johnsonville quickly learned that it was dangerous outside the confines of the depot. Lt. Walter Howland, Henry's brother, rode the rails with a satchel holding $20,000 in pay for the men inside the entrenchments.

---

18 Atwood, October 31, 1864.

19 Ibid., October 19, 1864.

Trace Creek Trestle and Blockhouse, Nashville and Northwestern Railroad near Denver, Tennessee, 1864. *Tennessee State Library & Archives*

When he returned, he fully acknowledged that it "was not quite safe to venture out."[20]

The Blockhouse

Trains could not enter Johnsonville's 90-acre compound without passing a small blockhouse sitting atop a steep knob on the left side of the tracks. Richard Wagner, acting first assistant engineer aboard the gunboat USS *Key West*, remembered the fortification as "a small blockhouse, unfinished and unmanned."[21]

20 Samuel D. Smith, Benjamin C. Nance, and Fred M. Prouty, *A Survey of Civil War Era Military Sites in Tennessee* (Nashville, 2003), 133. Detail from Jacob Coonley's photographic image of Johnsonville's south view of the supply depot and Fort Johnson taken in November 1864, at Johnsonville, Tennessee; Walter Howland, September 23, 1864.

21 *The Official Atlas of the Civil War*, Plate XIV; Testimony of Acting 1st Assistant Engineer for the USS *Key West*, Peter Wagner, regarding the destruction of government

By 1864, blockhouses had replaced the more popular spike-topped military log stockades. Johnsonville's blockhouse would have followed military specifications of "30 feet square and designed to hold about 30 men: a sufficient guard for the less important railroad bridges," but no details seem to exist describing it other than it looked "small." Almost certainly the square log stronghold boasted shuttered windows and loop holes—small openings in the walls that allowed soldiers inside to slide their rifle barrels out and fire while protected from the enemy.

The blockhouse roof consisted of a "layer of logs laid side by side and covered with earth. On top of that was a roof of shingles or boards and battens. It was very important to keep the block house dry so the garrison could live comfortably inside. Blockhouses were supplied with ventilators, cellars, water tanks, and bunks." Blockhouse guards had a clear view of anyone traveling on the road within a mile of the post, and could spot incoming trains from about the same distance.[22]

It is clear that Johnsonville boasted fairly significant defensive lines, but a report by Henry Howland, captain and assistant quartermaster, indicated otherwise. "I should here remark that at this time," he later wrote, "that we had nothing worthy [of] the name of fortifications, only one small block-house and a little earthwork thrown up on two hills overlooking the town and river, where were mounted the six 10-pounder Parrotts of the First Kansas Battery, the only guns then here." As we will see, the "little earthwork thrown up on two hills" was in fact two strong redoubts that helped anchor a long line of entrenchments.[23]

---

property at Johnsonville, Tennessee on November 4, 1864, for the Court of Inquiry at Mound City, Illinois, for the Court Martial case of Acting Volunteer Lt. Commander Edward M. King, May 15, 1865, *U.S. Navy Records 1864-65, Courts Martial*, RG 11-86, U.S. Navy Department, 75.

22 *OR* 16, pt. 2, 178; Smith, Nance, and Prouty, *A Survey of Civil War Era Military Sites in Tennessee*, 144-48. Battens are cut boards that provide the fixing point for other roofing materials, such as shingles.

23 *ORN* 26, 621.

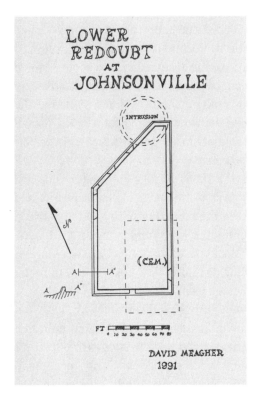

LOWER
REDOUBT
AT
JOHNSONVILLE

DAVID MEAGHER
1991

Footprint drawing of Redoubt No. 1
(Lower Redoubt), Johnsonville,
Tennessee, 1992. *Courtesy of David J. Meagher*

Fort Johnson
(Redoubts No.1 and No. 2)

Johnsonville's land defenses were anchored by two earthen redoubts collectively called Fort Johnson, after Gov. Andrew Johnson. For reasons that remain unexplained, the Federals often referred to both forts collectively as "Fort Johnson," even though many references to "Fort Johnson" are actually a reference to the lower redoubt closer to the Tennessee River. Unfortunately, very little information exists regarding the upper redoubt.

A redoubt is a square, polygonal, or circular fortification enclosed on all sides and reinforced with artillery. Engineers usually erected redoubts on top of a hill or some form of high or rising ground to help strengthen related lines of earthworks. Johnsonville's redoubts were 350 yards apart. Each was atop a hill overlooking the supply depot and enjoyed a commanding two-mile view up and down the Tennessee River.

Fort Johnson's lower redoubt (Redoubt No. 1) sat atop a lower hill close to the center of the supply depot. The name "lower" redoubt referred to its proximity to the river. Built of earth, Redoubt No. 1 was 210 feet long by 100 feet wide with walls 10 feet high (measured from the bottom of the outer ditch). It was designed with six embrasures, or openings, so artillery could be rolled forward, aimed, and fired.

Fort Johnson's upper redoubt or, Redoubt No. 2, sat 350 yards southeast behind the lower redoubt on a higher hill overlooking the Tennessee River. Also made of earth, Redoubt No. 2 was 255 feet by 120 feet, with walls 15 feet high. The general shape and layout, however, was more circular in shape

Footprint drawing of Redoubt No. 2
(Upper Redoubt), Johnsonville,
Tennessee, 1992. *Courtesy of David J. Meagher*

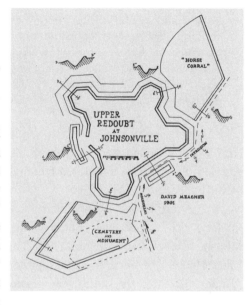

than Redoubt No. 1. The ground
was raised and prepared in each
circular "corner" so gunners
could position their artillery
pieces to fire above the parapet.[24]

Both fortifications were
identified by officers and
soldiers as "forts," "redoubts,"
and even collectively as "Fort
Johnson," as illustrated in
personal letters and in the official correspondence. Col. J. C. Peterson,
commander of the U.S. 2nd Infantry Regiment (mounted) wrote that "my
command was posted in Fort Johnson and remained under arms during the
night."[25] Maj. Gen. Thomas referenced both redoubts in his correspondence:
"I do not see how the enemy can cross the river to attack the forts." Lt. Col.
William Sinclair offered a revealing description of the lower redoubt, but
doesn't mention the upper redoubt (Redoubt No. 2) at all: "on the hill, near
the river, there was an earth-work, the artillery being posted in and about this
work. Part of the infantry was posted in this work, and part in rifle-pits that
had been thrown up on the flat north of the railroad."[26]

Theodore Gardner, a sergeant in the 1st Kansas Battery, remembered
two different locations for his battery. In his description of Redoubt No. 1,
Gardner recalled:

24 Deputy State Historic Preservation Officer "National Register Nomination,
Johnsonville Historic District," Humphries County, Tennessee, Section 7, 1990, 1.

25 *OR* 52, pt. 1, 656.

26 Ibid, and *OR* 39, pt. 1, 859; *ORN* 26, 621. Sinclair's failure to mention a word about
Redoubt No. 2 is difficult to explain. Perhaps it was simply an oversight. However, artillery
and infantry forces were posted there as well, and Redoubt No. 2 was in sight from
Sinclair's observation point in Redoubt No. 1.

At the southern edge of the village in a round knob some seventy-five feet above the river and a few hundred feet east of it . . . was constructed an earthwork with embrasures in which were installed the six guns of the First Kansas battery, giving them a commanding position, covering the village and the great warehouses on the levee, which were filled with supplies for the Army of the Cumberland. Just south of this redoubt was our camp, a few yards away.[27]

Gardner also provided details about the possible position of Redoubt No.2 when he added, "at the back of this knob about a thousand feet was a second ridge, perhaps a hundred feet higher. This second ridge was dubbed by the battery boys "Mt. Pisgah."[28]

Kansas artillerists manned their pieces inside Redoubts No.1 and No. 2. In fact, the 1st Kansas Battery camped at several locations inside Johnsonville's defensive perimeter. The "six 10 pd'r parrots of the 1st Kansas battery," Henry Howland reported "were stationed in the small fort." A report filed after the Battle of Johnsonville by Capt. Charles H. Lovelace, one of many assistant quartermasters at Johnsonville, suggests a third possible defensive position. According to Lovelace, "on the range of hills between the fortifications before mentioned, here the 1st Kansas Battery of Six Guns was stationed," meaning at some point the battery was not at either redoubt.[29]

The accounts by Gardner, Howland, and Lovelace all agreed the 1st Kansas Battery participated in the Johnsonville battle of November 4-5, 1864. Exactly where the 1st Kansas Battery was located at the time is

---

27 Theodore Gardner, "The First Kansas Battery: An Historical Sketch, With Personal Reminiscences of Army Life, 1861-65," in *Collections of the Kansas State Historical Society, 1915-1918: Together with Addresses at Annual Meetings, Memorials and Miscellaneous Papers*, vol. XIV, ed. William E. Connelley (Topeka, 1918), 277.

28 Ibid., 276. Pisgah is a Hebrew name for mountain, often referring to Mount Nebo as illustrated in the Book of Deuteronomy (34:1-4): "Then Moses climbed Mount Nebo from the plains of Moab to the top of Pisgah, across from Jerico."

29 AQM Henry Howland to Brigadier General James S. Donaldson, November 16, 1864, Johnsonville, Tennessee, RG 94, Carded Records Relating to Civil War Staff Officers, National Archives, Washington, D.C.; Affidavit account provided by Captain Charles H. Lovelace regarding the destruction of government property at Johnsonville, Tennessee on November 4, 1864, for the Board of Survey at Nashville, Tennessee, in the Court Martial case of Acting Volunteer Lt. Commander, Edward M. King, December 29, 1864, *U.S. Navy Records 1864-65, Courts Martial*, RG 11-86, U.S. Navy Department, National Archives, Washington, D.C.

unclear. The Gardner and Lovelace accounts make it likely the Kansas battery relocated during the battle from the area of Redoubt No. 2 ("Mt. Pisgah") to a more strategic position somewhere to the left and outside of Fort Johnson's Redoubt No. 1. This makes sense because most other accounts have Battery A, 2nd U.S. Colored Light Artillery occupying the upper fortification, or Redoubt No. 2.[30]

According to Lovelace, "we had a fortification on the hill, I think four Brass 12 pdr's manned by a Colored Battery [Battery A], the two 20 pd'r Parrotts taken from the steamer 'Venus.'" Gardner firmly remembered that the 1st Kansas Battery was positioned inside Redoubt No. 1, but after fighting on November 4 relocated to Redoubt No. 2. "The small earthwork in which our battery was located, being within easy range of the enemy's guns," explained Gardner,

> caused us, on the night of the 3rd [4th] to move them back to the higher ground of Mt. Pisgah, where we were out of their range and yet within effective range of our own. The morning of the 5th was damp and a dense fog hung upon the river. We were up bright and early having bivouacked on the high ground beside our guns.[31]

Infantry and cavalry soldiers from the 12th, 13th, 40th and 100th USCT regiments, the 43rd Wisconsin Volunteer Infantry, the 8th Iowa Cavalry, and the 2nd and 11th Tennessee Infantry (mounted) deployed in and near each redoubt in support of the artillery. Additionally, as Colonel Thompson recalled, armed civilian employees from the Quartermaster's Department in Nashville helped defend Redoubt No. 1, perhaps as guards.

Gardner recalled that "the battery [inside Redoubt No. 1] recruited a number of civilian men from the quartermaster's department," which suggests the civilian employees helped the 1st Kansas Battery in some capacity. Gardner also remembered being ordered to Nashville to retrieve civilian quartermaster employees who had been assigned to assist the

30 Affidavit account provided by Captain Charles H. Lovelace, December 29, 1864, *U.S. Navy Records, 1864-65, Courts Martial*, RG 11-86, U.S. Navy Department, National Archives, Washington, D.C.

31 Theodore Gardner, "The First Kansas Battery: An Historical Sketch, With Personal Reminiscences of Army Life, 1861-65," in *Collections of the Kansas State Historical Society 1915-1918: Together with Addresses at Annual Meetings, Memorials and Miscellaneous Papers, Vol. XIV*, ed. William E. Connelley (Topeka, 1918), 277.

battery, and return with them to Johnsonville. Some of the civilians never made it: "The train ran out fifty miles from Nashville, when it was ditched by guerrillas and burned, the passengers being murdered in cold blood."[32]

Entrenchments

A continuous arc of earthen entrenchments encircled the depot like a giant horseshoe. Company G, 13th USCT, together with other companies from other regiments, spent July and August 1864 constructing this outer line, in addition to an inner line connecting Redoubts No. 1 and No. 2.[33]

The entrenchments were substantial at approximately six feet deep and ten feet across, and included strategically placed traverses. Head logs— medium-sized trees felled, de-limbed, and positioned to offer soldiers added protection and concealment when firing at the enemy—lined the top of the trenches. The makeup of the troops manning the outer line of entrenchments—recorded by Cpl. Atwood as "being 5 miles in extent" —changed every six hours.[34]

A line of entrenchments "5 miles in extent" is substantial and would have given any enemy pause. Asst. Quartermaster Henry Howland, whose quarters where he and his brother Walter were "quite comfortably settled" and had "a very comfortable little house," curiously made no mention of this extensive line in his letters, reports, or other communications. Thankfully, others did. Capt. Samuel J. McConnell, acting assistant-inspector general for the District of Tennessee, had orders to rotate his employees "in the intrenchments" below Redoubt No. 1. "I commenced to improve the works we occupied," reported Col. John C. Peterson, commander of the Second Regiment of Quartermaster's Department employees. "The works erected were of sufficient strength to resist field artillery, and they were well protected from a flank fire by heavy traverses every fifteen feet."[35]

---

32 *OR* 39, pt. 1, 865-66; Gardner, "The First Kansas Battery: An Historical Sketch, With Personal Reminiscences of Army Life, 1861-65," 277.

33 Atwood, October 19, 1864; *OR Supplement*, vol. 77, 495.

34 Atwood, October 19, 1864.

35 *ORN* 26, 626; Walter Howland, September 23, 1864; Henry Howland to mother, October 23, 1864, Johnsonville, Tennessee; *OR* 52, pt. 1, 656.

Based on these descriptions, which describe the earthworks located around and inside Johnsonville's perimeter, it is difficult to understand why Howland, who was "in charge of this quartermaster's depot," appeared unaware of the outer defenses, or didn't think them worth mentioning.[36]

Johnsonville's earthen defenses were well-positioned on high terrain, but Col. Thompson's undersized and inexperienced ground forces were expected to defend an important supply depot with a five-mile perimeter. For the first many months of its existence, Johnsonville rarely had more than 500 defenders. Only after November 1, 1864, just three days before the battle, could the depot boast a defense force of 2,500 men. More than once Thompson, Howland, and King appealed to Maj. Gen. Thomas for more troops, but none were made available until early November.

Except for the 1st Kansas Battery, the mounted Tennessee commands, and some of the USCT men, Johnsonville's garrison was wholly inexperienced and left the depot vulnerable to capture from its land side. Even after Thompson arrived in mid-October, his correspondence revealed that he could not defend the warehouses or hold the perimeter around the depot in an organized effort against a determined enemy. Thompson knew Johnsonville was threatened by Maj. Gen. Nathan Bedford Forrest and his cavalry, and was fully aware of the very real danger they posed.

By this stage of the war, most Union field officers in Tennessee understood that Forrest often used mounted troops to lay siege to static posts in an effort to force their surrender. He had done so at Murfreesboro, Union City, and Fort Pillow, Tennessee, as well as Paducah, Kentucky, and Athens, Alabama. If he came for Johnsonville, every soldier and civilian at the post would be put to the ultimate test.

---

36 Henry Howland to mother, October 23, 1864, Johnsonville, Tennessee.

CHAPTER 7

Confederates on the Move

AFTER the fall of Atlanta in early September 1864 and Confederate Gen. John B. Hood's decision to move north with his battered Army of Tennessee, the Union high command came to believe posts like Johnsonville were now on the periphery of the war. Confederate commanders felt differently. Federal bases housed massive stores of supplies, and interfering with or wrecking Union logistics was always a top Confederate objective.[1]

The West Tennessee/Johnsonville Expedition

In mid-September, Maj. Gen. Nathan Bedford Forrest set off on a major cavalry raid into northern Alabama and central Tennessee in an effort to reduce supplies flowing to Maj. Gen. William Sherman's command around Atlanta. The raid ended in October in northern Mississippi with the cavalryman exhausted and the Union general's supply situation unaffected. Forrest needed a lengthy rest, and while at Cherokee Station, Alabama, wrote his commanding officer to request one. "I have been constantly in the field since 1861, and have spent half the entire time in the saddle," Forrest

---

1 Francis C. Kajencki, "The Man Who Beat the Devil," *Civil War Times, Illustrated* (October, 1998), No. 5, vol. 37, 40; John F. Marszalek, *Sherman: A Soldier's Passion for Order* (New York, 1993), 261.

Major General Nathan B. Forrest, ca. 1864. *Library of Congress*

informed Lt. Gen. Richard Taylor, commander of the Department of Alabama, Mississippi, and East Louisiana. He continued:

> I have never asked for a furlough for over ten days for which to rest and recruit. My strength is failing and it is absolutely necessary that I should have some rest. I desire if possible to get my command together and with General Chalmers as senior

Brigadier General James R. Chalmers, Forrest's First Division commander, ca. 1864.
Library of Congress

officer feel that it would be safe to leave the command for a short time, which in my present state of health is absolutely necessary.[2]

Taylor replied the next day, October 9, requesting that before he take leave, Forrest inform him "of the condition of affairs . . . in West Tennessee." Taylor went on to explain that Sherman's response to Hood's move north against his logistical lifeline (a dispersal of his command to maintain his lines of communication and chase down Hood) offered a rare opportunity in the state. "Western Tennessee will be left unprotected or [un]occupied by the enemy," he wrote, and he urged the cavalry commander to strip the area clean of "all the supplies you can, making necessary arrangements before you leave."[3]

Being the soldier he was, Forrest set aside his leave request and replied to Taylor three days later, "I avail myself of the first leisure moment to comply with your request. I move with my command into West Tennessee in a few days." Two days later, Forrest wrote Taylor again, this time proposing a three-fold plan that included a raid into West Tennessee for the purpose of securing the much-needed supplies and new recruits Taylor wanted extracted from the exposed part of the state.[4]

First, Forrest recommended repairing the railroads accessing West Tennessee, vital for transporting men and supplies. These repairs, he urged, should commence immediately on the Memphis and Charleston Railroad from Cherokee, Alabama, to Corinth, Mississippi. He also suggested the

2 *OR* 39, pt. 3, 807; Berry Craig, *Kentucky Confederates: Secession, Civil War, and the Jackson Purchase* (Lexington, 2014), 231, 234-36.

3 James Harvey Mathes, *General Forrest* (New York, 1902), 296; *OR* 39, pt. 3, 810.

4 *OR* 39, pt. 3, 815.

"entirely destroyed" Mobile and Ohio Railroad, from Bethel to Jackson, Tennessee, should be completed and better protected for "Hood's army moving on Middle Tennessee, and to afford an avenue of retreat if necessary."[5]

The second part of Forrest's plan involved two coordinated movements into West Tennessee. Forrest's First Division under Brig. Gen. James R. Chalmers would ride from the vicinity of Memphis to Jackson while his Second Division under Brig. Gen. Abraham Buford rode north from Corinth to Lexington, Tennessee. Forrest, with his escort and Col. Edmund W. Rucker's brigade (temporarily under Lt. Col. David C. Kelley), would connect with Chalmers at Jackson.

From Lexington, Buford's division would move to Huntingdon, Tennessee, and then on to Paris until Chalmers' division came close enough to provide support. Buford would then advance from Paris to the Tennessee River and establish batteries between the Big Sandy River and Paris Landing. Buford intended to leave artillery and Brig. Gen. Tyree Bell's cavalry brigade at Paris Landing and continue on with the rest of his division into Western Kentucky with Brig. Gen. Hylan B. Lyon's brigade and occupy Fort Heiman, a deserted Confederate fort five miles across the Kentucky state line on a high bluff overlooking the Tennessee River. Once Chalmers reached Paris, he was to establish a perimeter and ride to the Tennessee River with Col. Rucker's and Col. Robert McCulloch's brigades to support Buford at the river. "It is my present design," Forrest explained to Taylor, "to take possession of Fort Heiman, on the west bank of the Tennessee River below Johnsonville and thus prevent all communication with Johnsonville by transports."

The third and last prong of Forrest's plan involved gathering new recruits, food, and horses, and, if possible, the capture of supplies from trains running on the Nashville and Northwestern Railroad, "which are shipped up the Tennessee River and thence to Johnsonville and Nashville."[6]

Although familiar with the logistical challenges and meager state of sustenance in West Tennessee, Forrest remained unconvinced that a cavalry

5 Mathes, *General Forrest*, 296.

6 *OR* 39, pt. 3, 815-17; Mathes, *General Forrest*, 296-97; General Thomas Jordan and J. P. Pryor, *The Campaigns of General Nathan Bedford Forrest and of Forrest's Cavalry* (New Orleans, 1868), 586-87.

Brigadier General Abraham Buford,
Forrest's Second Division commander,
ca. 1864. *Library of Congress*

sweep into the region would
yield the results Taylor
envisioned. "From what I have
seen in West Tennessee," he
explained,

> I am satisfied the amount of
> supplies in that region has been
> greatly exaggerated. I can subsist
> my command there, and will be
> able to gather up some wheat and hogs, but not in amounts large as has been
> supposed. To hunt up and press the needed supplies will require much time and will
> take all of my command to accomplish much.[7]

Forrest's concerns notwithstanding, Taylor knew that new recruits and
supplies would go a long way to help matters within his ailing department.
He approved Forrest's complex plan and offered the cavalry leader any
logistical support Forrest needed that could be made available. While Taylor
ordered repairs on the railroads, Forrest followed through with the second
phase of his plan.

On October 12, Forrest ordered Gen. Chalmers, who was operating
below Memphis near Grenada, Mississippi, to "report to me at Jackson,
Tenn., with all the available men you have except enough to picket your
front, fetching the two batteries with you. Telegraph me how much artillery
ammunition you will want for the two batteries," he added. "I will supply
you at Jackson. Fetch your wagons with you." Four days later Chalmers,
whose depleted division included Mabry's and McCulloch's brigades, a
combined force of about 550 mounted infantry, and Thrall's and Rice's

---

7 Jordan and Pryor, *The Campaigns of General Nathan Bedford Forrest*, 587.

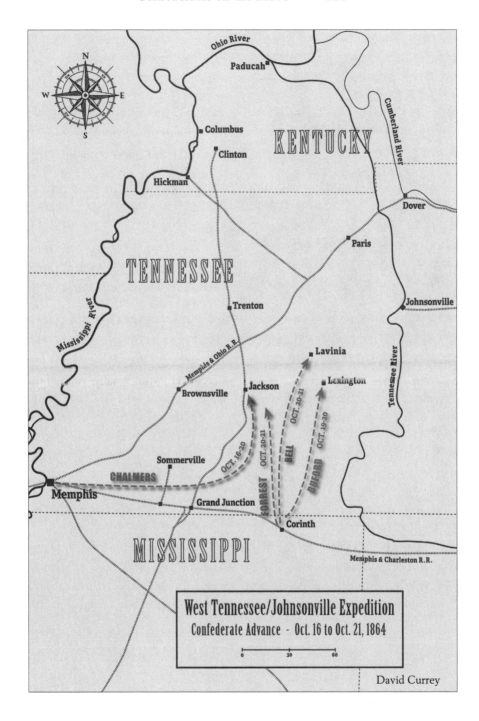

West Tennessee/Johnsonville Expedition
Confederate Advance - Oct. 16 to Oct. 21, 1864

David Currey

Captain John W. Morton,
Forrest's Chief of Artillery, ca. 1864.
Tennessee State Library & Archives

batteries of eight guns and 200 men, left the Memphis area and moved east toward Jackson across the lower portion of the state.[8]

The next day, Forrest ordered Buford to depart Corinth with his division and move north to Lexington. Buford, who had recently returned from observing Federal movements along the Tennessee River, instructed his men to re-shoe and refit their horses as soon as possible. Around noon, Buford ordered Bell's brigade, with 650 mounted infantry, to ride north to Lavinia, Tennessee, to serve as the division's vanguard. Two days later, on October 19, the remainder of Buford's division departed Corinth and moved north. Buford's command included Lyon's brigade of 750 mounted infantry, Morton's 90-man battery under Forrest's 24-year-old chief of artillery, Capt. John W. Morton, and Hudson's Mississippi battery (Walton's battery) of 80 men, commanded by Lt. E. S. Walton.[9]

Chalmers' division arrived at Jackson on October 20. The following day, Rucker's brigade joined Chalmers along with Forrest and his escort. Meanwhile, Buford's division, with Lyon's brigade and Morton's and Walton's batteries, rendezvoused with Chalmers at Jackson. Capt. Morton

8   *OR* 39, pt. 3, 817, 837; Jordan and Pryor, *The Campaigns of General Nathan Bedford Forrest*, 588.

9   Jordan and Pryor, *The Campaigns of General Nathan Bedford Forrest*, 589, 690; John Allan Wyeth, *That Devil Forrest: Life of General Nathan Bedford Forrest* (New York, 1959), 455; Captain James Dinkins, "Destroying Military Stores and Gunboats," *Confederate Veteran*, 34, No. 5 (May 1926), 455.

recalled that while at Jackson "recruits and absentees were gathered in" and his artillery was divided with "one section being assigned to Chalmers' Division, another to Bell's Brigade, while Morton's and Walton's Batteries were sent with Buford's Division."[10]

After Forrest rallied his troops at Jackson, he reported his total strength as follows: Buford's division (Lyon's and Bell's brigades) numbered about 2,000 plus artillery; Chalmers' division (Rucker's, McCulloch's, and Mabry's brigades) about 1,300 plus artillery; and Forrest's own staff and escort totaled some 100 men. Forrest's effective strength during entire Johnsonville campaign never exceeded 3,400 troops.[11]

On October 24, Forrest ordered Buford to take his division and move north to Huntingdon, and from there to Paris, and finally on to the Tennessee River as planned. At the same time, Chalmers was to move his division northeast from Jackson to McLemoresville. Both generals were carefully instructed to be especially alert, and "interpose no obstacle whatsoever, if the enemy attempts to pass to the west bank of the Tennessee." They were also to pay special attention to the "collection of absentees in their respective neighborhoods."

That night at his headquarters in Jackson, Forrest took a few minutes to update Lt. Gen. Taylor on his campaign and its relationship to Gen. Hood's recent move out of northern Georgia and into Alabama. "I shall do the best that can be done, and in every way do all in my power to create a diversion in favor of General Hood," he carefully explained. "I left a regiment at Corinth, and feel some solicitude for its protection, as the preservation of the Mobile and Ohio road may prove to be of great importance, especially so should it,

10 John Watson Morton, *The Artillery of Nathan Bedford Forrest's Cavalry* (Nashville, 1909), 245. The sources are unclear about when Chalmers' division arrived at Jackson and whether Buford's orders were to move to Lexington or Jack's Creek, as primary sources claim both locations as destination points. One primary source claimed Chalmers arrived at Jackson on October 16, two others claim he arrived there on October 20, and two more on October 17. There is no doubt Forrest arrived at Jackson, via Purdy and Henderson Station, and established his headquarters there on October 21. Additionally, some primary sources claim Buford joined Chalmers at Jackson, whereas other credible accounts have him remaining at Lexington until October 24, when Forrest ordered him move north to Paris, Tennessee via Huntingdon.

11 *OR* 39, pt. 3, 838, Jordan and Pryor, *The Campaigns of General Nathan Bedford Forrest,* 589; Wyeth, *That Devil Forrest,* 456.

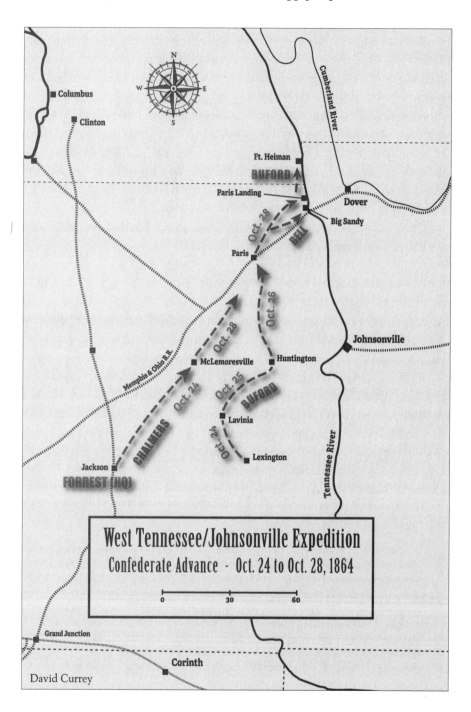

West Tennessee/Johnsonville Expedition
Confederate Advance - Oct. 24 to Oct. 28, 1864

David Currey

in any event, be necessary in transporting supplies to the Army of Tennessee."[12]

Paris Landing and Fort Heiman

Forrest's raid was thus far unfolding as planned. On October 28, Buford reached the mouth of the Big Sandy River where it flows into the Tennessee River just below Paris Landing. Forrest had instructed Buford that when he reached the Tennessee, he should establish gun positions there and continue riding north into southern Kentucky to occupy Fort Heiman.[13]

Buford did as ordered. After a careful reconnaissance he selected artillery positions, with Capt. Morton's assistance, to command the river from both directions. The men placed a section of guns above and below the landing. The first section of two pieces north of the landing belonged to Lt. Joseph M. Mason of Morton's battery. They were under the command of Sgt. Lemuel Zarring because Mason had fallen sick at Jackson. The second section was positioned "1000 yards above Paris Landing" near the mouth of the Big Sandy River. These guns belonged to Lt. Milton H. Trantham of Walton's battery, under Sgt.-Maj. Orlando M. Crozier. Bell's brigade of mounted infantry assisted the gunners by helping prepare the positions at each of the locations so they could hold "about four or five" 3-inch Ordnance Rifles.[14]

Buford divided his division at Paris Landing, leaving Bell's brigade and two sections of Morton's and Walton's batteries behind while Lyon's

---

12 Jordan and Pryor, *The Campaigns of General Nathan Bedford Forrest,* 590.

13 Ibid, 591; Dinkins, "Destroying Military Stores and Gunboats," 177; Mathes, *General Forrest*, 297; Lonnie E. Maness, *An Untutored Genius: The Military Career of General Nathan Bedford Forrest* (Oxford, 1990), 309; Morton, *The Artillery of Nathan Bedford Forrest's Cavalry*, 245. Accounts vary of when Buford's division reached the Tennessee River. Capt. James Dinkins, one of General Chalmers' staff officers, wrote: "on the 26th, Buford moved to the mouth of the Big Sandy River." Capt. John W. Morton, however, who was with Buford, claimed to have reached the mouth of the Big Sandy River on October 28.

14 *ORN* 26, 601; Jordan and Pryor, *The Campaigns of General Nathan Bedford Forrest*, 591-92; Dinkins, 177; Morton, *The Artillery of Nathan Bedford Forrest's Cavalry*, 245; Mathes, *General Forrest*, 297; Captain John W. Morton, "Raid of Forrest's Cavalry on the Tennessee River in 1864," *Southern Historical Society Papers*, Vol. X, No. 6 (June 1882): 261-62. Note to reader: The naval reference "above" means upriver, which in this case, because the river winds, about, is south down the Tennessee River toward Johnsonville.

brigade and the rest of his guns continued five miles north just over the Kentucky line to occupy the abandoned Fort Heiman. Buford arrived there late on the afternoon of October 28 and ordered Walton's battery (formerly Hudson's Mississippi Battery), commanded by Capt. Edwin S. Walton, to oversee the positioning of a pair of 20-pounder Parrott Rifles that had been captured and transported from Mobile, Alabama. Walton assisted Lt. William O. Hunter in positioning the powerful rifled guns in the upper area of Fort Heiman.[15]

The remainder of Morton's battery—a section of 3-inch Rodman guns under Lt. John W. Brown—was concealed in thick underbrush along the river bank about 800 yards south of Fort Heiman. Forrest's orders were to "prevent all communication with Johnsonville by transports," and one way to help bring this about was to camouflage the guns. "[E]ach of these sections was masked," recalled Morton, "and each commanded the river about a mile from either direction." Lyon's brigade of primarily mounted infantry protected both artillery sections at Fort Heiman from any approach by the enemy on land.[16]

Meanwhile, that same evening five miles farther south, Bell's mounted infantry assisted Sgt.-Maj. Crozier in planting his artillery section near the mouth of the Big Sandy River. They were doing so when a Federal gunboat and two empty transports, having recently unloaded their cargo at Johnsonville, steamed north around a bend heading toward Paducah. Bell's orders were to "not to disturb any transports or gunboats until the batteries were thoroughly prepared for action," so he directed his men to keep out of sight and allow the boats to pass. Later, when the same gunboat and transports reached the vicinity of Fort Heiman, the masked Rebel batteries there also held their fire.[17]

---

15 Jordan and Pryor, *The Campaigns of General Nathan Bedford Forrest*, 591; Dinkins, "Destroying Military Stores and Gunboats," 177.

16 Jordan and Pryor, *The Campaigns of General Nathan Bedford Forrest*, 592; Morton, "Raid of Forrest's Cavalry on the Tennessee River in 1864," 262; Morton, *The Artillery of Nathan Bedford Forrest's Cavalry*, 245.

17 Dinkins, "Destroying Military Stores and Gunboats," 176; Morton, "Raid of Forrest's Cavalry on the Tennessee River in 1864," 262; *ORN* 26, 684-85.

Capturing the *Mazeppa*

By the time dawn arrived on Saturday, October 29, Buford's division was prepared to disrupt traffic on the Tennessee River. The first victim steamed into view around 9:00 a.m.

The Union transport and supply vessel *Mazeppa* had left Cincinnati, Ohio, three days earlier on her maiden voyage. She was now approaching Fort Heiman heading upriver (which at this point on the Tennessee meant moving south) toward Johnsonville towing a barge loaded with 700 tons of freight. The *Mazeppa* was chugging her way closer to Fort Heiman (on her right), recalled Capt. Morton, "unaware of the lurking danger." The steamship was "allowed to pass Brown's three-inch 'Rodmans,' and when well above us, I ordered Brown to run his guns from under cover up close to the water's edge and open on her." Walton's guns opened about the same time. The *Mazeppa* was a sitting duck in a deadly crossfire. Both sections fired two volleys without visible effect when Morton's section of 3-inch Rodman's under Lt. Brown fired a third volley. The iron balls sliced one of the *Mazeppa's* steam pipes in half. Walton's heavy Parrotts followed suit "with such effect that her machinery was speedily disabled."[18]

With her steering capability limited and her iron plating punctured, the wounded *Mazeppa* staggered to the opposite side of the river in an effort to put distance between herself and the enemy artillery. The *Mazeppa's* pilot turned the boat toward shore and ran her by the head into a sandbar. The barge being towed by the *Mazeppa* continued moving and the river's northbound current wrapped it around the stern, trapping the *Mazeppa* against the bank. Once frozen against the sandbar, and with the barge jammed up against her, the *Mazeppa's* crew disembarked as fast as possible and dispersed into the woods lining the eastern bank.[19]

Confederate Capt. Frank P. Gracey, an officer in the 3rd Kentucky Infantry (mounted), part of Lyon's brigade, was "concealed on the bank of the Tennessee," and recalled in detail the shelling and capture of the *Mazeppa*:

18 *ORN* 26, 604.

19 Jordan and Pryor, *The Campaigns of General Nathan Bedford Forrest*, 592; Jack Hurst, *Nathan Bedford Forrest: A Biography* (New York, 1993), 225.

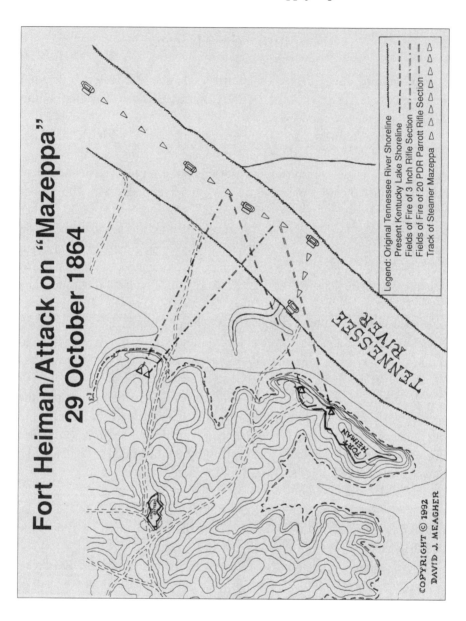

Fort Heiman/Attack on "Mazeppa"
29 October 1864

Legend: Original Tennessee River Shoreline
Present Kentucky Lake Shoreline
Fields of Fire of 3 Inch Rifle Section
Fields of Fire of 20 PDR Parrott Rifle Section
Track of Steamer Mazeppa

TENNESSEE RIVER

FORT HEIMAN

COPYRIGHT © 1992
DAVID J. MEAGHER

About 9 a.m., a boat was reported ascending the river. She soon appeared around the point below us, heavily laden with a barge in tow. She proved to be the *Mazeppa*, a new steamboat on her first trip. As soon as she had passed above us a few hundred yards, I had the pleasure of seeing how Forrest's Artillery would work, and am glad to say that it was served with a skill and precision I had not seen surpassed during three years of almost constant strife. In ten minutes her machinery was wrecked, and she, by the impetus she had when the fatal shot struck her, was driven aground on the opposite shore.[20]

With the *Mazeppa* incapacitated on the opposite side of the river, Capt. Gracey and another officer, Capt. John Horn, volunteered to hazard the heavy current to capture the boat. One of the witnesses of this feat, Col. A. R. Shacklett of the 8th Kentucky Infantry (Mounted), recounted the extraordinary exploit. The captains "each selected a log and rolled it into the river, throwing off their clothes, put their pistol belts around their necks, mounted their logs, and paddled to the boat."[21]

The *Mazeppa's* captain was still aboard his doomed ship, a "white flag flying from her bow," when the officers began crossing the river. Once his crewmen had made good their escape, the captain elected to remain behind "to try to save the boat for the owners." That hope ended once the Confederate captains boarded his vessel. As Col. Shacklett recalled, "after lowering the yawl, they loaded in the cable, and one pulled the oars and the other played off the line to our side of the river." With the *Mazeppa* now "warped by a hawser across to the west bank of the river," wrote the proud colonel, "one hundred men of my regiment—the Eighth Kentucky—seized the rope, made a check post of a tree, and hauled the boat and barge across the river" just beneath Fort Heiman. Gen. Buford's Confederates worked much of the afternoon unloading the captured supplies from the *Mazeppa*

---

20 *ORN* 26, 604; Captain F. P. Gracey to Capt. J. W. Morton, "Capture of the *Mazeppa*," *Confederate Veteran*, vol. 13, No. 12 (December 1905), 567.

21 Colonel A. R. Shacklett to J. F. Gracey, "Capture of the *Mazeppa*," 568. There are various accounts and disagreements of who actually swam the Tennessee River and commandeered the *Mazeppa*. Jordan and Pryor, in *The Campaigns of General Nathan Bedford Forrest*, claim that Captain Gracey of the 3rd Kentucky was the sole person who accomplished the feat. However, witnesses Morton, Young, and Hancock, claimed that Pvt. "Clabe" West of the 2nd Tennessee Cavalry was the swimmer. A third source was Capt. James Dinkins, who named Pvt. Dick Clinton of Walton's battery as the captor of the *Mazeppa*. However, Dinkins was on Chalmers staff, whose division did not show up at the Tennessee River until after the capture of the *Mazeppa*. A variety of commentaries by men who witnessed the boat's capture appeared in issues of the *Confederate Veteran* and continued the ongoing arguments. A majority of accounts from later witnesses, however, positively claimed that it was indeed Capts. Gracey and Horn who swam the Tennessee and commandeered the *Mazeppa*.

Captain Frank P. Gracey,
3rd Kentucky Infantry, Cobb's battery.
Courtesy of Daniel Taylor

and the barge. The valuable stores included shoes, blankets, food, and clothing.[22]

Around 4:00 p.m., while the Confederates were hurriedly unloading the vessels, "three gunboats appeared from below and began to shell the men who were actively engaged in removing the stores." To prevent the recapture of the *Mazeppa*, Gen. Buford ordered Hunter's 20-pounder Parrott's to return fire. A heated twenty-minute engagement followed before the gunboats thought better of the effort and withdrew out of range downriver. Buford, who fully expected "a return of the gunboats in greater force," ordered Col. Shacklett to "take command of the boat" and set the *Mazeppa* on fire even though a significant portion of the captured supplies were still aboard. Shacklett directed "Captain Charles W. Jetton and Private James W. King," members of Company H, 3rd Kentucky Infantry (mounted), to "apply the torch to the steamer" at the shoreline.[23]

The Federal gunboats reappeared, but after the *Mazeppa* was set ablaze, assumed a "position out of range of the Confederate guns" and, after a time, withdrew to Paducah. Once it was safe to do so, Buford's men worked

---

22 T. E. Crutcher, "Witness to the Capture of the Mazeppa," *Confederate Veteran*, Vol. 37, No. 11 (November 1929): 71; Jordan and Pryor, *The Campaigns of General Nathan Bedford Forrest*, 593; Shacklett to Gracey, "Capture of the *Mazeppa*," 568; *ORN* 26, 620.

23 Mathes, *General Forrest*, 299; Henry George, *History of the 3rd, 7th, 8th, and 12th Kentucky, C.S.A.* (Louisville, 1911), 128.

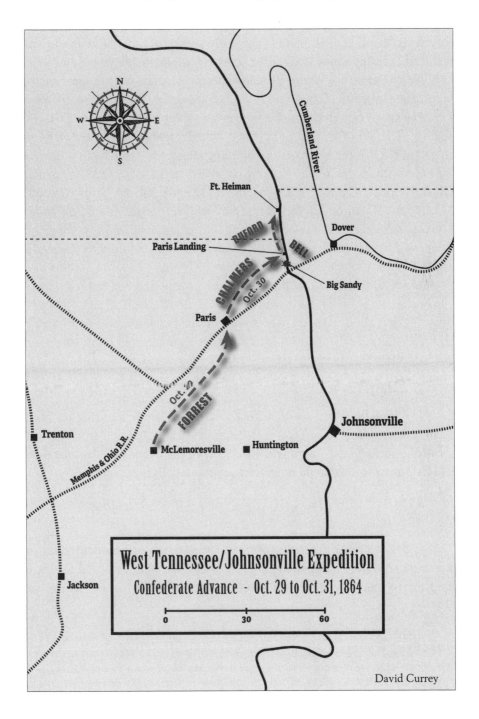

Ft. Heiman

Cumberland River

Dover

BUFORD

Paris Landing

BELL

CHALMERS

Oct. 30

Big Sandy

Paris

Oct. 29

FORREST

Johnsonville

Trenton

McLemoresville   Huntington

Memphis & Ohio R.R.

Jackson

West Tennessee/Johnsonville Expedition
Confederate Advance - Oct. 29 to Oct. 31, 1864

0   30   60

David Currey

feverishly "hauling the captured supplies to a place of security, with wagons and teams mainly impressed for the service from the neighborhood."[24]

The *Mazeppa's* crewmen, meanwhile, made their way to the Federal outpost at Pine Bluff, Tennessee, two miles above the old site of Confederate Fort Henry. When the Union commander at Pine Bluff, Lt. Col. T. R. Weaver, learned of the *Mazeppa's* fate, he telegraphed Henry Howland at Johnsonville to inform him of the disturbing attack. Howland, in turn, shared the news with Johnsonville's ranking naval officer, Lt. Edward M. King, and telegraphed Lt. Cmdr. Le Roy Fitch, commander of the Tenth District, Mississippi Squadron, at Paducah. There was no longer any doubt about Forrest's whereabouts. He was operating in strength, with artillery, along the Tennessee River, and the ability to interdict traffic to and from Johnsonville posed a major problem.

Earlier on the same day the *Mazeppa* was captured and burned, James Chalmers reined in at Paris with Mabry's, McCulloch's, and Rucker's brigades, and all his artillery. The arrival of the division protected Buford's rear and coalesced the main body of Forrest's command. At Paris, Chalmers wasted little time ordering Mabry's brigade, together with Thrall's battery, to remain there and establish a defensive perimeter while he continued east with McCulloch's and Rucker's brigades to connect with Bell's command at Paris Landing. Later that same evening, October 29, Forrest and his staff and escort arrived. Before he went into camp at Paris a dispatch from Buford arrived describing the morning's success with the capture of the *Mazeppa* and its cargo. Forrest could not have been more delighted.[25]

Naval Charades

Sunday, October 30, found Buford's troops in position and ready to attack more Union transports and gunboats on the Tennessee River. They didn't have long to wait. About 10:00 a.m., Sgt. Maj. Crozier's section of

---

24 Morton, *The Artillery of Nathan Bedford Forrest's Cavalry*, 247; Jordon and Pryor, *The Campaigns of General Nathan Bedford Forrest*, 593; Richard R. Hancock, *Hancock's Diary: or, A History of the Second Tennessee Confederate Cavalry, with Sketches of First and Seventh battalions; also, Portraits and Biographical Sketches. Two volumes in One* (Nashville,1887), 496-97.

25 Ibid.

Walton's battery spotted the Federal transport *Anna* steaming north downriver toward Paducah. Like the *Mazeppa*, she was also towing a barge. Unlike the prior day's situation, however, the *Anna* was escorted by the USS *Undine*, one of Johnsonville's four gunboats.

The *Undine* was a "tin-clad"—a lightly armored converted steamboat that was faster, more maneuverable, and drew less water than a conventional ironclad. Tin-clads were perfect for patrolling inland rivers and could serve as effectively as transports and as support for infantry. The *Undine* was built in Cincinnati in 1863 and commissioned there the following April of 1864. "The boat I am on now carries 2, 24 pound Dahlgren boat howitzers, brass bow chasers," explained Frank Drake, a crewman aboard the *Undine*, to his sister on July 1, 1864. "They are the most exquisite pieces of workmanship. This is a "tin" clad," he continued,

> covered with iron of sufficient thickness to resist rifle balls and perhaps grape and canister though old "salts" say that the gun deck when greased will glance a 32 pound shot. This is. . .the fastest one in the squadron. We made 25 miles per hour the other day coming down the river. We started up from Paducah July 1st—8 am with 3 convoys. I don't think we will come up here many more times as the river is so low that we can hardly move [26]

Three months earlier on this same river the *Undine*, under the command of Acting Master John L. Bryant, ran into an underwater obstruction and sank. She was refloated a week later. Bryant retained his command.

That same Sunday, October 30, the USS *Undine* was about 600 yards astern of the *Anna*. "I saw her safely below Sandy Island," reported Bryant. "No firing was heard at that time, when I gave orders to head the ship upsteam and proceed back toward Johnsonville." Once the *Undine* turned about and headed south, the *Anna*, now without her escort, continued north downriver. She was passing Crozier's section of 3-inch Ordnance Rifles just south of Paris Landing when the guns opened fire. Bryant immediately ordered full steam ahead and the *Anna* escaped the iron balls. She continued downriver unaware that more concealed artillery under Lt. Zarring was

---

26 Frank Drake to Clemma Drake Smith, May 16 and July 2, 1864, Frank Drake Letters, Ralzemond Parker Collection, Clarke Historical Library, Central Michigan University (hereafter Drake Letters). In fact, the *Undine* had eight 24-pound Howitzers, four on each side.

waiting for her. The *Anna* approached Paris Landing as close to the western bank as prudence would allow.[27]

A Confederate officer suddenly appeared on horseback and ordered the boat to steer toward the bank. The *Anna's* pilot rang the ship's bell and shouted back, "I will come to, at the lower landing!" The *Anna* was approaching the bank when she went to full steam in an effort to escape an obvious trap, and used the river current to increase her speed and aid her escape. Confederate gunners opened fire and struck her multiple times, inflicting serious but not fatal damage. Her narrow escape brings to mind Frank Drake's letter to his sister about how "old salts" bragged "the gun deck when greased will glance a 32 pound shot." Somehow, greased sides or otherwise, the *Anna* escaped the Confederate batteries at Paris Landing and Fort Heiman and safely reached Paducah.[28]

Master Bryant aboard the *Undine*, meanwhile, heard the heavy firing behind him, turned his gunboat about, and steamed downriver toward Paris Landing. By doing so he fell into the same trap sprung on the *Anna*. Once in front of Paris Landing, a Confederate officer (likely the same one who had called out to the *Anna*) boldly repeated his performance. "[W]hen abreast of Paris Landing, I was hailed by a man on the bank, 'Halloo, there, gunboat,' or some such words," Master Bryant later reported. "I immediately stopped my engines. At that instant, was opened on from the west bank by a heavy artillery and infantry fire about 50 yards from shore."[29]

The *Undine* immediately returned fire from her four port-side 24-pounder howitzers "for 55 minutes up to 700 yards distance." At some point the *Undine* was temporarily crippled when a shot penetrated her side and extinguished the fire powering her boilers. Bryant ordered the pilot to steer the gunboat to the opposite bank as far away from the enemy batteries as possible. Once out of effective range, Bryant dropped anchor along the eastern shore and began repairs. A short time later a "heavy fire of musketry from the west bank" opened on the stationary gunboat. Bryant ordered his

---

27 *ORN* 26, 602.

28 Dinkins, "Destroying Military Stores and Gunboats," 177; Maness, *An Untutored Genius*, 310; Irion and Beard, *Underwater Archaeological: Assessment of Civil War Shipwrecks*, 32; *ORN* 26, 602; *OR* 39, pt. 3, 550.

29 *ORN* 26, 602.

gunners to return fire, and the port-side howitzers hammered the distant shore for about an hour until the Confederate infantry disengaged.

It was about 2:00 p.m., while the *Undine* sat anchored along the east bank engaged with Bell's Confederates, when the *Venus*, another Federal transport, appeared two miles above the *Undine* steaming downriver from Johnsonville. Bryant realized the *Venus* was about to enter the same gauntlet of Confederate batteries and "warned her by signals to keep out of danger." Despite several attempts to warn her off, the *Venus* ignored the signals and steamed within range. Confederate artillery fire struck her and small arms fire peppered her sides, but the *Venus*'s wheel remained functioning. The transport moved to the opposite bank and anchored under the protection of the *Undine's* howitzers.[30]

Twenty minutes later, a third Federal transport towing two barges appeared from the same direction as the *Venus*. The *J. W. Cheeseman* was a large transport loaded with supplies including pickled pork, bacon, coffee, crackers, candies, flour, and furniture. As the *J.W. Cheeseman* approached the enemy batteries at Paris Landing, the Rebels opened fire and "completely disabled [her machinery] in a short time." With her steering capacity gone, the *J. W. Cheeseman* began "turning around in the stream," and could not escape to the eastern shore. Instead, to the horror of her crew and the delight of the Confederates, she ended up on the western bank just below the Paris Landing batteries near Sandy Island. Incapacitated and without the means of waging any credible defense, the crew dropped the gangway and Confederates clamored aboard, with the first being "Captain Lawler, Company C" of the 7th Tennessee Cavalry. Within a few minutes, the *J. W. Cheeseman's* crewmen were officially prisoners and ordered to begin unloading the vessel's abundance of supplies into captured yawls to haul ashore.[31]

30 Ibid, 602-03.

31 Morton, *The Artillery of Nathan Bedford Forrest's Cavalry*, 248; Dinkins, "Destroying Military Stores and Gunboats," 177; J.P. Young, *The Seventh Tennessee Cavalry-Confederate* (Dayton, Ohio, 1976), 114; Mathes, *General Forrest*, 299.

Taking the USS *Undine* and Transport *Venus*

Following Forrest's directive that he "must be prompt," Chalmers ordered his men to assist the *Cheeseman's* captured crew in unloading supplies from the grounded vessel. As these duties commenced, Mabry's brigade and Thrall's artillery arrived from Paris and rejoined the rest of Chalmers' division at Paris Landing. Rucker ordered Lt. Col. D. C. Kelley of the 3rd Tennessee Cavalry and the 15th Tennessee Cavalry under Lt. Col. T. H. Logwood to "make a reconnaissance, and if found practicable, to take Walton's two 10-pounder Parrott guns and two Howitzers of Thrall's battery, and move as near the *Undine* and *Venus* as he could and attack them."[32]

Meanwhile, as Rucker's men opened fire with artillery and small arms on the *Venus* 350 yards distant, a small contingent of new recruits from the 34th New Jersey Infantry poured out of the interior and lined the rails of the boat. A Union lieutenant gave the orders and the line of men returned fire, engaging the barely visible Confederates across the river. An hour of steady firing ground to a fitful halt from the New Jersey barrels when the men realized that two of their own, together with the *Venus's* captain, had been killed.[33]

As Rucker's men kept up their relentless barrage against the *Venus*, other Confederates turned their attention to the *Undine*, raking the unlucky boat from bow to stern. The men aboard had no way to return fire because they had closed the gun ports to protect their gunners from Kelley's deadly sharpshooters. A shell from one of Thrall's guns struck the *Undine's* stern and damaged her rudder. By this time it was obvious to everyone aboard both vessels that the situation was hopeless. Out of every option but one, the men aboard the *Undine* and *Venus* abandoned their boats and escaped into the woods, leaving their dead and wounded aboard ship. The survivors eventually made their way to the Federal garrison at Fort Donelson.[34]

---

32 *OR* 39, pt.3, 868.

33 "Tennessee River Raid," *The Nashville Appeal*, June 29, 1902, 5; *OR* 39, pt. 3, 868-72; *ORN* 26, 605, 624.

34 Dinkins, "Destroying Military Stores and Gunboats," 177; Mathes, *General Forrest*, 299.

One of the men aboard the *Undine* who escaped that afternoon was crewman Frank Drake. His father, Dr. Flemon Drake, penned a letter a few months later to his daughter Clemma detailing her brother's escape. "The suspense that has hung over us so long in regard to Frank is at last dispelled," he began. "One of his shipmates has arrived home at Detroit & written to me such statements within his knowledge that leaves us no room to doubt but what Frank was killed by the Guerrillas after escaping from the boat." Dr. Drake continued:

> He says that all of those who escaped from the boat arrived in safety at Ft. Davidson [Donelson] & that the day after Frank with a number of the crew started to go to Johnsonville a distance of 32 miles & that when 15 miles out they were overtaken by Guerillas and Frank & an other man from Toledo were killed.[35]

Now, with both the *Undine* and *Venus* abandoned along the eastern bank north of Paris Landing, Forrest ordered Chalmers to "burn nothing unless you are compelled to do so; save all the blankets and shoes as we will need them for McCulloch's Brigade and Mabry's Brigade." Chalmers directed two companies under Col. Kelley to construct makeshift rafts and cross the Tennessee to commandeer the abandoned vessels. Neither the *Undine* nor the *Venus* were heavily damaged, and Kelley's men worked quicky to repair what they could. The Rebels then "raised steam, and carried both gunboat and transport to Paris Landing."[36]

Forrest arrived with his escort at Paris Landing on Monday morning, October 31. With the captured *Undine* and *Venus* now safely in his possession, Forrest examined the *J. W. Cheeseman* with Chalmers and determined that she was "so badly damaged, it was not thought possible to put her in service." Forrest would later write that considering the *J. W. Cheeseman's* poor condition "she was ordered, with the two barges, to be burned." With a small "fleet" of captured Federal vessels under his command, Forrest planned an attack against Johnsonville. The cavalryman enjoyed experimenting with artillery, so he asked Capt. John Morton, "how would you like to transfer your guns to these boats and command a gunboat

---

35 Dr. Flemon Drake to Clemma Drake, February 2, 1865, Drake Letters.

36 *OR* 39, pt. 3, 868; Hancock, *Hancock's Diary*, 500.

Lt. Col. William A. Dawson, 15th
Tennessee Infantry, ca., 1864.
Courtesy of Daniel Taylor

fleet?" Morton declined the
offer, but agreed to accompany
the boats by land.

Forrest gathered his officers
and conveyed his plan. The
captured vessels would steam
toward Johnsonville accompanied by a land force. The infantry
would move south along the
western bank in synchronization with the boats serving as protection.
Chalmers' division would lead the contingent with Morton's artillery close
behind serving as a screen against any Federal gunboat attacks. Buford's
division would bring up the rear "to cover them from any gunboats which
might come from the direction of Paducah."[37]

That afternoon, Forrest ordered Buford to have some of his men practice
piloting the recently captured *Undine* and *Venus*. Many of Buford's infantry
("horse marines," as they were later called) boarded the vessels (some while
still mounted) and practiced maneuvering the boats along the five-mile
stretch of river between the batteries at Paris Landing and abandoned Fort
Heiman. Capt. Frank Gracey, who had experience operating steamboats
prior to the war, piloted the *Undine*. Lt. Col. William A. Dawson of the 15th
Tennessee Infantry of Rucker's brigade, who had also operated steamboats
in West Tennessee waters before the war, volunteered to pilot the *Venus*.[38]

---

37 "Tennessee River Raid," *The Niashville Appeal*, June 29, 1902, 5; *ORN* 26, 682-683;
Morton, 248; Jordan and Pryor, *The Campaigns of General Nathan Bedford Forrest*,
596-597.

38 Morton, *The Artillery of Nathan Bedford Forrest's Cavalry*, 249; Maness, *An
Untutored Genius*, 311; Jordan and Pryor, *The Campaigns of General Nathan Bedford
Forrest*, 597; "For Whom Dawson Camp was Named," *Confederate Veteran* (April, 1901),
vol. 9, No. 4: 149.

Some of the Confederate artillerists aboard the *Undine* practiced rapid-fire drills with the captured 24-pounder howitzers, and by the end of the day were comfortable operating the pieces. Walton's two 20-pounder Parrotts were loaded onto the *Venus*, but not placed into battery for use. As night arrived on the final day of October—a month that had produced nothing but success for Forrest—the Confederates slept soundly in dry conditions as storm clouds slowly darkened in the west.

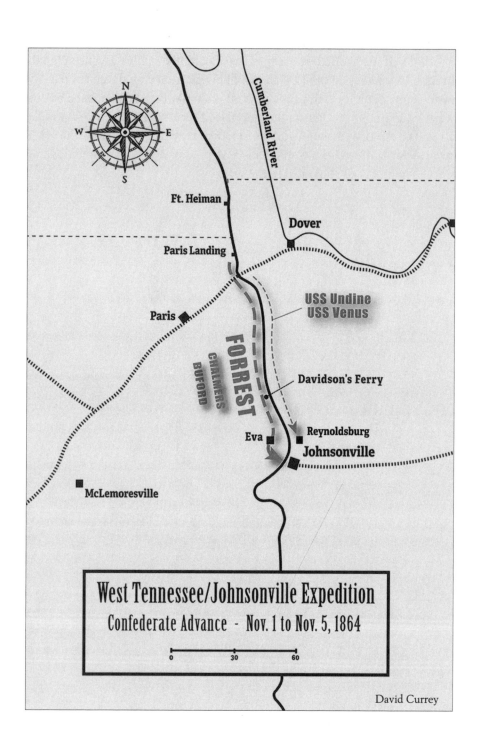

West Tennessee/Johnsonville Expedition
Confederate Advance - Nov. 1 to Nov. 5, 1864

David Currey

CHAPTER 8

The Noose Tightens:
The Battle of Reynoldsburg Island

$\mathbf{A}$T 4:00 a.m., on Tuesday, November 1, Abraham Buford's Confederate troops vacated their positions at Fort Heiman and joined James Chalmers' division at Paris Landing. For the first time in more than a week Nathan Bedford Forrest had his entire force assembled and prepared to move south against Johnsonville.

The Confederates were organizing their ample train of wagons, now heavy with captured Federal supplies, when a local Southern sympathizer named Jack Hinson appeared. Hinson, who lived between the Tennessee and Cumberland rivers in Stewart County, offered to show Forrest "the road the guns should take through the Cypress Creek Swamp to get into good positions for the bombardment of Johnsonville." Forrest understood tall the task that lay ahead for his troops, who would be marching along the muddy shoreline in conjunction with the captured gunboats, and agreed to Hinson's offer. He allowed the old man to accompany Chalmers' men as they moved south.[1]

---

1 Jill Knight Garrett, "Guerillas and Bushwhackers in Middle Tennessee during the Civil War," in Jill Knight Garrett collection, Box 11, F1, manuscripts, TSLA, Nashville, Tennessee. Just before departing Paris Landing, the wounded Federal soldiers and crewmen from the *J. W. Cheeseman* and *Undine* were gathered and left to fend for themselves, without medicine or care. Two days later, after the Confederates had departed the area, the wounded were discovered by the U.S. Navy gunboat USS *Moose* under Lt. Comdr. Le Roy Fitch, who provided medicine and bandages and a surgeon. Most of the wounded were

A light rain that began falling at 11:00 a.m. steadily increased throughout the day. By the middle of the afternoon Forrest's men were marching through one of heaviest rain storms of the year in Tennessee. The cold pelting water slowed their advance along roads that became muddier by the hour. Hauling artillery, caissons, limbers, and wagons was soon nearly impossible for the overworked horses and mules. Chalmers' men, who hugged the sticky shoreline at the head of the column, struggled to keep up with the captured *Undine* and *Venus*, which slipped ahead of the land force by almost two miles.[2]

Exhausted, soaked, and cold, Chalmers' troopers only made it twelve miles to Danville before setting up camp near the ruins of a burned railroad bridge that had once crossed the Tennessee River. Artillery officers positioned their guns along the riverbank to protect the *Undine* and *Venus*, which anchored just offshore. Buford's men, meanwhile, served as a rear guard and camped three miles behind (north) of Chalmers' position.[3]

A "Good Prize"

The Confederates continued south on the morning of November 2 along the western shore of the Tennessee River. Earlier that morning, the heavy rain that had stopped for a while during the night commenced once more. Forrest, who accompanied Chalmers' command along the shore, directed Capt. Frank P. Gracey, commanding the *Undine*, and Lt. Col. William A. Dawson, commanding the *Venus*, to guide the boats to the western shore. Chalmers, meanwhile, was to halt his command just above Davidson's Ferry, where the river made a gradual turn southwest seven miles north of Johnsonville. There, the entire column rested briefly before continuing its coordinated advance with the *Undine* and *Venus*, which moved upriver about 100 yards from the bank. Prior to departing, Forrest ordered Mabry's brigade and Thrall's battery to move farther upriver ahead of the main column and establish concealed gun positions across from Johnsonville.

---

rescued and carried aboard the vessel. Some, however, were too ill or badly injured to be moved and were left at various houses in the community to be cared for by the local citizenry. *ORN* 26, 612.

2 Ibid; Dinkins,"Destroying Military Stores and Gunboats," 178; *ORN* 26, 612.

3 *ORN* 26, 685-86; Hancock, diary, 503.

U.S. Navy Mississippi Squadron near Cape Girardeau, Missouri, with U.S.S. *Key West*
(Gunboat No. 32) at far left, ca. 1863. *Library of Congress*

Like they had the previous day, the *Undine* and *Venus* once again moved
faster than the land-bound troops, who struggled through nearly impassable
terrain.[4]

While Forrest was approaching Johnsonville, naval officer Lt. Edward
King spent much of the day re-supplying the *Key West* and *Tawah*. He
departed from the Johnsonville wharf with both gunboats at 2:30 p.m. and
steamed downriver with the intention of recapturing the *Undine* and *Venus*.
Six and a half miles from Johnsonville, King's gunboats rounded the bend
near Green Bottom Bar, a large sand bar that hugged the eastern side of the
river half a mile south of Davidson's Ferry—and ran directly into the *Undine*
and *Venus*, both of which were loaded with Confederate troops.[5]

It didn't take long to figure out that the ships in front of them were
enemy vessels under a different flag, and the *Key West* and *Tawah*
immediately engaged the *Undine*, which was serving as escort to the *Venus*
500 yards astern. The Federal gunboats turned so their broadsides faced
downriver and opened fire. The *Undine* returned fire with its 24-pounder
howitzers. After what one eyewitness described as a "sharp engagement for
some twenty minutes," the *Venus*, trailing the *Undine*, lost control of its
steering and struggled to stay on course. As it turned out, the *Venus*'s tiller

---

4 Ibid; Jordan and Pryor, *The Campaigns of General Nathan Bedford Forrest,* 598-99;
Maness, *An Untutored Genius*, 312-13; *ORN* 26, 685.

5 *ORN* 26, 621.

rope, which controlled the rudder, had been severed and the vessel was now unmanageable. Lt. Col. Dawson realized that his vessel could not escape downriver. By some means, he managed to turn the *Venus* around to face north and, with the current pushing the boat, struck the north end of Green Bottom Bar along the eastern bank while "under a hot fire" from the *Tawah*.[6]

With the *Venus* run aground, Dawson ordered his troops to abandon ship while under under fire from the *Tawah*. The Confederates had no choice but to leave behind the pair of 20-pounder Parrott Rifles and captured cargo from the *Mazeppa* and *J. W. Cheeseman*, which included "300 rounds of ammunition, 100 boxes of shoes, two bales of blankets, and 576 boxes of hard bread." Because of shelling from the *Tawah*, Dawson's men did not even have time to set fire to the *Venus*, choosing instead to escape into the woods lining the riverbank. Capt. Gracey's *Undine* made several attempts to rescue the *Venus* and pull her off the sandbar, but the relentless fire from the *Key West* and *Tawah* made the task impossible, and she withdrew downriver leaving the *Venus* to her fate. Around dusk, the *Tawah* moved in and, according to an after-action report filed by Lt. Comdr. Fitch a few days later, "captured the *Venus*, with two 20-pounder rifles and some 300 rounds of ammunition." The *Tawah's* crew attached a hawser to the *Venus* and towed her safely back to Johnsonville with the *Key West* providing escort.[7]

6 Jordan and Pryor, *The Campaigns of General Nathan Bedford Forrest*, 598; *ORN* 26, 613, 615-17. According to Jordan and Pryor, 598, it was suggested that since the Confederates retained some of *Venus'* original crew, including the boat's "old engineer," the cutting of the tiller-rope was likely sabotage, especially considering the bow of the boat faced the Union gunboats and was 500 yards astern of the *Undine*. During the Civil War, boats were still being steered by a wheel and transmitted via tiller ropes and tackles to the rudder, as it had been for centuries. The protection of these tiller-ropes (also called wheel-ropes and steering chains) was important and ships were designed to protect them as much as possible. If they were cut, the ship was often as good as lost. As one writer noted: "The USS *Louisville* had her tiller ropes shot away at Fort Donelson and drifted away down the river, out of control. The CSS *Tennessee's* steering chains were for some indecipherable reason left exposed in grooves on the afterdeck, covered only by a thin sheet of boiler iron, and they were soon shot away by the USS *Chickasaw*, leaving her unmanageable." Mark F. Jenkins, "The Technology of the Ironclads," *Naval Gazette*, vol. 3, No. 1 (1998), 1-3.

7 Wyeth, *That Devil Forrest*, 462; Jordan and Pryor, *The Campaigns of General Nathan Bedford Forrest*, 598-99; Morton, *The Artillery of Nathan Bedford Forrest's Cavalry*, 251; *ORN* 26, 613, 615. Dinkins, "Destroying Military Stores and Gunboats," 178. The exact whereabouts of Chalmers' division during the fight of the *Undine* and *Venus* with the Federal gunboats on November 2 is not exactly clear. No known accounts, except a few words by Dinkins, go into detail about what the Confederates witnessed. What is known, however, is that Capt. Dinkins was with Chalmers' division on the wet and muddy march to

That evening, Lt. King sent a telegram to his superior, Lt. Comdr. James W. Shirk, commander of the Ninth District, Mississippi Squadron, that because of the "misty and dark" weather, he had decided not to pursue the *Undine*, which "got away with shot through her. *Venus* is now here; good prize. We feel sore about the escape of *Undine*, but did not like to leave this place uncovered. She went down river faster than ever before. We won't let this place fall into enemy's hands." King later sent a message to Lt. Comdr. Fitch at Paducah to send his fleet of six gunboats, which included the *Paw-Paw*, *Moose*, *Fairy*, *Victory*, *Curlew*, and *Brilliant* to reinforce him at Johnsonville.[8]

While the gunboats battled it out in the middle of the Tennessee River, Chalmers and Morton's men, camouflaged by the dense river cane lining the edge of the Tennesse River, were moving south of Davidson's Ferry and came upon the action. Peering from the shoreline in anticipation of a "horse marine" victory over the practiced and precise marksmanship of the Union naval gunners, the Rebels watched in amazement as the battle commenced in earnest. Once the *Venus* was lost, the wet and exhausted Confederates continued pushing south toward Johnsonville.

Late that night, Lt. King, along with Peter Wagner, an engineer aboard the USS *Key West*, and Col. Thompson met aboard the *Key West* at Johnsonville's levee to discuss "the course to be pursued in case of an attack." As Wagner later recalled, they all agreed that "in the event the gunboats were destroyed it would probably be necessary to destroy the transports to prevent their falling into the enemy's hands." In a decision that would later have significant consequences, the officers decided the property entrusted to them should be destroyed rather than captured.[9]

Johnsonville, and that Dinkins described seeing the loss of the transport *Venus* as "Colonel Dawson ran her ashore." Ibid. Dawson's men who escaped onto the eastern shore of the Tennessee eventually rejoined Forrest in front of Johnsonville on the evening of November 3. After constructing makeshift rafts from driftwood, remembered John Morton, and using the cover of darkness, they "crossed on logs and rude rafts" to transfer back to the western shore. Morton, *The Artillery of Nathan Bedford Forrest's Cavalry*, 251.

8 Wyeth, *That Devil Forrest*, 462; Jordan and Pryor, *The Campaigns of General Nathan Bedford Forrest,* 598-99; Morton, *The Artillery of Nathan Bedford Forrest's Cavalry*, 251; *ORN* 26, 613, 615.

9 Irion and Beard, *Underwater Archaeological: Assessment of Civil War Shipwrecks*, 35.

After the meeting ended, King told Asst. Quartermaster Henry Howland about the decisions agreed upon and expressed that "in the event of the gunboats being attacked to night & disabled, I think it will be well for now to make preparations for destroying by fire all the transports now here so that they may not fall into the enemy's hands." Howland passed along this information to his Acting Assistant Quartermaster, Samuel W. Treat, who would have to be aware of the plan and follow through with the order "to destroy by fire all the transports now here" in case something happened to Howland. Howland also informed the transport boat pilots at the levee to keep "steam-up" overnight in anticipation of an attack.[10]

Late that evening and under a torrential downpour, Chalmers' division went into camp along the western bank of the Tennessee River a mile below (north of) Reynoldsburg. Forrest, with his staff and escort, continued riding another four miles south past Chalmers using a branch of the Paris-Reynoldsburg Road, a community road that ran through Beaver Dam Valley along its eastern ridge, and camped near Eva, Tennessee. Buford's division, meanwhile, slowed by the same mud as their comrades ahead of them, continued bringing up the rear of the column. By nightfall on November 2, the division had made it to the vicinity of Davidson's Ferry, where they bivouacked the night under an even heavier rain.

Testing the Limits

Forrest's Confederates were up at dawn on November 3. Mabry's brigade with Thrall's artillery moved south through the small town of Eva, and were joined by Lt. Col. William F. Taylor's 7th Tennessee Cavalry before noon. Forrest had previously ordered Mabry (who was farther south than any other unit) "to establish his command as nearly opposite to

---

10 Acting Volunteer Lt. Edward M. King to AQM Henry Howland, letter, November 3, 1864, and AQM Henry Howland to AAQM Samuel W. Treat, letter, November 3, 1864, both in Johnsonville, Tennessee, RG 94, Carded Records Relating to Civil War Staff Officers, National Archives, Washington, D.C. Excerpt from proceedings of the Board of Survey, in Nashville, Tennessee, for the investigation into the destruction of government property at Johnsonville, Tennessee, on November 4, 1864. Testimony provided by Johnsonville AAQM Lieutenant Samuel W. Treat, January 4, 1865, *U.S. Navy Records 1864-65, Courts Martial*, RG 11-86, National Archives, Washington, D.C., page # not provided; *ORN* 26, 621-23.

Johnsonville as possible . . . keeping carefully out of sight of the enemy." The remainder of Forrest's troops, which included the rest of Chalmers' division and Buford's division riding in the rear, moved in Mabry's wake. Chalmers ordered Col. Edmund Rucker to assist Capt. Morton in concealing a battery of four guns along the west bank of the river near the head of Reynoldsburg Island, a large tree-covered shoal a mile and a half long in the middle of the Tennessee and about three miles from Johnsonville.[11]

The river across from the head of Reynoldsburg Island, where Rucker and Morton concealed the artillery, was a narrow curve full of sandbars and shoals. Riverboat pilots familiar with this stretch called the obstacle "the chute." The average depth was only about five feet at the head of the island and double that at the end. Terrain always matters, and "the chute" would play a key role in the upcoming naval actions.[12]

After the previous day's engagement with the *Key West* and *Tawah*, the *Undine* had withdrawn downriver and anchored for the night under the protection of Chalmers' land batteries just below Reynoldsburg Island. At noon, the *Undine* increased steam and moved upriver "for the purpose of decoying" the Federal gunboats into range of the concealed Confederate shore batteries. When the *Undine* once again appeared a mile downriver from Reynoldsburg Island, Lt. King—who had anticipated the ruse— boarded the *Key West*, and, together with the *Tawah* in support, steamed downriver to engage her.[13]

As the *Key West* and *Tawah* approached the *Undine* and moved into range, Morton's battery and Rucker's sharpshooters lining the western bank opened fire. King's gunboats returned a hailstorm of shells into the Confederate land positions. While the *Key West* concentrated its fire on Morton's guns and Rucker's sharpshooters, the *Tawah* pursued the *Undine* and twice attempted to recapture her. Captain Gracey, however, deftly

11 Hancock, diary, 504; Jordan and Pryor, *The Campaigns of General Nathan Bedford Forrest,* 598-99; Affidavit account provided by First Class Pilot, Thomas J. Thornton, of the USS *Tawah*, May 17, 1865, in Nashville, Tennessee, regarding the gunboat battle between the USS *Key West*, *Elfin*, and *Tawah*, with the Confederate occupied USS *Undine* at Reynoldsburg Island, Tennessee, on November 4, 1864, *U.S. Navy Records 1864-65, Courts Martial*, RG 11-86, U.S. Navy Department, National Archives, Washington, D.C.

12 *ORN* 26, 630: Irion and Beard, *Underwater Archaeological: Assessment of Civil War Shipwrecks*, 35; Affidavit, Thornton, May 17, 1865.

13 *ORN* 26, 621-25.

maneuvered the *Undine* and kept enough distance between his ship and King's gunboats to prevent any Union effort to board her. After a brisk thirty-minute engagement, the *Undine* withdrew to the protection of the land batteries while King's gunboats returned upriver to Johnsonville to await the arrival of Fitch's fleet from Paducah.[14]

That evening, the Union defenders at the supply depot worked through the night in preparation for the larger battle they were certain was about to fall upon them. King took particular caution to ensure that the Confederates would not try to board the transport boats at the wharf during the night by ordering the *Tawah* to head downstream and protect the channel "with her 30-pounders."[15]

On the Confederate (western) side of the river, Forrest's troops remained hindered by some of the worst mud they had experienced thus far during the war. The rare opportunity to strike an important Union supply depot, however, coupled with the equally rare addition of naval support, had encouraged the men and helped push the column along on its advance toward Johnsonville. Chalmers' men had made camp and were doing their best to get as comfortable as possible when Lt. Comdr. Fitch's gunboat flotilla from Paducah arrived. "Just below Green Bottom Bar, about 30 miles above Fort Hindman [Heiman], I came up to a large encampment about 9:30 p.m.," reported Fitch. When he realized the camp could only be the enemy,

> we at once opened fire and drove them back, but I suppose not entirely away, as they could be heard during the night. After shelling the encampment for a time, causing the rebels to extinguish their fires, I dropped down a little below the camp, and to where there was no road by which they could bring artillery on the bank abreast of me, and anchored for the night.[16]

Capt. James Dinkins, a member of Chalmers' staff, never forgot the surprise bombardment that night and wrote about it decades later for *Confederate Veteran*. "The intensity of the shelling was like nothing most of the men had ever witnessed or endured," he began. The staffer continued:

---

14 Irion and Beard, *Underwater Archaeological: Assessment of Civil War Shipwrecks*, 35;

15 *ORN* 26, 616.

16 Ibid., 612.

Shells from 32-pounder rifles were thrown fully for three miles. They crashed through the woods with great din and uproar, but, happily, without harm. Every old soldier who was ever under fire from gunboats understands how dreadful the roar and how little the damage—except to the tops of the trees.[17]

Forrest and his staff, who the night before had camped at Eva, returned north that evening to check on the progress of those troops still strung out along a distance of three miles between Johnsonville and Reynoldsburg Island, slowed by rain and muddy roads. That night, Forrest bivouacked with his escort along the shore near the anchored *Undine*, only a mile south of Fitch's gunboat flotilla anchored at the northern end of Reynoldsburg Island. Late that evening, the cavalry commander wrote to Gen. Taylor about his plans for the following day, and his strategy to connect with Gen. Hood's Army of Tennessee:

GENERAL: Having advised you, by previous dispatch, of the capture of the U.S. gunboat 55 [*Undine*] and three transports and barges, and also of the damage to steamer *Anna*, which, in consequence of damage from our batteries, is reported to have sunk, I have now the honor to state that my command is in front of Johnsonville, at which place there are three gunboats and seven transports and quite a number of barges. I have batteries above and below the boats, and am to-night fortifying and placing a battery directly opposite them, and will to-morrow endeavor to sink or destroy them.

Johnsonville, he continued, "is strongly fortified, with heavy siege pieces in their works, and is garrisoned by a heavy force." Forrest continued:

We still have the gunboat in possession, but she is out of coal and it being impossible to supply her or to get her by Johnsonville, I may have to burn her. Will make the attack on the transports to-morrow at Johnsonville, and will, day after to-morrow, if necessary to do so, burn the gunboat, and move to join General Hood.[18]

17 Dinkins, "Destroying Military Stores and Gunboats," 178.

18 *ORN* 26, 683-84. Forrest's report that Johnsonville was "strongly fortified, with heavy siege pieces in their works, and is garrisoned by a heavy force," was inaccurate, and likely the result of unreliable intelligence. In fact, the depot was not all that "heavily fortified," as Col. Thompson and Lt. King revealed in several telegrams requesting more troops to defend it. Additionally, there is no evidence that any siege guns, 32-pounders or larger, were present in the forts or entrenchments at Johnsonville. Every gun present was a field artillery

Black Friday-November 4

On Friday, November 4, the weather at Johnsonville dawned cloudy. A light mist hung in the air from lingering rain that had been "falling incessantly" for three days, complained Cpl. Lorenzo Atwood of the 43rd Wisconsin. "[I]t has rained nearly all of the time night and day for the last 3 days, mud from ankle to boot leg deep. A good deal of thunder with the rain." As if to find a silver lining in the weather, he added, "We have had but one frost yet."[19] Lt. Walter Howland described similar conditions in a report and concluded, "I would have clung to my native hills with devotion which several men I have just met [carpenters and laborers] wish they had experienced before they left their Mass. Homes for the mud of Tenn."[20]

As unpleasant as the weather conditions were for the Federals, the Confederates had it even worse. Forrest's men had been operating in the field for months without much time to rest and refit. The men and horses were exhausted, the regiments understrength, and their morale lower than normal. Despite the mud, rain, and extremely trying outdoor conditions, the raid would move forward as planned. "It had been raining continuously and was very cold," wrote Captain Dinkins, "but General Forrest never postponed anything."[21]

While Forrest's men shivered under the rainy conditions, the Union commander at Johnsonville worried—and rightly so. Col. Thompson received a dispatch the evening before from Lt. King that the Confederates had withdrawn from around Reynoldsburg Island, and "that a large portion

---

piece, such as 3-inch Ordnance Rifles, 10- and 20-pounder Parrott Rifles, and 12-pounder Napoleons. The U.S. gunboats at Johnsonville, however, did have 24-pounder howitzers that were cause for concern for Forrest, who many times during the war had experienced the effects of naval artillery.

19 Jordan and Pryor, *The Campaigns of General Nathan Bedford Forrest,* 599; Atwood, letter, November 8, 1864.

20 Jordan and Pryor, *The Campaigns of General Nathan Bedford Forrest,* 599; Atwood, letter, November 8, 1864; Walter Howland, letter, November 20, 1864. The "carpenters and laborers" were civilian workers who traveled to Johnsonville for employment after reading advertisements in their local newspapers requesting workers for the Quartermaster's Department at the depots in Nashville, Chattanooga, and Johnsonville.

21 Dinkins, "Destroying Military Stores and Gunboats," 178-79.

of Forrest's command had crossed to the east side of the river and that an attack would be made on Johnsonville the next morning."[22]

In fact, none of Forrest's men were on the same side of the river as Johnsonville, but Thompson had no reason to doubt King's warning. Thompson suspected the engagements with the *Undine* on November 2 and 3 had been designed to draw the gunboats away and thus remove their more than two-dozen cannon he so desperately needed to defend the depot and town. Thompson also suspected that the diversion made by the *Undine* would have allowed time for Forrest's troops to cross to the eastern bank, surround Johnsonville from the land side, and, when the hour arrived, force a surrender. Thompson ordered increased security around Johnsonville's perimeter and waited. There was little else he could do.

Late on the evening of November 3 and into the early hours of November 4, a majority of Forrest's troops relocated from around Reynoldsburg Island to positions across the river from Johnsonville. Their front stretched for about three-quarters of a mile and included five prepared cannon positions for a surprise attack on the supply depot. Captain Morton, as might be expected, was especially busy that night. Guiding his horse through the sloppy Tennessee mud, Morton recalled finding "Forrest and Bell at a point half a mile below Johnsonville, opposite the mouth of Trace Creek. Some holes had been cut into the bank of the river for the guns." According to the gunnery officer, Rucker's men had carved out the position, and Morton was none too happy about it:

I objected to putting my guns into these holes, and asked Forrest to allow me to pass up the river and examine the position opposite Johnsonville. He at first hesitated, but told me to "hurry up" as he had issued orders to open all along the line at 12 o'clock. I galloped up the slough in rear of the river bank and took in the situation. A gunboat was plying about fifty yards out in the river. I could have thrown a stone

22 Affidavit account provided by Col. Charles R. Thompson regarding the actions of the U.S. forces at Johnsonville, Tennessee, that resulted in the destruction of government property on November 4, 1864, for the Board of Survey at Nashville, Tennessee, in the Court Martial case of Acting Volunteer Lt. Commander, Edward M. King, December 29, 1864, *U.S. Navy Records 1864-65, Courts Martial*, RG 11-86, U.S. Navy Department, National Archives, Washington, D.C.

onto the boat. I slipped back to my horse and rode back to where Forrest was and asked him to allow me to carry my old battery to the position I had located.[23]

Morton advised his commander that, even though his reconnaissance had been quickly performed, "I have examined the location well. The fort is so elevated that they can't depress their guns sufficiently to affect me, and the gunboats are so much below in the river that they will fire over me, and I'll be in an angle of comparative safety." At first Forrest declined Morton's proposal because he was concerned the position was too close and his guns would be discovered before the barrage could begin. Instead, Forrest wanted his artillery officer to deploy his guns farther away from the western levee and out of direct range of the Union gunboats. Morton, however, continued pressing his case until the general obliged his young artillery chief to "carry two guns forward" to the recommended position. Morton immediately ordered a detail "to cut out logs, remove driftwood, and help the guns through the mud."[24]

The mud-caked rebels labored well into the early morning hours of November 4 hauling guns by hand into position, digging chambers to settle cannon trails deeper into the ground for more elevation, carving embrasures into the natural levee, and cutting underbrush to camouflage each gun position. Morton recalled just how difficult it was to properly deploy the guns in such a short period of time. "It took two hours of infinitely toilsome work to get the guns in position," he recalled. "Every step of the road had to be made, and in many places the guns had to be carried over fallen timber by hand. The underbrush was dense and the mud sticky." In order for the Confederate surprise attack to succeed, complete silence was required. Forrest instructed his officers to demand precisely that from their men while working on embrasures and getting everything ready. Doing so would ensure that noises from the cutting of wood and the clattering of chains against cannon carriages would not alert the Federals, who were only 400 yards away.[25]

23 John W. Morton, "Tennessee River Raid: An Interesting Communication to Captain S. R. Latta," in *Dyer County Herald*, March 14, 1896.

24 Morton, *The Artillery of Nathan Bedford Forrest's Cavalry*, 254; Morton, "Tennessee River Raid," 5.

25 Morton, "Tennessee River Raid," 5.

Brig. Gen. Hylan B. Lyon had been an artillery officer before the war, and used his past experience to help Thrall's artillerists position their guns 100 yards south of Warehouse No. 2. Thrall's guns (four 12-pounder howitzers), represented the extreme right flank of Forrest's extended line, or the farthest point south of all the Confederate artillery positions. There, recalled Forrest, "the river bank fell-off rapidly westward, and formed a natural rampart, behind which Lyon sunk chambers for his guns, and cut embrasures through the solid natural parapet in his front." Thrall's artillerists worked all night under a steady rain and in the kind of wet smelly mud only a river bottom can produce. The battery, Forrest wrote approvingly, "was completely shielded from the gunboats."[26]

The next battery position was about 300 yards north, or downriver, from Thrall's place of deployment. There, Col. Rucker's men helped establish Sgt. Lemuel Zarring's section of Morton's battery (two 3-inch Ordnance Rifles) just opposite Johnsonville. Three more artillery positions were established along the river north of Thrall's and Morton's guns.

The third position included another section of Morton's battery (two 3-inch Rodmans) under the command of Lt. J. W. Brown. These guns were opposite the mouth of Trace Creek about 100 yards north of Zarring's section. A fourth position included a section of Walton's (Rice's) battery (two rather rare 14-pounder James Rifles) 100 yards north of Brown's section under Lt. H. H. Briggs. The fifth and final artillery position was another section of Walton's (Rice's) battery (two 10-pounder Parrott Rifles) under Sgt. Maj. Orlando M. Crozier, positioned a mile and a half downriver between Reynoldsburg and Johnsonville to protect "a crossing of a shallow bar." Once the artillery positions were established, the Confederates had a total of twelve guns located between five heavily camouflaged positions.[27]

The Union forces at Johnsonville had a tactical advantage over their Confederate rivals considering that their artillery and infantry were positioned primarily on higher ground that overlooked the western river bank. But there were disadvantages to the position as well. The busy supply depot was a noisy place, with saw mills constantly running and train and

---

26 Ibid; Jordan and Pryor, *The Campaigns of General Nathan Bedford Forrest,* 599, 601.

27 Jordan and Pryor, *The Campaigns of General Nathan Bedford Forrest,* 599, 601; Dinkins, 178; Morton, *The Artillery of Nathan Bedford Forrest's Cavalry,* 254; *OR* 39, pt. 2, 883-84.

steamboat engines, with their high-pitched, hissing steam from pressure valves on steam boilers, overpowering even the loudest shouts of an officer. All of this combined to help muffle any noises coming from across the river, whether from rattling chains, squeaking wheels, or axes and shovels doing their laborious work. The Confederate gunners did not finish positioning themselves under cover of the high natural levee until noon, and were only 400 yards away across the river. Although there is evidence that the Unionists on the far side of the river knew or suspected the enemy was up to something, they seem to have had no idea that approximately 3,400 Confederates were laboring so intensely and so near to bring about their destruction.

The Union gunboats *Elfin*, *Key West*, and *Tawah* spent the early morning hours of November 4 firing fitfully (and blindly) into and beyond the wooded embankment across the river. The Confederates were somewhere in the vicinity, so lobbing shells might force them to show their hand or at least slow down and perhaps disrupt their plans. At worst, it would keep them from getting a good night's sleep. "The gunboats shelled the woods: the big beer-keg like shells crashed through the trees and created quite a commotion among the cavalry," confirmed Capt. Morton. "A good many amusing things occurred that night." Horses tied up behind the troops along the river bank, for example, broke out of their hitches and ran out of control in every direction because of the thunderous noise created by the gunboat shells.[28]

While the artillerymen were camouflaging their positions, Chalmers and Buford were moving their infantry into position and carefully concealing them in the underbrush and behind logs between the five artillery positions. After overseeing the positioning of his troops into the early morning hours of November 4, Forrest took refuge with his staff in a cypress swamp near the river and rested there for a short time. When daylight arrived, he was pleased that his generals had fulfilled his orders and that "all the guns were sunk," and the batteries "completely shielded from the gunboats."[29]

The Federal gunboats present at Johnsonville that morning included the *Elfin*, *Key West*, and *Tawah*, all of which had been instructed to keep "steam

---

28 Morton, "Tennessee River Raid," March 14, 1896.

29 Ibid.; Jordan and Pryor, *The Campaigns of General Nathan Bedford Forrest,* 601; Morton, *The Artillery of Nathan Bedford Forrest's Cavalry,* 254; Dinkins, 178.

up" overnight in the event of an attack. Acting Assistant Quartermaster Treat remembered a wide variety of "steamers and barges lying at our levee." The eight "steamers" (transports) included the *Arcola, Aurora, Doane #2, Duke, Goody Friends, J.B. Ford, Mountaineer*, together with the recaptured transport *Venus*.

Treat also recalled the eleven barges "clustered around" at the wharf. These barges included the *Celeste, Chickamauga, Eagle Coal Co. No. 20, Guthrie #36, J.H. Doan, Josephine, Kentucky, T.H. U.S. 57, U.S. 11, U.S. 44*, and *Whale #8*. Twenty-two riverine vessels were moored at Johnsonville's wharf when the sun rose on November 4. The only vessels owned by the United States Navy included the gunboats *Elfin, Key West*, and *Tawah* (the captured USS *Undine* was in Confederate hands.) All of the other boats or vessels at the wharf, mainly transports and barges, were privately owned vessels leased to the Navy.[30]

While Forrest's Confederates hunkered down and waited, business at Johnsonville carried on pretty much as usual. "A number of barges clustered around; negroes were loading them, officers and men were coming and going, and passengers could be seen strolling down to the wharf," was how Capt. Morton recalled the idyllic scene as he watched the activity from just across the wide Tennessee. "The river banks for some distance back," he continued,

> were lined with quantities of stores, and two freight trains were being made up. It was an animated scene, and one which wore an air of complete security. The Federals evidently thought General Forrest had accepted his loss of the day before and retired.[31]

---

30 AAQM Samuel W. Treat to Colonel L. B. Parsons, Chief Quartermaster of West River "transp," letter, November 24, 1864, Johnsonville, Tennessee (National Archives), 1; *Vessels Bought, Sold, and Chartered by the United States, 1861-1868: Report by the Quartermaster General Relative to Vessels Bought, Sold, and Chartered Since April 1861*, 40th Congress, 2nd Session, House Executive Document No. 337, 114-17, 124-25, 160-61, 164-65, 172-75, 182-83, 194-95, 200-01, 220-21; Morton, *The Artillery of Nathan Bedford Forrest's Cavalry*, 253; Treat to Parsons, Vessels Bought, Sold, and Chartered by the United States, 1861-1868: Report by the Quartermaster General Relative to Vessels Bought, Sold, and Chartered Since April 1861, 1.

31 Morton, *The Artillery of Nathan Bedford Forrest's Cavalry*, 253.

The Battle of Reynoldsburg Island

At 7:00 a.m., on November 4, local workers informed one of Johnsonville's acting assistant quartermasters, Capt. James E. Montandon, to expect a Confederate attack the next day (November 5.) Montandon, a New Jersey-born painter who served earlier in the war with Assistant Quartermaster Henry Howland in the 51st Illinois Infantry, reported this information to Lt. King, and the two officers discussed their course of action in the event of an attack. When later asked about his conversation with the naval officer and his estimation of the value of Johnsonville's stores, Montandon replied, "[A]bout three million dollars. He [King] desired to know my idea of the probabilities of saving the property in case of an attack, with the defence on hand. I said that if we were attacked by a large force, we could save nothing."[32]

Montandon's local source was right: The threat of a Confederate attack was real. At 8:00 a.m., the *Undine*, still manned by Confederate troops, made another appearance about one-half mile downriver from Johnsonville. The gunboat cautiously approached, turned broadside in the middle of the river, and fired several rounds to let the Federals know she had not retreated. The gunboats *Elfin*, *Key West*, and *Tawah*, which had been ordered to keep "steam-up" in anticipation of an attack, prepared to pursue the *Undine* once again. Just prior to their departure, King invited Montandon to travel with him aboard the *Key West*.[33]

Once he had their full attention, Capt. Gracey turned the *Undine* around and moved slowly downriver toward Reynoldsburg Island to return within range of the waiting masked Confederate shore batteries dug in near "the

32 Affidavit account provided by AAQM Captain James E. Montandon regarding the actions of the U.S. forces at Johnsonville, Tennessee, that resulted in the destruction of government property on November 4, 1864, for the Board of Survey at Nashville, Tennessee, in the Court Martial case of Acting Volunteer Lieutenant Edward M. King, December 29, 1864, *U.S. Navy Records 1864-65, Courts Martial*, RG 11-86, U.S. Navy Department, National Archives, Washington, D.C.

33 Affidavit account, Colonel Charles R. Thompson, December 29, 1864; Account provided by First Class Pilot, Thomas J. Thornton, of the USS *Tawah*, May 17, 1865, in Nashville, Tennessee, regarding the gunboat battle between the USS *Key West*, *Elfin*, and *Tawah*, with the Confederate occupied USS *Undine* at Johnsonville, Tennessee, on November 4, 1864, *U.S. Navy Records 1864-65, Courts Martial*, RG 11-86, U.S. Navy Department, National Archives, Washington, D.C., page # not provided; *ORN* 26, 626.

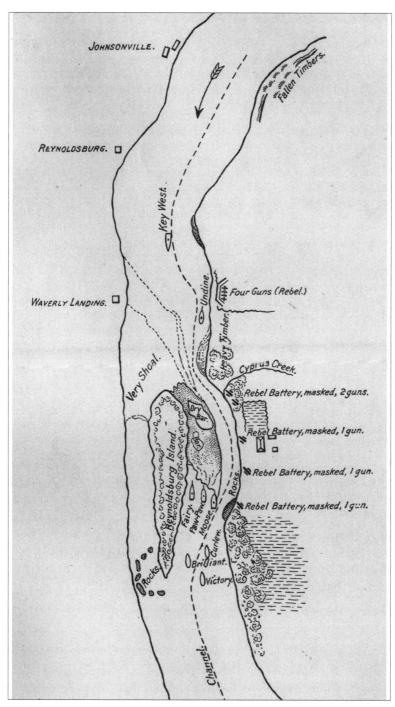

Sketch of the Battle of Reynoldsburg Island, November 3-4, 1864, by Lt. Cmdr. Le Roy Fitch, 10th District, Mississippi Squadron. *Official Records*

Lt. Commander Le Roy Fitch,
10th District, Mississippi Squadron,
ca. 1864.

*Official Records of the Union and
Confederate Navies in the War of the Rebellion*

chute." The three Union gunboats, meanwhile, quickly backed away from the wharf in unison, and, with the *Key West* steaming in the lead, drove after the *Undine*, her deck guns loaded and fully prepared for the battle everyone confidently believed was now upon them. "About 8:00 a.m., the *Undine* came in sight below near the Island. The *Key West*, *Tawah*, and *Elfin* started down towards her," recalled Thomas J. Thornton, the *Tawah*'s pilot. "We had gone about half way to her when a battery opened on the *Key West*. She and the *Tawah* replied. We were about two hundred yards astern of the Key West."[34]

The previous evening, Lt. Comdr. Fitch had arrived from Paducah at the northern end of Reynoldsburg Island with a flotilla of six gunboats. Rather than enter the hazardous "chute" from below, Fitch ordered his gunboats to commence a long-range bombardment beyond their vision into the thick foilage lining the river banks where he thought the Confederate batteries were located.[35]

Lt. King, meanwhile, kept up speed in an effort to move his gunboats farther downriver and connect with Fitch's flotilla at the northern end of Reynoldsburg Island. However, each time the *Key West*, which was well ahead of the *Elfin* and *Tawah*, advanced and attempted to slip past the Rebel land batteries along "the chute," the enemy fire became too heavy and she turned back upriver. "She received nineteen shots from 20 pdr guns which passed entirely through her before she could escape from this newly

---

34 Account provided by First Class Pilot, Thomas J. Thornton, of the USS *Tawah*, May 17, 1865.

35 Irion and Beard, *Underwater Archaeological: Assessment of Civil War Shipwrecks*, 35; Maness, *An Untutored Genius*, 313; *ORN* 26, 610, 612, 630.

discovered battery," explained one of the depot's acting assistant quartermasters in a letter after the battle. Three times the *Key West* tried to run the gauntlet, and three times she was turned away. Lt. Comdr. Fitch confirmed the gunboat's damage in a report when he noted, "The *Key West*, in advance, ran into a battery within 2 miles of Johnsonville and received nineteen shots before she was able to escape." Fitch was unable to get his own gunboats upriver through "the chute" to better engage the land batteries or offer the embattled gunboat protection. "Five of our gunboats came up the river and engaged the rebel batteries near the foot of Reynoldsburg Island, about 5 miles below Johnsonville," he explained, "but were not able to get up."[36]

Although from a distance it might have looked as though Forrest's artillery was having its way with the hapless Union gunboats, such was not the case. By this time the *Undine* had been struck three times and was trapped between King's Johnsonville warships coming down from above and Fitch's six gunboats up from Paducah and was now just below Reynoldsburg Island. Capt. Gracey knew he was trapped and increased his rate of fire at King's gunboats in a last ditch effort to save the *Undine*. He soon realized the hopelessness of his situation. "It was now perfectly evident that we could not save our vessel. The only question was, should we surrender, or blow her up, taking our chances for escape?" wrote Gracey after the war. "Having no one to consult with, I soon determined to blow her up."

Gracey ordered his men to gather the boat's mattresses, which were stuffed with wood shavings, cut them open, and toss them into the *Undine's* magazine. The men cracked open a barrel of oil and liberally poured the contents on top. "A man stood by with a burning lamp to touch it off when I gave the word, and not before." Gracey took what he described as a "wistful look along the shore for Forrest," fired a final round in King's direction, "and the order was given to head her hard down for shore." The *Undine*

---

36 *ORN* 26, 625; Capt. Henry Howland to Col. James Donaldson, letter, November 16, 1864, RG 94, Carded Records Relating to Civil War Staff Officers, National Archives, Washington, D.C.. Henry Howland's claim that the USS *Key West* received 19 shots "from 20 pdr guns" in inaccurate. The Confederates were firing two 10-pounder Parrott Rifles and two rare 14-pounder James Rifles from Morton's and Walton's batteries at the gunboat. Howland was also mistaken when he wrote that "five" gunboats came up the river. There were six in Fitch's flotilla: the USS *Paw-Paw, Moose, Fairy, Victory, Curlew*, and *Brilliant*.

struck a shallow sandbar in "three feet of water, and about seventy-five yards from shore," along the western bank below a high ridge called Pilot Knob.

The final moment had arrived, and Gracey gave the order:

> The torch was applied, and almost before you could jump into the water, the flames burst through the hurricane roof. Soon our side batteries, that were left heavily loaded, were fired by the heat of the burning vessel, quickly followed by the magazine. The boat, in five minutes of being fired by the torch, was in total ruins, and Forrest's fleet was dissolved forever more.[37]

With the *Undine* destroyed, Gracey and his erstwhile crew members joined the rest of Forrest's troops on land.

Lt. King's *Key West* was also in serious trouble, though nothing nearly as dire as that which had overtaken the *Undine*. The heavily damaged Union gunboat turned and, together with the *Elfin* and *Tawah*, steamed upriver for Johnsonville, which the *Key West* reached in "a disabled condition." Once at the wharf, King jumped off the *Key West* and immediately boarded the *Tawah*, with Pilot Thornton still at the wheel. King had no intention of abandoning the fight. "Capt. King came on board and wanted to go down and engage the battery again," recalled the *Tawah's* Acting Ensign Joseph Sawyer. Instead, the intrepid lieutenant steamed back downriver and resumed shelling the irksome Confederate batteries.[38]

"Captain King came aboard the *Tawah* and we went down to engage the battery alone," recalled Pilot Thornton. The Confederate gunners were skilled at their craft, but apparently did not inflict any additional serious damage to the *Tawah* this time around. "We fired a few shots when it was reported to the Captain that she was leaking so fast from the firing that she could not be kept clear," testified the pilot. "The concussion of our bow guns started her to leaking," confirmed Ensign Sawyer, "and we had to come back. The exchange between the Confederate artillerists and the *Tawah* maybe have consumed an hour before the leaking gunboat turned upriver

---

37 Capt. Henry Howland to Col. James Donaldson, letter, November 16, 1864.

38 Affidavit account provided by Acting Ensign, Joseph Sawyer, regarding destruction of government property on November 4, 1864, for the Board of Survey at Nashville, Tennessee, in the Court Martial case of Acting Volunteer Lt. Edward M. King, May 16, 1865, *U S Navy Records - Courts Martial*, RG 11-86, U.S. Navy Department, National Archives, Washington, D.C.

and heaved her way back to the safety of Johnsonville around 11:00 a.m. "We went back and made fast to the *Key West*, put the syphon pump in, and tried to pump her out," was how the boat's pilot described the event. The *Tawah's* retreat officially ended the Battle of Reynoldsburg Island.[39]

The arrival of the pummeled Union gunboats at Johnsonville's wharf made it clear to anyone who was still uncertain that the Confederates meant business, and that the depot was in serious trouble. It was "at this time," wrote Assistant Quartermaster Henry Howland to his superior in Nashville, that "Col. Thompson directed that we arm and place in the intrenchments five hundred of our citizen employees."[40]

Col. Thompson took advantage of the lull in the action and telegraphed Capt. A. H. Plummer, the acting assistant adjutant general, in Nashville, that Lt. Comdr. Fitch's gunboats were unable to pass upriver past the Rebel batteries, and that Lt. King's gunboats were damaged in the engagement. "I sent four 10-pounder Parrotts, with 500 infantry support, to Reynoldsburg to engage the rebel battery," continued Thompson. "Am secure here."[41]

Although it was not yet noon, there was much worse to come.

---

39 Account provided by First Class Pilot, Thomas J. Thornton, of the USS *Tawah*, May 17, 1865; Affidavit, Acting Ensign Joseph Sawyer, May 16, 1865.

40 Howland to Donaldson, letter, November 16, 1864.

41 It composition of the 500 infantry Thompson sent to Reynoldsburg is unclear, but the only sizeable infantry regiment at Johnsonville was the 43rd Wisconsin Infantry, which was about 700 strong.

CHAPTER 9

Reckless and Wholesale Destruction: The Battle of Johnsonville

$\mathbf{A}$FTER exhausting marching in terrible weather and extensive preparation, Gen. Forrest had his forces in position and ready to attack by noon on November 4. The Rebels had waited patiently as Johnsonville's three gunboats steamed away that morning to engage the *Undine*. The time to strike was rapidly approaching.

Forrest rallied with his officers behind Capt. Morton's batteries to discuss the forthcoming battle. He had the men synchronize their watches with the understanding that the bombardment would commence at 2:00 p.m. with an opening volley by Sgt Lemuel Zarring's guns positioned directly across from Johnsonville.[1]

"The Firing Was Terrific"

About the same time Forrest was holding a counsel of war with his chief subordinates, Acting Ensign Joseph Sawyer was aboard the *Tawah* anchored at the wharf. His gunboat had just returned to Johnsonville after the morning's engagement with the *Undine*. It was only matter of time before

---

1 Morton, *The Artillery of Nathan Bedford Forrest's Cavalry*, 254; *OR* 39, pt. 3, 883-84; Jordan and Pryor, *The Campaigns of General Nathan Bedford Forrest*, 601-02; Maness, *An Untutored Genius*, 314. Forrest noted a start time of 3:00 p.m. in his official report, but all of the other evidence points to 2:00 p.m.

someone in Union blue figured out there were thousands of Rebels and artillery batteries just across the river. And that time had arrived.

"When we got back up to the neighborhood of Johnsonville, and came to anchor," reported Ensign Sawyer, "we got orders to shell the woods on the opposite side where the rebels were placing a battery and to shell the sharp shooters on that bank—all the boats shelled the bank." After randomly shelling the western bank of the river, the *Tawah ,*"being along-side the 'Key West' which was at anchor," continued Sawyer, "the rebels opened on us from the lower battery below Johnsonville on the opposite side [and] almost simultaneously two other batteries, one below and one above us, we answered all their batteries. . . ."[2]

Capt. Howland agreed with the ensign's recollection, for he, too, believed the gunboats opened the ball. "At about 2 o'clock p.m. the enemy were discovered planting batteries directly opposite, also above and below our warehouses and levee," he wrote in a letter twelve days later. "The gunboats opened fire upon them, as did also our batteries upon the hill. The cannonading was the most terrific I have ever witnessed."[3]

The opening of the battle was remembered somewhat differently from the Confederate side of the Tennessee. It was just before 2:00 p.m., recalled Morton, when "one of the steamers seemed to get wind of the movement on the opposite shore and steamed toward it." The steamer was the *Key West*, Lt. King's flagship. According to Forrest's artillery chief, the gunboat eased into the middle of the river running parallel to, and about 150 yards from, the western shore. The opportunity was too ripe to pass up, and Morton was more than willing to take full advantage of it. The artilleryman ordered Sgt. Zarring to focus on the gunboat and open fire. A pair of unnamed artillerists each yanked a lanyard in unison, sending 9.5-lb. iron balls through tongues of flame and clouds of bluish-gray powder smoke in a crisp volley from the pair of 3-inch Ordnance Rifles. The deep-throated reverberations echoed up

2   Affidavit account provided by Acting Ensign, Joseph Sawyer, regarding destruction of government property on November 4, 1864, for the Board of Survey at Nashville, Tennessee, in the Court Martial case of Acting Volunteer Lt. Edward M. King, May 16, 1865, *U.S. Navy Records 1864-65, Courts Martial*, RG 11-86, U.S. Navy Department, National Archives, Washington, D.C.

3   AQM Henry Howland to Brigadier General Jacob Donaldson, letter, November 16, 1864, Johnsonville, Tennessee, RG 94, Carded Records Relating to Civil War Staff Officers, National Archives, Washington, D.C.

and down the river bottom. It was a bit ahead of Forrest's schedule, but it was also the signal the other batteries along the entire Confederate line were waiting to hear. Rapid thunder-like booms erupted along Forrest's lengthy front.[4]

However it began, once the firing was underway all hell broke loose. Aimed with care, the furious cannonade from seasoned gunners raked the boats bobbing lazily on the Tennessee, the town, and the supply depot. "As if a magician's wand had been suddenly waved over it," marveled Morton, "spurts of steam broke from the boats, the crews dropping their washing, hauling and packing, and jumping into the water like rats deserting a sinking ship. The passengers who had been sauntering around in the neighborhood of the wharf," he continued, "rushed wildly up the hillside, and everybody made for shelter."

The first shots from Zarring's and Thrall's sections targeted the steering mechanisms of the gunboats to knock them out of commission. It worked. "We commenced to get underway," reported Ensign Sawyer, "when we were told the 'Key West's' wheel was disabled." Caught in the middle of the river between Thrall's four howitzers and Zarring's three-inch Ordnance Rifles, the *Key West* had tried to slip her anchor and move out of range. Thanks to the confusion generated by the thunderous cannonade and King's own misfortune, the gunboat's anchor buoy got caught in the stern paddle wheel and disabled the boat.[5]

Whatever its exact genesis, the Battle of Johnsonville had begun.

According to Forrest's post-battle report, the Federals immediately "returned fire from 28 guns on their gunboats and 14 guns on the hill. About 50 guns were thus engaged at the same time, the firing was terrific."[6]

While under heavy fire, the *Tawah*, which had only recently left the wharf to steam closer to the *Key West*, pulled alongside and tossed a rope to the crippled boat, hitched it to the bow, and towed her back to a more remote part of the levee not as easily reached by the Rebel guns. During the daring

---

4   Morton, *The Artillery of Nathan Bedford Forrest's Cavalry*, 255.

5   Morton, *The Artillery of Nathan Bedford Forrest's Cavalry*, 255; Affidavit account provided by Acting Ensign Joseph Sawyer regarding destruction of government property on November 4, 1864, for the Board of Survey at Nashville, Tennessee, in the Court Martial case of Acting Volunteer Lt. Edward M. King, May 16, 1865, U.S. Navy Records 1864-65, Courts Martial, RG 11-86, U.S. Navy Department, National Archives, Washington, D.C.

6   *OR* 39, pt. 1, 871.

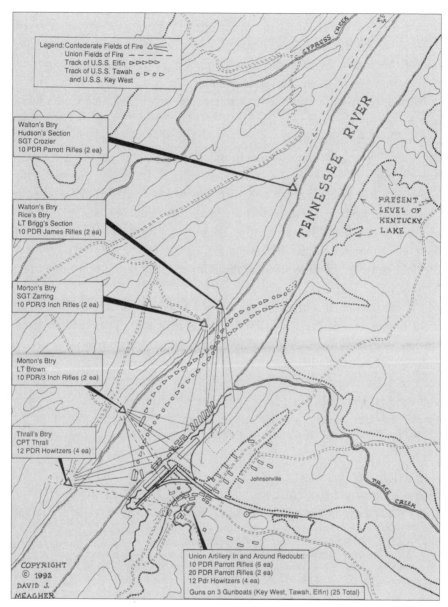

The Confederate Attack on Johnsonville, Tennessee,
November 4, 1864, (1992). *Courtesy of David J. Meagher*

rescue, the *Tawah* was struck multiple times in the stern and began taking on water. She suffered additional damages when defective ammunition caused one of the bow guns to malfunction, creating a powerful concussion that dismounted one of them from its carriage.[7]

About twenty minutes into the cannonade, with his boat taking on water and Rebel shells dropping dangerously close, the *Tawah's* commander ordered his embattled crew to abandon ship. "The gunboats fought magnificently," remembered Howland, and "continued firing for more than twenty minutes after they were all disabled." Lt. King did not fully appreciate the extensive damage suffered by his own *Key West* and the *Tawah* until both had returned to the levee. The gunboats sustained fifty-nine combined hits. Likely recalling his meeting with Col. Thompson two days earlier about destroying the boats in the event Johnsonville faced capture, King ordered the crews of the *Elfin* and *Key West* to set fire to their vessels, along with the crippled *Tawah*.[8]

Those present at Johnsonville's wharf when the gunboats and transports were ordered to be burned offered various accounts of what took place. Ensign Sawyer thought the *Tawah* was "in good working order as far as I am aware." When questioned about the destruction of the *Key West*, the ensign seemed to backtrack a bit by declaring, "the *Key West's* wheel was disabled and the *Tawah* would have soon sunk. I would have burnt them—for they would have been easily raised if sunk and they were not under the protection of the forts." Sawyer even claimed the Confederates "would sing out to us not to burn the boats as they wanted to use them."[9]

"While laying there a battery opened on us from the left bank just below," explained the *Tawah's* pilot, Thomas Thornton, in his effort to recall the afternoon's events. "We towed the Key West in to the shore and

---

7 *OR* 39, pt. 1, 871; Irion and Beard, *Underwater Archaeological Assessment of Civil War Shipwrecks*, 42-42; *U.S. Navy Department Records, 1865*, RG 11-86, National Archives, Washington, D.C., 150-58, 169-171.

8 AQM Henry Howland to Brigadier General Jacob Donaldson, November 16, 1864, Johnsonville, Tennessee, RG 94, Carded Records Relating to Civil War Staff Officers, National Archives, Washington, D.C.; *ORN* 26, 611.

9 Affidavit account provided by Acting Ensign, Joseph Sawyer, regarding destruction of government property on November 4, 1864, for the Board of Survey at Nashville, Tennessee, in the Court Martial case of Acting Volunteer Lt. Edward M. King, May 16, 1865, *U.S. Navy Records 1864-65, Courts Martial*, RG 11-86, U.S. Navy Department, National Archives, Washington, D.C., page # not provided.

she made fast to a barge and we to another just below her. Captain [Lt.] King," he continued,

> called out to our commanding officer to put his head down stream and engage the battery. While we were trying to get out from the barge a battery a little above us opened on us. Captain Williams who commanded the *Tawah* ordered me to put her alongside the barge again and come down out of the pilot house. I did so and came down. I saw nothing more until the Captain came in some 20 minutes later and ordered us to go ashore. I left her then and she was set on fire and was blazing in 15 minutes after.[10]

Cmdr. Fitch and his six-gunboat flotilla were still at the northern end of Reynoldsburg Island when the Confederate cannon fire broke out upriver opposite Johnsonville. The Confederates, he believed, still held a strong position somewhere within the 500 yard stretch of "the chute" which made it too risky to move his valuable ships in that direction. "Johnsonville," he concluded, "was in all probability surrounded by the enemy." Unable to help King and Thompson, Fitch moved his flotilla down to Paris Landing and anchored there for the night.

Later, in his report of the battle, Fitch claimed he intended to enter "the chute" and come to the garrison's rescue, but there were too many complications in doing so. "The vessels would have to go very slowly and one after the other," he explained, adding,

> and had there been a chance of my getting through [the chute] with the loss of only one or two boats, and then dislodging the enemy, I should have attempted it, but having no force on shore to cooperate with me. . . I did not see what I could accomplish; for even had I got through. In fact, I firmly believe, had I made the effort, not a single boat would have gotten out of the river. The *Key West*, *Tawah* and *Elfin*, fought desperately and were handled in magnificent style, but it is impossible for boats of this class, with their batteries, to contend successfully against heavy rifled field batteries in a narrow river full of bars and shoals, no matter with what skill and desperation they may be fought.[11]

10 Affidavit account provided by First Class Pilot, Thomas J. Thornton, of the USS *Tawah*, May 17, 1865, in Nashville, Tennessee, regarding the gunboat battle between the USS *Key West*, *Elfin*, and *Tawah*, with the Confederate occupied USS *Undine* at Johnsonville, Tennessee, on November 4, 1864, *U.S. Navy Records 1864-65, Courts Martial*, RG 11-86, U.S. Navy Department, National Archives, Washington, D.C., page # not provided.

11 *ORN* 26, 614.

Johnsonville, Tennessee, 1864. Soldiers and officers of Battery A, 2nd U.S. Colored Light Artillery with unlimbered 12-pounder howitzers and tack sitting on limbers with corral in background. *Library of Congress*

With the gunboats neutralized, Gen. Forrest ordered all his batteries except Walton's to concentrate their fire on the warehouses, transports, and supplies spread out along the wharf. Morton was studying the conflagration through his field glasses when a nearby rebel gunner exclaimed it was like "shooting pickerel in a barrel."[12]

The USCT gunners returned fire from Fort Johnson (Redoubt No. 1). Col. Reuben D. Mussey, a thickly bearded New Hampshire commander of the newly raised 100th USCT, took delight in the manner in which Josiah Meigs' Battery A, 2nd U.S. Colored Light Artillery, handled itself. "A section of Meigs' battery, temporarily there, made excellent practice," he boasted, "dismounting one of the guns of a battery placed by the rebels on the opposite bank of the river and causing the battery several times to change

12 Dinkins, "Destroying Military Stores and Gunboats," 175.

their location. The rebel battery, he continued, "devoted its attention to this section, shelling it furiously."[13]

Assistant Quartermaster Henry Howland reported to Col. Thompson that he had received distressing reports "from trustworthy and reliable men who were captured from the transports" who had since escaped. These boatmen, explained Thompson later, had told Howland that a Rebel force of "13,000 men under Generals Forrest, Chalmers, Buford, Bell, and Lyon, with thirty-six pieces of artillery, twenty of them 20-pounder Parrotts, on the opposite bank of the river . . . would endeavor to cross sufficient force under the cover of their guns to obtain possession of their transports." He directed Howland "to destroy by fire all the transports." Howland dutifully passed the orders on to his officers, soldiers, sailors, and civilians, who boarded the boats with torches and set them afire, including the barges.[14]

While the men were burning the boats and barges, the Confederates continued firing at the target-rich environment along the lengthy wharf and inside the depot itself, creating panic and chaos everywhere. "I arrived at about 2 p.m. and was immediately put in command of about 550 Government employees, and directed to put them in the intrenchments," Captain Montandon later reported. "Our battery was firing over the left of the line," he continued,

> where my employees were stationed, one of the 20-pounder guns going off and killing twenty mules in the corral near where the employees were stationed, completely demoralizing them and causing them to stampede immediately. About this time the gunboats were set on fire, and Captain Howland told me that he had ordered the transports to be burned.[15]

---

13 *OR* 39, pt. 1, 868. In all likelihood, the disabled gun was one of Zarring's pieces, which were the closest Confederate guns to Meigs' Battery A. As a testament to the accurate fire conducted by Meigs' Battery A., authors Jordan and Pryor, *The Campaigns of General Nathan Bedford Forrest*, 603, drawing from the accounts of Confederate participants in the battle, wrote, "the guns of the redoubt, soon getting the range, threw their shells so accurately, that several were dropped into the sunken gun chambers, but without further harm than breaking the rammers in the hands of the gunners in two instances, for they sunk so deep before they exploded that they did no injury."

14 *OR* 52, pt. 1, 123.

15 Ibid., 39, pt. 1, 865.

"Their sharpshooters were firing at the levee very briskly, and we were not replying," admitted Montandon. "The transports were burned by order of our own men. One of my men, William Everett, an officer of Co. "B" 3rd Regt. Q.M. Forces, under promise of a large fee from Capt. Howland," continued the captain, "went in an open boat under a severe fire and fired two Transports. I do not think the destruction of the Gunboats and Transports there was a necessity, in a military point of view, for their being destroyed."[16]

About this time the Confederates turned their artillery against the large stockpiles of freight that had recently been unloaded. One particular area included stacks of barrels covered with white canvas tarps that presented a giant target. The gunners sighted their pieces on the barrels and soon discovered they contained whiskey, because they "burst with a loud explosion . . . the burning liquor ran in torrents of livid flame down the hillside; spreading a flame in its course toward the river and filling the air with the blended yet distinct fumes of burning spirits, sugar, coffee, and meat."

Many Confederates watched all this from just 400 yards away. While flames consumed the enormous stockpiles of freight on the wharf, Capt. Thrall watched in amazement as the burning gunboats "drifted against some loaded barges, and . . . were quickly in flames." The wind was picking up and helped spread the flames from the burning transports across the entirety of the wharf for a distance of some 600 yards.[17]

By 4:00 p.m., it became apparent to Johnsonville's commanders that the spreading fires could consume the entire wharf area, including the transports, barges, buildings, and small mountains of supplies. Howland, who endured much of the battle under artillery and small arms fire, continued overseeing the burning of the transport boats but ordered everyone else at the wharf (mainly Quartermaster's Department employees and navy personnel), to do their best to extinguish other fires. "The flames

16 Affidavit of AAQM Captain James E. Montandon, January 16, 1865, from the proceedings of a Board of Survey about the destruction of Army Stores at Johnsonville, Tennessee, Nov. 4-5, 1864, RG 11-86, Roll 159, *U.S. Naval Records, Court Martial*, National Archives, Washington, D.C., page # not provided.

17 *OR* 39, pt.1, 862, 871; Jordan and Pryor, *The Campaigns of General Nathan Bedford Forrest*, 604; Hurst, *Nathan Bedford Forrest: A Biography*, 227.

spread rapidly," Lt. Col. Sinclair wrote, "and soon communicated to the small transfer building which with its contents was speedily consumed and which contained six hundred and fifty tons of provisions." The intense heat from the conflagration made it impossible to get close enough to battle the flames, so "very little was done toward complying with the order." Peter Wagner, chief engineer aboard the transport USS *Volunteer*, later explained that even if they had wanted to save they transports, it was impossible to do so. "We could not get a man to remain on the transports," he later testified. "They had all left sometime before the transports were burned."[18]

Available personnel to battle the flames "would no sooner make their appearance [at the wharf] than the rebel batteries and sharpshooters would fire upon them," reported a Kentucky newspaper. Johnsonville's garrison troops, civilians, and navy personnel, did their best to return fire to suppress the devastating rain of iron and lead, to little avail.[19]

"As soon as we got the range of their guns we sent some 20 lb. pound shells howling down to them," recalled Cpl. Lorenzo Atwood of the 43rd Wisconsin Infantry in a letter home. "One company stood a little to the left of the battery watching the effect of our shells not thinking that the rebs would turn their fire from the gunboats, but to our surprise," he continued,

> they paid us a compliment in the shape of a 20 lb shell which burst just in front of our company, one piece that we picked up some 2 inches square passed between Capt. Stockwells legs and mine and we stood within 2 feet of each other, one piece brushed the shoulder of one man, no one was hurt.[20]

---

18 Howland to Donaldson, November 16, 1864, Johnsonville, Tennessee, RG 94, records relating to Civil War staff officers, National Archives, Washington, D.C.; *Louisville Democrat*, November 8, 1864; *OR* 39, pt.1, 862; Testimony of Peter Wagner, USS *Volunteer*, Case No. 4, Acting Volunteer Lieutenant E.M. King, lately of the USS "*Key West*," May 8, 1865 in *The Abandonment and Destruction of the USS Key West, Tawah, and Elfin*, RG 11-86, Roll 159, *U.S. Naval Records, Court Martial*, National Archives, Washington, D.C., 76.

19 *Louisville Democrat*, November 8, 1864.

20 Atwood, November 8, 1864. The only 20-pounders were the two guns captured from the *Venus*, which were mounted in Redoubt No. 1 (the lower redoubt). This meant Atwood and his fellow 43rd Wisconsin soldiers had to have been on the hill by the fort, or underneath the brow of the fort at its base, where many of the USCT and 43rd soldiers stood and fired at the Rebels with their Enfields and Springfields. In all likelihood, Atwood was below the base of the fort and the guns were firing over him.

While the Wisconsin troops faced the potentially lethal iron shells, Captain Montandon and his men battled the intense flames and spreading conflagration in the wharf area. "The boats when burning were not more than twenty five or thirty feet from the line of stores on the levee which were mostly subsistence stores and forage," he began. "There was some salt and pork on the levee. Most of the hard bread was in the transfer building 150 to 200 feet from the river. Most of the steamers lay directly opposite the transfer building or Warehouse No. 1. I do not know whether the stores took fire from the burning boats or Rebel shells," he continued,

> but the intense heat set fire to the stores on the levee. It was impossible with our facilities to have extinguished the flames. The transports were not fired by the burning gunboats. No stores were thrown into the river to my knowledge. Some of the boats were used as storehouses. There were more Goods sent to Johnsonville than our means of transportation would allow to be sent away. We were obliged to allow stores to accumulate in Warehouses, Transports and on the levee. We could have loaded four hundred cars per day and we only received about sixty. I do not know who ordered such immense amounts of supplies.[21]

Darkness crept over the hellish landscape about 5:00 p.m. By this time the inferno had consumed the smaller warehouse (Warehouse No. 1) and all of its machinery and supplies. Even though the fires were now out of control, the Confederates had no intention of ending or slowing their attack. Instead, they attempted to set fire to the larger freight transfer warehouse (Warehouse No. 2). Despite heavy shelling, it failed to ignite.

Under this umbrella of pandemonium, another form of destruction broke out. According to Lt. Col. Sinclair, as the fires consumed the wharf, a number of civilian employees inaugurated "a general system of theft," looting the stores and boats as fast as they could. After the soldiers and Quartermaster's Department employees at the wharf realized what was happening, Sinclair reported that they too "came in for their share of the plunder."[22]

---

21 Affidavit of AAQM Captain James E. Montandon, January 16, 1865, from the proceedings of a Board of Survey about the destruction of Army Stores at Johnsonville, Tennessee, Nov. 4-5, 1864, RG 11-86, Roll 159, *U.S. Naval Records, Court Martial*, National Archives, Washington, D.C., page # not provided.

22 *OR* 39. pt. 1, 862.

While the uncontrollable looting was underway, Lt. Col. Sinclair also reported that Johnsonville's railroad agent, Charles H. Nabb, arrived with a locomotive and attached "a train of cars loaded with clothing and some 400 men from the gun-boats. The boxes on this train were broken open and a considerable amount of clothing stolen." Agent Nabb left the supply depot with a train full of stolen military supplies. According to an appalled Sinclair, when the train reached Waverly, Nabb "cut off the engine and tender and run right to Nashville, leaving his trainload of refugees to fend for themselves."[23]

Col. Thompson was less concerned about the looting than he was about the horrific state of affairs under his oversight. The Army officer telegraphed Capt. A. H. Plummer, acting assistant adjutant-general in Nashville, at 6:00 p.m., that "artillery firing has ceased. Lieut. Commander Le Roy Fitch says he cannot get up with the fleet from below." Thompson continued:

> The enemy has several 20-pounder Parrotts, not less than twenty guns in all. The firing supposed to be in the enemy's rear was, I think, fired by our skirmishers. Send ammunition for 10-pounder Parrotts and Napoleon guns, under strong guard. We must have ammunition to fight with. Have you orders to give, other than to fight? That I will do without orders.[24]

At least some good news reached Thompson that evening in the form of a telegram from Maj. Gen. Thomas at 8:00 p.m. The commander in Nashville urged Thompson to "hold on to your position. I will send the Twenty-third Corps, or a portion of it at least, to your assistance, either to-morrow or in the evening. You must not let the enemy have your position, but must hold on to it till re-enforcements reach you." Maj. Gen. John M. Schofield, commander of the XXIII Corps at Stevenson, Alabama, replied to Thomas that he "expect[ed] to reach Nashville some time to-night. One brigade only is ahead of me, another is moving to-day."[25]

Earlier that afternoon and without Col. Thompson's knowledge, Lt. King had telegraphed a desperate message to Lt. Comdr. Shirk at Paducah:

23 Ibid; Garrett, *The History of Humphreys County, Tennessee*, 107.

24 *OR* 39, pt. 3, 637. In truth, the young colonel had no reliable intelligence regarding Forrest or his own forces. At most Forrest fielded 12 field pieces, with the largest being two 14-pounder James Rifles. There were no Union men in the "enemy's rear."

25 Ibid., 638.

"My officers and crew I have ordered to the fort. Johnsonville can only be saved by a large force and ironclads. Seven transports and our prize *Venus* are set on fire. We have done what we could. With a heavy heart I close this dispatch." Thirty minutes later, Maj. Gen. Thomas received a calmer, and more professional telegram from Col. Thompson: "Three gun-boats were disabled at Johnsonville to-day and abandoned, and destroyed by fire by rebel batteries on the western bank of the Tennessee River . . . the gun-boats and transports captured by enemy a few days since were all destroyed."[26]

It is unknown whether King or Thompson were at Johnsonville when they telegraphed Shirk and Thomas. Neither telegram addressed the destruction of the massive wharf, transport boats, or tons of stores that had been set ablaze under the direct orders of King, Howland, and Thompson. Eleazer A. Greenleaf, a civilian employee who worked at the depot and was present at Johnsonville on November 4, recalled that "not one person in charge could be found." Greenleaf attributed much of it to plain cowardice. "Where were the authorities?" he demanded in letter to Andrew Johnson just two months after the battle. "They were neither fighting the enemy nor protecting the Government property." After "considerable" search, he continued,

> I found they had fled for safety out by some Negro shanties behind a hill near the R. Road, perhaps half a mile from the River—Here I found Quarter Masters Henry Howland, & J. E. Montandon with several other gentlemen whom I took to be officers of the burning boats . . . whoever counselled or ordered the destruction did not know what he was about. . . . Never did I witness so sad a sight as the burning of our stores that night—our successes in Tennessee appeared to me utterly hopeless and our own authorities as our worst enemies.[27]

Across the river, meanwhile, Forrest studied the effects of his attack. "[T]he wharf for nearly one mile up and down the river presented one solid

---

26 *ORN* 26, 611,619.

27 Eleazer A. Greenleaf to Governor Andrew Johnson, Janaury 13, 1865, in Graf and haskins, *The Papers of Andrew Johnson*, vol. 7, 401-02. Eleazer Greenleaf (1809-1878) was an Episcopal minister from Stillwater, Maine, who had come to Tennessee in 1864 to work for the Union cause. He had answered an advertisement for employment with the U.S. Quartermaster's Department, and, upon his arrival in Nashville, was assigned to work at Johnsonville as a sawyer at Saw Mill No. 2. J. E. Greenleaf, *Genealogy of the Greenleaf Family* (Boston, 1896), 414.

sheet of flame," he reported. "The enemy continued a furious cannonading on my batteries." Now that darkness was fully upon them, the cavalry commander ordered his guns to cease fire and his troops to withdraw from the riverbank areas except for Rucker's brigade and an artillery section of Walton's (Rice's) battery, which would remain in place to cover the withdrawal. The movement was efficiently conducted and the men marched six miles "by the light of the enemy's burning property" along two sloppy roads in the direction of Perryville, Tennessee. "Having completed the work designed by the expedition," explained Forrest, "I moved my command 6 miles during the night by the light of the enemy's burning property. The roads were almost impassable, and the march to Corinth was slow and toilsome." During the withdrawal, Walton's artillery continued a brisk cannonade, which by this time acted more as a diversionary tactic than an intent to destroy anything else of value. Federal artillerymen inside Fort Johnson (Redoubt No. 1) blindly returned fire into the inky darkness.[28]

By 11:00 p.m. the cannon fire on both sides of the river ceased and the riverfront was once again silent. Forrest remained on the field, but having had almost no sleep for two full days had pushed himself beyond the point of exhaustion. When the opportunity offered, he took refuge in one of Morton's muddy but vacated artillery positions and rested as he watched for any retaliatory actions that might come his way. It soon became clear that nothing else was going to interfere with his command that night. The madness and confusion of November 4 was finally at an end.[29]

"Nothing to Compare to this"—November 5

The following morning, Saturday, November 5, "dawned misty and foggy." At 7:30 a.m., after the fog raised, the Confederates opened a "brisk fire upon the hill where the colored battery was stationed." As Walton's (Rice's) battery opened the day, the gunners in Meigs Battery A, 2nd U.S.

---

28 *ORN* 26, 683. Gen. Chalmers' after-action report was written from Perryville, Tennessee, on November 8, which they likely reached the previous day after waiting for Rucker, who remained on the field November 5 with Rice's battery, firing into the town of Johnsonville. *OR* 39, pt. 1, 871-72. See also Mathes, *General Forrest*, 303.

29 Mathes, *General Forrest*, 303.

Colored Light Artillery, replied with their 12-pounder howitzers almost immediately.[30]

Describing the fury of the morning, Captain William W. Likens, Company H, 43rd Wisconsin, depicted the battle on the second day at Johnsonville:

> Saturday morning at 7 ½ o'clock, firing commenced with cannon on both sides—shells of the rebels quite thickly—continued until 9 ½ o'clock when firings on the part of the rebels ceased. Andrew Hudson of Co. B. 43. Reg. Wis. Vol.—struck by shell in thigh at 7.40 A.M.—died in afternoon.—Frederick D. Starin, Company Clerk of Co. "H." 43. Reg. W.V.—wounded severely, one leg off and heel of other foot at 8 O'clock A.M. Nov. 5. 1864—Both legs amputated. one just below the knee. the other just below the ankle—At this time he is doing well—physicians think he will live—All the suffering borne with truly heroic fortitude by fine noble young man.[31]

Around 9:30 a.m., the Confederates ceased their cannonade and waited about half an hour before resuming. A reporter with the *Louisville Democrat* at Johnsonville that morning, provided a rare civilian account of the battle:

> The citizens and non-combatants commenced to leave the town in the morning, and as they went out on the road they were shelled by the rebel batteries and a number of them were killed. At about 10 o'clock, the cannonading was again commenced, and lasted some thirty minutes. All remained quiet for the next eight and a half hours until seven o'clock in the evening when the cannonading resumed.[32]

Col. Thompson, meanwhile, was still unsure of Forrest's whereabouts and remained concerned that he was about to assault the land-side of Johnsonville. "Colonel Gallup has arrived with 1,000 men, thank God," he

---

30 Testimony of A.A.Q.M. Lieutenant S.W. Treat, January 4, 1865, from the proceedings of a Board of Survey about the destruction of Army Stores at Johnsonville, Tennessee, Nov. 4-5, 1864, RG 11-86, Roll 159, *U.S. Naval Records, Court Martial*, National Archives, Washington, D.C., page # not provided.

31 Captain William W. Likens, Company H, 43rd Wisconsin Infantry, November 6, 1864, various correspondence of U.S. Army Officers, Civil War, RG 94, National Archives, Washington, D.C.

32 *Louisville Democrat*, November 8, 1864.

telegraphed Maj. Gen. Thomas in Nashville. "Is General Schofield on his way here, as reported?"

"Have you any new movements on the part of the enemy to report this morning?" Thomas shot back bruskly."General Schofield's troops are being forwarded you as rapidly as possible, and some of the trains should reach you by the time you receive this. A greater portion of the corps will reach you today. Hold on to your position till the re-enforcements reach you," he ordered once again, "when you will have enough force to drive the enemy off."[33]

Confederate sharpshooters from Rucker's command spent the entire day firing from mostly concealed positions across the Tennessee River at anything worth a pull of the trigger while Walton's guns did likewise. Seventeen-year old Alfred Redfern, the personal assistant and messenger for Henry Howland, provided a detailed account of the shelling. "The Rebs opened fire at 7 O'Clock AM on the 5th. Just as I was Eating Breakfast I had a Can of Peaches in one hand and some Dried Beef and Crackers in the other & a Cup of Coffee," he began. "Well I can't tell you how the shells did fly," he continued,

> they knocked the Roof off of the house I was in, Vicksburg or any other Place was nothing to Compare to this. So I thought it was time to Evacuate so I dropped everything but my Peaches and I carried them till I found a N Soldier hid behind a stump I gave them to him the shells whistling Past my ears all the time, they kept it up for one hour, But I came off all right so far today we have been Reinforced by 2000 men & before 12 O.Clock tonight we expect 1000 more so I consider my self & Johnsonville all safe . . . I cant hardly Believe my self how I came to escape some of them shells they went within a foot of me Lots of them . . . the Rebels still hold their Position on the opposite side of the river, so I can't tell you anymore. I am getting used to Bombardment by this time this all News I can send you.[34]

Capt. Likens of the 43rd Wisconsin confirmed Redfern's account of the devastating artillery that day when he wrote, "Heavy damage done to the town by rebel shells. Shells bursted in afternoon of Friday into Saturday

---

33 *OR* 39, pt. 3, 653.

34 Alfred Redfern to Mother and Father, November 5, 1864, Johnsonville, Tennessee, by permission of Friends of Johnsonville State Historic Park.

forenoon in all parts of the camp-our government employees killed and several wounded in town."[35]

Around 3:00 p.m., Forrest finally ordered Rucker to withdraw with his brigade and Walton's (Rice's) guns and rejoin the rest of his command, which was now at least seven miles south moving in the direction of Perryville. The Confederates were preparing to depart when troops from one of the black regiments appeared and "displayed themselves on the opposite shore in amusing, irate antics. Throwing off their coats and shaking their clutched fists at the hated rebels they hurled across the river their arsenal of explosives, epithets, maledictions."

Col. Rucker ordered Lt. Briggs to unlimber his guns and send a reply to the animated enemy. According to one of Rucker's men, "one volley dispersed the capering crowd and sent those not killed or wounded scampering away in the wildest confusion." It is unknown how many of the soldiers were killed or wounded, but eyewitnesses remembered "a number were left dead or wounded upon the river-bank."[36]

Gen. Forrest and his remaining men withdrew around 10:00 p.m. Hampered by more rain, the smaller Rebel column followed the same route Gens. Buford and Chalmers' troops had taken the previous day to Perryville. The Battle of Johnsonville was over.[37]

*   *   *

As far as Civil War standards go, the losses incurred on both sides during the West Tennessee–Johnsonville expedition, which included the actions along the Tennessee River and the fighting at Johnsonville (Nov. 4-5, 1865) were quite low.

According to Nathan Bedford Forrest's after-action report, "my loss during the entire trip was 2 killed and 9 wounded and [150 prisoners]. . . .

---

35 Captain William W. Likens, Company H, 43rd Wisconsin Infantry, November 6, 1864.

36 Jordan and Pryor, *The Campaigns of General Nathan Bedford Forrest*, 605; Mathes, *General Forrest*, 303-04; Dinkins, "Destroying Military Stores and Gunboats," 179.

37 Jordan and Pryor, *The Campaigns of General Nathan Bedford Forrest*, 605.

That of the enemy will probably reach 500 killed, wounded, and prisoners."[38]

James Chalmers, in his preliminary report penned on November 8, 1864, claimed, "Our loss in this affair was very small, but as official reports have not been received, it cannot now be stated with accuracy." He updated his report when more information arrived. Including all the actions *prior* to November 1 (at Fort Heiman and Paris Landing), he reported, "Our loss in this affair was 1 man of Rucker's brigade severely wounded; that of the enemy as far as we have been able to ascertain it, was 5 killed and 6 wounded on the *Venus*; 3 killed and 4 wounded on the *Undine*, and 1 wounded on the *Cheeseman*; total, 8 killed and 11 wounded. We also captured 43 prisoners, among whom was 1 officer and 10 men of the United States Infantry. The others belonged to different boats." Regarding the main battle on November 4, expounded Chalmers, "The enemy kept up a heavy fire from their gunboats and land batteries . . . but without inflicting any serious injury upon us or forcing any part of our troops to abandon their positions. . . . Our loss in this engagement was very small." Forrest's other commanders do not seem to have filed casualty reports, or, if they did, they have not been located.[39]

Union losses were reported by Lt. Col. William Sinclair, assistant inspector-general. According to Sinclair, and speaking only on behalf of the Army losses, "our force sustained a loss of 8 men killed and wounded during the attack. Colonel Thompson and Captain Howland are responsible for the destruction of the boats and other property at Johnsonville."[40]

The campaign's low casualties appear impossible, but can be attributed to the fact that opposing ground forces never came into direct or close-quarters contact. In this rather rare combat, the fighting took place on the Tennessee River with gunboats, or with the wide river dividing each side. The Union troops were mostly hidden inside earthworks or fortifications, as were the Rebel artillerists in their sunken gun pits. In fact, other than clouds of powder smoke or other evidence that demonstrated the area from which they were firing, the Confederates remained mostly invisible to Union eyes.

38 *OR* 39, pt. 1, 871, *ORN* 26, 683. As experienced as he was by this time in the war, Forrest's estimate of Union losses was wildly off the mark.

39 *ORN* 26, 683, 686. Chalmers's division's casualties were so insignificant that he did not even break down his killed, wounded, and missing/prisoners.

40 *OR* 39, pt.1, 863.

Aftermath

Early on November 6, Maj. Gen. Thomas telegraphed Maj. Gen. Schofield urging him once again to send reinforcements to Johnsonville as quickly as possible. Schofield assured Thomas that the two brigades he had previously dispatched were expected to arrive there after daylight. Right on time, around 6:00 a.m. that morning, the first wave of reinforcements—Col. George W. Gallup's men, First Brigade, Schofield's XXIII Corps—reached Johnsonville by rail. Two hours later, 300 more from the 2nd Tennessee Infantry (mounted) rode into Johnsonville to further reinforce the post. Thomas had ordered the Tennesseans the day before to move from Centreville and assist Schofield's reinforcement effort. The last wave of reinforcements, Col. Orlando H. Moore's men, Second Brigade, XXIII Corps, arrived around 3:00 p.m. Regardless of what the Confederates were planning, Johnsonville was now safe.[1]

Reinforced and Abandoned

John Schofield, who had been ordered by Thomas to personally go to Johnsonville and oversee its affairs, pulled into the supply depot aboard a military locomotive at 7:00 p.m. "I have just arrived at this place," he reported. "I think Colonel Gallup's brigade will be quite sufficient, but I will

1 *OR* 39, pt. 3, 673-75.

Major General John Schofield, commander, XXIII Corps.
Library of Congress

examine the ground early in the morning and report definitely." The arrival of Schofield's men left quite an impression on Cpl. Atwood, who thought the reinforcements totaled "some 7000 men, and 3 batterys." In reality, the actual number of reinforcements totaled 2,300 men (parts of two brigades), 300 mounted infantry, and a single battery of artillery.[2]

On Monday, November 7, the troops from Gallup and Moore's brigades began enhancing the existing fortifications and extended Johnsonville's entrenchments by half a mile. The arrival of reinforcements provided a much-needed spark to the garrison and the additional protection Thompson had so desperately sought. Maj. Gen. Thomas wrote his superior, Maj. Gen. Henry Halleck in Washington, that "General Schofield's presence at Johnsonville has had the effect of quieting excitement among the troops at that place, and they are now busily engaged constructing works for better defense of the position. He will leave Johnsonville to-morrow." The same day, Maj. Gen. Sherman, operating around Kingston, Georgia, uttered one of his most famous statements in a telegram to Lt. Gen. Grant at City Point, Virginia, when his telegraph operator tapped out, "that devil Forrest was down about Johnsonville and was making havoc among the gun-boats and transports."[3]

On November 8, Election Day 1864, citizens across the Northern states re-elected President Lincoln for a second term. This time, Andrew Johnson

2 Ibid; Atwood, Nov. 8, 1864.

3 Jacob D. Cox, *The Battle of Franklin, Tennessee, November 30, 1864: A Monograph* (New York: Charles Scribner's Sons, 1897), 9-10, 24; *OR* 39, pt. 3, 659, 685.

was on the ticket as his vice-president. While people cast their ballots, Schofield's men lifted shovels of earth or swung pick axes in their continued efforts to make Johnsonville impregnable to further attacks. The reinforcements also helped by cutting underbrush and felling trees across the river. "At present all danger at Johnsonville seems over and past," Capt. James Rusling, an assistant quartermaster at the Nashville Depot, reported to Maj. Gen. Meigs. "The woods about the post," he continued,

> are being cut down and the bank of the river opposite the town is being fortified as to prevent a repetition of the cannonading, as in the last attack. We shall have ample time from present appearances to clear away the debris there and prepare for future operations.[4]

"Notwithstanding the many reports in the papers the place stands and is likely to," penned Walter Howland. "There is a large force here now part of the 23rd Corps—but it is rumored part will be withdrawn."[5]

By mid-November, any immediate threat by Forrest had evaporated. However, now that Gen. John B. Hood had entered Tennessee with his Army of Tennessee, the possibility of a large-scale attack against Nashville had suddenly materialized. Thomas recognized the need to begin making preparations to move government property, stores, and personnel from Johnsonville to Nashville so that, in the event of an attack, the needed supplies would be readily available to the defending forces. On November 24, Donaldson, now a brevet brigadier general, ordered Capt. Rusling to inform Howland to begin preparations for abandoning supply operations at Johnsonville. That same day, Thomas ordered Schofield's men to depart Johnsonville—Gallup's men by road to Centerville and Moore's men by train to Nashville.[6]

"Henry received a telegram to forward all gov't stores [from Johnsonville] to this place as rapidly as possible," penned Walter Howland on November 26 from Nashville. "I presume for the present—as I learn that

---

4 *OR* 52, pt. 1, 121.

5 Walter Howland Letters, November 20, 1864.

6 Captain James Rusling to Henry Howland, November 23, 1864, Nashville, Tennessee, RG 94, Carded Records Relating to Civil War Staff Officers, National Archives, Washington, D.C.; *OR* 45, pt. 1, 1,100, 1,021.

Johnsonville will probably be evacuated tomorrow. It seems rather rough to be turned out of home just as we had got pleasantly located for the winter."[7]

After evacuation procedures commenced, Col. Thompson carried on with his responsibility of defending Johnsonville and patrolling the surrounding areas. On November 27, he ordered the 2nd Tennessee Infantry (mounted) and mounted men of the 12th and 13th USCT regiments to patrol outside Johnsonville to the north bank of the Duck River.[8]

On the morning of November 29, one day before Hood's disastrous battle at Franklin, Tennessee, Thomas telegraphed Thompson at Johnsonville, "The Forty-third Wisconsin will be used as guards to the trains of quartermaster's stores coming to this place [Nashville]. If everything has been sent away from Johnsonville you may withdraw from the place with your force, marching in the direction of Nashville along the railroad, picking up your guards as you come along." The "guards" Thomas referenced were men from the various USCT regiments who had been assigned to protect sections of the Nashville and Northwestern Railroad.

"All the valuable stores have been sent except the machinery," Thompson replied to Thomas, "which is being loaded and will be ready to be sent out by 2 o'clock this p.m. There will be about twenty car-loads of stores left . . . of carpenter's tools and mess furniture, such as stoves, ranges, &c. We have switch engines here to send train with machinery." As far as the remaining armaments still in the Johnsonville redoubts, Thompson was instructed to "destroy the carriages of the 20-pounders and throw the guns in the river. The battery [1st Kansas Battery] will come along with you," directed Thomas. "You will withdraw your command from Johnsonville, leaving store-houses and other property undisturbed. Should you learn . . . that a heavy force of the enemy has crossed the Duck River, and there is a possibility of your being cut off from this place, then move promptly upon Clarksville and take post at that place."[9]

Walter Howland, who had been caught up in the harried evacuation activities, this time wrote from Johnsonville on November 29 to his mother. "I received a telegram from Henry to return and although rumors were plenty

---

7 Walter Howland to mother, November 26, 1864, Nashville, Tennessee,

8 *OR* 45, pt. 1, 1,100, 1,161-62.

9 *OR* 45, pt. 1, 1,161-62.

that Johnsonville was evacuated, I arrived here last night & found everything as quiet as ever. It may be given up for a time," he concluded, "although it does not look much like it to day."[10]

On November 30, while Hood's Army of Tennessee was being beaten back at Franklin by Schofield's XXIII Corps, Union forces finally evacuated Johnsonville. All personnel, stores, animals, and machinery were now en route to Nashville via the Nashville and Northwestern Railroad. "Johnsonville is evacuated," Walter Howland wrote on December 2 from Nashville. "We left on Tuesday and Wednesday. Military matters are quite stirring. Thomas entire Army is in & near the city."[11]

The November 30 evacuees included Cpl. Lorenzo Atwood and the 43rd Wisconsin Infantry. The Badger troops ended up performing garrison duty at Clarksville, Nashville, Dechard, and as their final assignment, served as guards of the Elk River Bridge on the Nashville and Chattanooga R.R. While there in April 1865, Lorenzo received a letter from his 10-year-old son Arthur informing him that wife Cordelia and daughter Leona had taken ill and died of diphtheria just four days apart.[12]

On December 30, two weeks after Hood's disastrous defeat at the Battle of Nashville on December 15-16, Thomas ordered the 13th USCT Regiment to establish guard posts along the Nashville and Northwestern Railroad. In early January 1865, Company E, 13th USCT Regiment, returned to Waverly and Johnsonville to guard sections of the Nashville and Northwestern Railroad, various military buildings, and partially man the fortifications. Navy vessels continued using the expansive wharf at Johnsonville as a base of operations on the Tennessee River.[13]

---

10 Walter Howland Letters, November 28, 1864.

11 *OR* 45, pt.1, 1,020-21, 1,049-50, 1,072, 1,085, 1,100; Walter Howland Letters, December 2, 1864.

12 Family information courtesy of Warren and Robin Atwood. In May 1865, the 43rd Wisconsin was mustered out of service on June 24, 1865. Lorenzo Atwood was ill, and spent time recovering before he could return home to Fayette, Wisconsin, and reunite with his son Arthur. With nothing left to keep them in Wisconsin, father and son returned to Hopkinton, New York, where Lorenzo married his late wife's sister, Paulina Phelps. He served as Justice of the Peace, Assessor, and Deacon of Hopkinton Congregational Church for 20 years before dying in 1899. Arthur, who worked as a teacher, salesman, and dairy farmer, died in 1923.

13 *OR Supplement*, vol. 77, 486-97.

On January 27, 1865, an unfortunate and deadly incident occurred at 6:00 a.m. when the transport *Eclipse*, docked at Johnsonville's wharf, exploded after her boilers overheated. Those aboard the steamer included members of the 9th Indiana Battery, who had just boarded en route to Paducah. The deadly explosion killed twenty-seven soldiers and wounded seventy-eight. Navy investigators concluded that the losses were the result of using, "in an emergency . . . an unsafe boat."[14]

Following the ill-fated explosion of the *Eclipse*, and unsure whether the event was an act of sabotage, Maj. Gen. Thomas ordered the 100th and 173rd Ohio regiments to occupy Johnsonville. On February 23, 1865, Col. J. R. Hurd of the 173rd Ohio stated that both Buckeye regiments "reported for duty 786 officers and men; Battery A, Second Missouri Artillery, 101 men; Battery F, of the same, 62 men: Battery I, of the same, 130 (Battery F armed with Enfield rifles). Total 1,079 officers and men."[15]

In early March, around the time Andrew Johnson took the oath of office as vice president of the United States, Thomas instructed Donaldson (now a brevet brigadier general and chief quartermaster for the Army of the Cumberland) to:

> Erect no buildings except a store house and office, and to make no accumulation of supplies there. From its position in a basin, with hills upon hills behind, Johnsonville is difficult to fortify, and will require a division at least to defend it. As a short line, however, to Eastport and the terminus of the Northwestern Railroad on the Tennessee, it is not without a certain value as an entrepot for Nashville during low water in the Cumberland, and therefore we shall have to keep it up.[16]

Parting Shots

In the two months following the disastrous attack against Johnsonville on November 4, inquiries about how such a thing could have happened inundated Union headquarters in Nashville. Military officials developed a better understanding about the wanton destruction of government property and privately leased transports and barges. The lapses in judgment by

14 *OR* 52, pt. 1, 714; *OR* 41, pt. 1, 600.

15 *OR* 49, pt. 1, 760-61.

16 Ibid., 871. The word "entrepot" is French for warehouse.

officers tasked with protecting the depot, which in turn had led to the unnecessary loss of lives and the destruction of government and civilian resources at Johnsonville, became a public embarrassment to the United States Army and Navy. It was now apparent to Montgomery Meigs and the Union high command structure that the self-destruction of invaluable government property, coupled with the financial losses incurred, were unparalleled.

The questionable actions of many officers and the looting of government stores at Johnsonville warranted an immediate and official investigation. Eventually, Army and Navy investigators determined that the burning of the military vessels and civilian transport boats and barges was the result of orders by Acting Volunteer Lt. Edward King, and not Col. Thompson or Capt. Howland, as many witnesses had claimed. King was ordered to appear in a court-martial hearing in Nashville under three naval court of inquiry charges: (1) Misconduct in action with the enemy; (2) Unnecessary destruction of government property, (3) Dereliction of duty.[17]

The court martial proceedings began on January 7, 1865, and concluded four months later on May 8, 1865. After weeks of sworn testimony from sailors, Quartermaster's Department personnel, civilians, and officers in charge on November 4—including Thompson and Howland—King was acquitted of all charges. Donaldson, however, disagreed with the outcome. Seven weeks after King's acquittal, Donaldson penned and sent off in his official report of operations of the Quartermaster's Department to General Meigs. "I think there was a want of judgement on the part of the officer who ordered the transports to be fired," he argued, firing a shot directly against the exonerated King. "It may be said he apprehended their falling into the hands of the enemy, but the answer to this is, the transports were under his fire and could have been destroyed at any time."[18]

In a rather odd twist, the court failed to bring a single charge against Thompson or Howland, who, according to official records, clearly issued orders that led to the destruction of the transports and government property.

17 Testimony of Acting Volunteer Lieutenant E.M. King, lately of the USS "*Key West*," May 8, 1865. *The Abandonment and Destruction of the USS Key West, Tawah, and Elfin*, RG 11-86, Roll 159, *U.S. Naval Records, Courts Martial*, National Archives, Washington, D.C., 4-7.

18 *OR* 52, pt. 1, 683.

Instead of being court-martialed Thompson was promoted to brevet brigadier general and Howland was assigned to a higher position at the Nashville Depot. In May 1865, Howland was promoted to lieutenant colonel.[19]

*   *   *

By early 1865 most military operations in the Western Theater had concluded, but supply operations continued apace at Johnsonville. In June 1865, after the collapse of the Confederacy, salvage efforts commenced at Johnsonville's wharf to raise the sunken transports and salvage equipment and armament from the destroyed gunboats. For the next eleven months, until March 1866, the Navy conducted recovery operations at Johnsonville using the salvage vessel USS *Kate* to retrieve the sunken boats and their valuable equipment.[20]

On June 30, Donaldson submitted his official report about the loss of government property at Johnsonville. "The value of the transports destroyed is estimated at $300,000," he concluded, and "of the barges—$35,000, total loss estimated at $1,500,000—$500,000 of which were commissary stores.

Nathan Bedford Forrest, in his after-action report written on January 12, 1865, provided a specific breakdown of the losses inflicted upon the Federal forces on the Tennessee River and at Johnsonville from October 28 through November 5, 1864—and perhaps a more accurate one. "I captured and destroyed 4 gunboats, 14 transports, 20 barges, 26 pieces of artillery, $6,700,000 worth of property, and 150 prisoners."

Regardless of whether the accumulated losses equaled $1.5 million dollars, as Federal officials claimed, or $6.7 million dollars, as Forrest estimated, both the monetary and physical losses to the Union war effort were astounding.[21]

19 Ibid, 683.

20 U.S. Navy Deck Log, USS *Kate* (salvage ship), April 2, 1865 - March 25, 1866 by Master Mates: J. H. Bentley, Spraque, and Cullbertson, RG 24, *Department of the Navy Deck Logs*, National Archives, Washington, D.C., 56-58.

21 Ibid; *ORN* 26, 683.

Postwar Improvements

For all intents and purposes, the Civil War concluded in the spring of 1865. Gen. Robert E. Lee surrendered in Virginia on April 9, Gen. Joseph E. Johnston in North Carolina later that month, and various other forces across the South put down their weapons thereafter. Johnsonville's civilian employees were released and many returned to their homes in the North. For the next six months, the Union army practically abandoned the supply depot's facilities. Some buildings were dismantled and the lumber re-purposed to construct houses in the town. The largest freight transfer building, Warehouse No. 2, remained intact with its machinery but was eventually dismantled and sold in the 1870s. A few new manufacturing buildings emerged along Johnsonville's wharf, but no records indicate how many structures were built.[22]

Several factors influenced how Johnsonville fared after the war. The most important factor was the provision of rail passenger service as a result of the bridging of the Tennessee River. The bridge shortened the travel time between Nashville and Memphis and the connection offered economic stability as visitors utilized the town's hotels, boarding houses, restaurants and mercantile stores. The *Nashville Republican Banner* described the impact and design of the Tennessee River Bridge in 1867:

> The new bridge over the Tennessee River is a splendid piece of workmanship. It is 1,900 feet long, resting upon seven stone pillars, neatness and durability, leaves nothing to be desired. From pillar to pillar leads a heavy wooden frame, joined by iron bolts, hanging on heavy blocks, and between the fourth and sixth pillar is the draw, which affords ample room for the passage of the largest steamers. The timber and ironwork of this bridge, the building of which took just ten months, was done at Chicago and brought by water to this place. It will enable us to reach Memphis to Nashville in nine hours.[23]

With the construction and opening of the new railroad bridge, the town blossomed as more merchants arrived and established businesses that catered to the bustling railroad passenger service. In Nashville, rail travelers purchased rail passes more frequently now that Memphis could be easily

---

22 *OR Supplement*, vol. 77, 486-97; Moore, "Farm Communities," 156, 162-163, 218-219.

23 *Nashville Republican Banner*, September 22, 1867, 4.

Burned Civil War transport boat ruins (foreground) and the Tennessee River Railroad Bridge at Johnsonville, Tennessee, 1914. *Confederate Veteran Magazine*

accessed, which increased the need for more hotels, taverns, and related merchants. In the middle of an economically depressed southern county devastated by the recent war, the bridge was the boost it so badly needed.

Another factor included Johnsonville's ability to maintain a significant population. Between March and November 1864, the town and supply depot had 2,900 occupants. Despite the loss of military personnel after the war ended, 1,000 white and black residents remained in Johnsonville. As a result, the town became the third most populated area in Humphreys County behind Waverly and McEwen.[24]

Two additional factors, both significant, included a shift in the town's image: terrorism and flooding. From its beginning, Johnsonville was popularized as a boat landing, military support operation, and sanctuary for

24 Byron and Barbara Sistler, eds., *1870 Census–Tennessee* (Nashville, 1985), 19, 31, 36-39, 55-65, 107-09.

Unionism. However, by 1867, terrorist activities routinely committed upon the town's black population tarnished its image. Stories of murder abounded in the region and greatly affected the town's economy. Travelers began avoiding the area. Additionally, flood damage earned regular headlines. Heavy flooding often submerged Johnsonville, which was built at river level. Concern by travelers of "the bridge being swept away" further impacted the town's already negative image as a sanctuary for free blacks who had been garrisoned at the Union army post in a region dominated by white secessionists.[25]

"The most doleful appearance." That is the dreary description that came to mind for one correspondent reporting on the Nashville and Northwestern Railroad when he visited Johnsonville. "The farm houses erected in great haste," he continued,

> are forsaken and forgotten; the stores once filled with goods of all kinds, are closed. Here and there you may still see, wandering among this desolation, a few of the former inhabitants, as if unwilling to forsake the place which offered them once so good an opportunity to make money fast. There they sit and bewail the evil days which have come upon them.[26]

Johnsonville's Black Population

Approximately thirty USCT veterans settled in Johnsonville after the war. The majority of these men had served in the 12th, 13th, 40th, 41st, 100th, 101st and 110th USCT regiments. Sixteen veterans of the 13th Regiment USCT who had served at Johnsonville established homes there in the remaining half of the 1860s. These men included Pvt. Dempsey Green, Company A; Pvt. Anderson, Company E; Pvt. Young (company unknown); Pvt. George Overall, Company C; and a man listed only as "George (Sutler Madison's)," Company D. Also, two USCT veterans with disabilities resided in Johnsonville: Sergeant Henry McWilliams, listed as having rheumatism, served in the 8th US Colored Heavy Artillery (company

25 *Nashville Daily Times and Press*, March 20-21, 1867, 1-2.

26 *Nashville Republican Banner*, September 22, 1867.

Private Adam Watkins (16th
U.S.C.T.) and his wife, ca. 1864
*Tennessee State Museum-Tennessee
Historical Society Collection*

unknown), and Cpl. Washington Carmack, Company H, 13th Regiment USCT, who had been shot in the hand during the Battle of Nashville.[27]

Employment opportunities in Johnsonville were limited after the war. Some whites found jobs farming and at various businesses in town such as Palmer's Saw Mill and at the river boat landing. However, whites commonly refused to hire blacks. The small contingent of black men who lived in Johnsonville were "chased and harassed by local desperadoes" and visited regularly by a secret anti-black society called the "Red Jackets," an organization similar to the Ku Klux Klan formed in Johnsonville in 1867. The persecution of Johnsonville's black population became so cruel that a Nashville correspondent noted "Johnsonville is bad news, its people, almost without exception, are void of all moral and religious sentiments."[28]

Blacks were unrecognized for their contributions to the Union victory and often blamed for causing the war. Because of this, Johnsonville's black population was marginalized through unfair employment practices,

27 Moore, "Farm Communities," 156, 162-163, 218-219; Byron and Barbara Sistler, eds., *1890 Civil War Veterans Census-Tennessee* (Evanston, 1978), 4, 6, 89, 119, 122, 197, 215, 239, 306, 312, 335. These pages list many of the black Union veterans from the 12th and 13th USCT as living in Johnsonville in 1890 from the *1890 Special Census Schedules, Civil War Union Veterans & Their Widows: West Tennessee*, MF 98, "Benton Co. through Weakley Co.," TSLA, Nashville, Tennessee. USCT veterans Green, Anderson, Young, Overall, "George," McWilliams, and Carmack were confirmed by examining muster rolls of the 12th and 13th USCT by permission of Dr. Wayne Moore, Assistant State Archivist, TSLA.

28 *Nashville Daily Press and Times*, February 4, 25, 1868, and October 29, 1868.

E. E. Martin Store, Johnsonville, Tennessee, 1910.
Johnsonville State Historic Park

segregated housing, and unpaid labor. These conditions did not improve until the arrival of a branch of the Bureau of Refugees, Freedmen, and Abandoned Lands, commonly known as the Freedmen's Bureau.[29]

In August 1867, the Freedmen's Bureau opened a school for blacks in Johnsonville and John Enoch accepted the appointment as its first agent. His replacement, John Wilson, arrived in November 1867 and enhanced the Freedmen's Bureau's services by ensuring that black children received a proper education. Wilson also helped legalize the marriages of former slaves and provided transportation for blacks who attempted to reunite with their families. Finally, he aided former black soldiers in their quest for back pay and pensions owed to them for their military service.[30]

29 Annual Reports of the Assistant Commissioner, Freedmen's Bureau of Tennessee, September 30, 1867, 5-6, and October 10, 1868,4, Records of the Commissioner, *Records of the Bureau of Refugees, Freedmen, and Abandoned Lands*, RG 105, National Archives, Washington, DC.

30 Letters of Johnsonville agents John Enoch and John L. Wilson to Assistant Commissioners Fisk, Lewis, Carlin, and Thompson of the Tennessee Freedmen's Bureau received from 1866-1869, *Records of the Tennessee field offices of the Bureau of Refugees,*

By 1868, the Freedmen's Bureau had significantly improved the quality of life for blacks and poor whites and facilitated an expansion of the black community. The Bureau distributed aid, including food and clothing, and helped blacks become self-sufficient by negotiating labor contracts between landowners and freedmen. In Tennessee alone, the Freedmen's Bureau issued more than 150,000 rations to both freedmen and white refugees. Additionally, several charitable organizations in Nashville and other towns near Johnsonville contributed significant amounts of corn, clothing, and fuel to aid the destitute. In 1869, the segregated black community in Johnsonville expanded. In addition to the school, a small congregation launched the Johnsonville African Methodist Episcopal Church, which would remain in operation until 1944.[31]

Johnsonville's Postwar Decline

Johnsonville's postwar population peaked in 1890 at about 2,800 residents, many of whom operated businesses that catered to railroad passengers. New operations included a general store, barber shop, coffin factory, lumber yard, a trio of hotels, and a peanut re-cleaning mill operated by the Barnhart Mercantile Company of St. Louis. The peanut operation employed hundreds of Humphreys County residents, including a large number of women.[32]

After a series of economic recessions and major floods in the 1890s and early 1900s, Johnsonville's economy suffered tremendously and its population decreased. In 1913, George Eric Moore and his family moved away from Johnsonville because of the recurring flooding, only to return in 1918. "We moved into a house ½ mile east of town," Moore recalled in discussing how hard life was there during the 1920s. "My dad," he continued,

---

Freedmen, and Abandoned Lands, 1865–1872, MF1911, RG 105, Reel 21, National Archives, Washington, D.C.

31 Ibid; Weymouth T. Jordan, "The Freedmen's Bureau in Tennessee," *The East Tennessee Historical Society's Publications*, 11 (1939), 54–55.

32 Garrett, *The History of Humphreys County, Tennessee*, 49-61; Robert G. Wyatt, "The Johnsonville Times: TVA Dam Brings Death of Old Town, Birth of New Johnsonville," in *The Nashville Banner*, 5 (March 1958), 1.

had gotten the night job at the elevator, watching, checking freight and pumping water for the trains. There was a coal chute across the track from the water tank where trains took the coal. In the early twenties a blight killed all the chestnut timbers. About 1926, they were cutting it for dye wood. I hauled dye wood off of Fort Hill [lower redoubt] and loaded it into box cars to ship.[33]

In the 1930s, the Tennessee Valley Authority (TVA) sought to bring hydro-electric power to the flood-ravaged Tennessee River Valley. In order to do this, it restrained the free-flowing Tennessee River by constructing a system of locks and dams. By 1941, as the Great Depression was coming to an end and World War II was beginning, Johnsonville's population had dwindled to just 300. The country's failed economy and employment crisis had devastated the small town. The TVA's last dam project utilized nearly 100 local laborers to help clear timber in advance of controlled flooding in that region. According to Robert Wyatt in *The Johnsonville Times*, "much good timber, fine oak, poplar, ash, walnut, gum, and other trees was raked up into huge piles by machinery and then the Tennessee Valley Authority gave men contracts at pleasing pay to burn them."[34]

The TVA's final dam project, the Kentucky Dam, located just below Paducah near Gilbertsville, finally opened in August 1944. The dammed Tennessee River below flood stage south of the new dam created the Kentucky Reservoir (better known as Kentucky Lake). Tennessee towns located at river level, such as Johnsonville, were practically submerged by the Kentucky Reservoir. Thankfully, Johnsonville's remaining Civil War earthworks had been constructed on higher ground and thus escaped the flooding.[35]

Johnsonville and the Lost Cause

Newspaper stories from 1867 to 1940 reveal little about Johnsonville's Civil War history beyond the reuse of a few military buildings or the brief

33 George Eric Moore, "Memories and Experiences of George Eric Moore" (self-published, 1977), 2-3.

34 Wyatt, "The Johnsonville Times," part 5, 1; Garrett, *The History of Humphreys County, Tennessee*, 57-67.

35 Tennessee Valley Authority, historical resource center for river depth levels on the Tennessee River at Johnsonville, Tennessee, online service.

mention of a business in town. Johnsonville's contribution to the Union victory all but disappeared from the collective memory of the Civil War. These omissions, particularly concerning railroad activities, are undeserved. After all, the Nashville and Northwestern Railroad terminated at Johnsonville and dramatically altered the landscape of four Middle Tennessee counties (Davidson, Cheatham, Dickson, and Humphreys), providing the commercial mechanism that rejuvenated the economies of those counties after the war.

Purposely forgetting the war was understandable especially in Humphreys County, where ninety-nine percent of its white population had supported secession in 1861. Geography likely explains Johnsonville's exclusion from the collective memory of the Civil War. The Union Army took advantage of its military occupation of Tennessee and built Johnsonville directly in the heart of a Confederate community. While the North celebrated its victory with parades, monuments, flags, and stage performances, Southerners, especially those near former military posts like Johnsonville, returned home to ruination and a constant reminder of the war they had fought and loss.[36]

At Johnsonville, the Civil War left in its wake burned warehouses, visible hulls of sunken transports and gunboats, abandoned sheds and saw mills, piles of scrap wood and stumps, and a devastated landscape practically immune to cultivation. One example of this ruination included a U.S. Army-built administration building, which was later converted into the popular Waggoner Hotel, named after Johnsonville resident Randolph Waggoner. Buildings like the Waggoner Hotel offered tangible reminders of the war. Northerners and Southerners alike used such relics to weave a narrative between 1865 and 1890 as a way to "contemplate the savage behavior of humans and the invasions of domestic privacy during wartime." When the historic town, various depot sites, and location of the Battle of Johnsonville became part of the Tennessee State Parks system in 1971, the Civil War history centered almost entirely on the Confederate side of the

36 Garrett, *The History of Humphreys County, Tennessee*, 53-55; Paul A. Shackel, *Memory in Black and White: Race, Commemoration, and the Post-Bellum Landscape* (Walnut Creek, 2003), 22-23; Gaines M. Foster, *Ghosts of the Confederacy: Defeat, the Lost Cause, and the Emergence of the New South, 1865-1913* (New York, 1987), 4-5, 55-57.

story. By doing so, it effectively excluded the contributions of the Union defenders.[37]

Johnsonville provides a classic example of an ethnographic landscape, where cultural expression influenced, as one writer put it, the "meanings, ideologies, beliefs, values, and world-views shared by a group of people." The Lost Cause, a ideology developed after the war by former Confederates during a period of postwar economic and racial uncertainty, also influenced Johnsonville. The Lost Cause romanticized the "Old South" and the Confederate war effort and its leaders, and distorted the history of the South's loss. Articles and books written after the war delivered heavy doses of the Lost Cause during the height of the "first" Lost Cause era from the late 1870s to the early 1920s. A more aggressive second generation of Lost Cause history resumed around 1940. Johnsonville's history is wrapped up in this ideology.[38]

Former Confederates, newspaper journalists, and fiction writers shaped the written influence of the Lost Cause. For example, a recurring theme associated with the Battle of Johnsonville regularly included Maj. Gen. Nathan B. Forrest and the Confederate victory there in early November 1864. Nearly all other actions taken by the Union forces during that battle other than the purported mass destruction of the supply depot and especially, the contributions from the United States Colored Troops, were intentionally omitted. For instance, one consistent story associated with the November battle recalled that, prior to the attack on November 4, the Union defenders were unaware of Confederate movements and thus completely overtaken by a surprise attack that resulted in the destruction of the supply depot and the

---

37 Megan Kate Nelson, *Ruin Nation: Destruction and the American Civil War* (Athens, 2012), 232; Richard H. Schein, ed., "Race and Landscape in the United States," in *Landscape and Race in the United States* (New York, 2006), 5-7; Garrett, *The History of Humphreys County, Tennessee*, 54. The building that would be the Waggoner Hotel is visible under construction in one of Coonley's photographs of Johnsonville. For years it was believed the hotel was a former military barracks, but the building was not in the area where the military barracks were once located. The Waggoner Hotel appears to have been an administrative building, especially since it was alongside the railroad tracks, which would have made it essentially impossible for troops to forma just outside its doors.

38 Donald Hardesty, "Ethnographic Landscapes: Transforming Nature into Culture," in *Preserving Cultural Landscapes in America*, eds. Arnold R. Alanen and Robert Z. Melnick (Baltimore, 2000), 172-80; Foster, *Ghosts of the Confederacy*, 4-5, 55-57; Shackel, *Memory in Black and White*, 26-29.

defeat of the Union forces. Both Union and Confederate sources reveal problems with this narrative.[39]

An examination of reports, telegrams, letters, and other primary sources reveal that the Union defenders knew about their enemy's presence, the Confederates directly inflicted very little lasting damage during the battle, and that the depot's own defenders caused the majority of the large-scale destruction at the wharf. Lost Cause authors, most of whom were former Confederate soldiers, popularized inaccurate stories of how Forrest's surprise attack created the wholesale destruction of the Union supply depot.[40]

The correspondence of three Union officers and an enlisted man explain in detail that the Union defenders were very much aware of the Confederate presence somewhere between Reynoldsburg Island and Johnsonville on the opposite river bank. In fact, on November 4, the Federals were at such a high level of alert that they acted to prevent the Confederates from occupying the western bank by removing brush and increasing shoreline gunboat patrols. Henry Howland's account of the battle, for example, varied considerably from the Southern accounts that peppered numerous issues of *Confederate Veteran* magazine. "At about 2 o'clock p.m the enemy were discovered planting batteries directly opposite also above and below our Warehouses and levee," wrote Johnsonville's assistant quartermaster. "The gunboats opened fire upon them, as did also our batteries upon the hill. After some twenty minutes firing, a reply was received from all the rebel batteries."[41]

The Lost Cause narrative notwithstanding, the result of the Johnsonville battle was but a minor setback with no strategic advantage for the Confederacy. The small but fascinating tactical Rebel victory at Johnsonville in November 1864 came so late in the war that there was no way for the Confederacy to capitalize on Forrest's achievement. In the end, the actual results of the Civil War remain at odds with Lost Cause rhetoric.

---

39 Shackel, *Memory in Black and White*, 27; David Blight, *Frederick Douglass' Civil War: Keeping faith in Jubilee* (Baton Rouge,1989), 228-29.

40 Shackel, *Memory in Black and White*, 27; David Blight, *Frederick Douglass' Civil War: Keeping faith in Jubilee* (Baton Rouge,1989), 228-29.

41 Henry Howland to Brigadier General Jacob Donaldson, November 16, 1864, Johnsonville, Tennessee, RG 94, Carded Records Relating to Civil War Staff Officers, National Archives, Washington, D.C.

Instead, the truth about what happened, especially at Johnsonville, indicates that wars are won from effective military planning, expert engineering methods, and by maintaining a consistent flow of supplies using networks of rivers and railroads.

The Rewards of History

The importance of Johnsonville during the Civil War cannot be overstated. Johnsonville evolved as the second largest supply depot in Tennessee during the Civil War: only the massive Nashville Depot was larger. Johnsonville's significance as a supply operation is important for three reasons. First, it provided Tennessee's Union forces with a better location for receiving supplies shipped from Northern bases. Second, the Nashville and Northwestern Railroad allowed a steady flow of supplies received at the Tennessee River to be connected to the important Nashville and Chattanooga Railroad, General Sherman's main line of supply. Without Johnsonville, Sherman's Army would not have received adequate ammunition, food, clothing, munitions and other supplies needed to conduct operations in Georgia. Third, Johnsonville established a permanent docking point for Union naval operations on the Tennessee River. With its central location, gunboats and transports had logistical advantage for conducting river operations either north or south of Johnsonville. Johnsonville proved to be more than just a logistical tool used to defeat the Confederacy in the waning days of the Civil War. Its legacy is still apparent today, not only as a State Park, but through the impact it had upon issues of supply, emancipation, and engineering during the Civil War.

*   *   *

Today, Johnsonville State Historic Park tells a broad range of stories associated with supply and logistics, emancipation and black troops, military railroads, naval actions, Quartermaster's Department activities, infantry and cavalry troops, artillery, battles, earthworks, animals, civilians, sickness, and death. These various themes help historical interpreters develop a wide variety of programs, walking tours, and exhibits about this remarkable site.

The Johnsonville Supply Depot Site today, with the Tennessee River
visible in the background. *Author*

Johnsonville's diversity, underpinned by three distinct perspectives: Federal, Confederate, and African American, offer a deep insight into how the war was waged and its manifest consequences.[42]

Three underlying themes drive the Johnsonville story. One is how the Union achieved massive change using supply and engineering mastery to help win the Civil War, and another is how race and Southern culture challenged Americans to negotiate loss with the true historical record. Last but perhaps the most important is that the true history of Johnsonville will forever remain a significant contribution to the history of supply operations in the Civil War and as a tribute to American ingenuity and bravery.[43]

42 James Broomall, "The Interpretation Is A-Changin: Memory, Museums, and Public History in Central Virginia," *The Journal of the Civil War Era* 1, Vol. 3 (March 2013, 114-122.

43 James Oliver Horton and Lois E. Horton, eds., *Slavery and Public History: The Tough Stuff of American Memory* (Chapel Hill, 2006), 166.

The Burden of Supply:
The U.S. Quartermaster's Department in Tennessee

JOHNSONVILLE was an excellent example of the Union's logistical mastery during the Civil War. The supply depot was the result of an ambitious president who understood the staggering logistical needs of a front line army. And without the exceptional efforts and expertise of the United States Quartermaster's Department, it would never have been successful.

Before the establishment of the current U.S. Quartermaster Corps in 1912, the Quartermaster's Department was designated by Congress as the agency responsible for the purchase, storage, and distribution of all military supplies. These supplies included food, weapons, clothing, ammunition, animals, and everything else required to sustain the military. Shortly after the start of the Civil War, the Quartermaster's Department also assumed the responsibility for burials and marking graves with government headstones.[1]

---

1 *General Orders No. 78*, July 25, 1873. The U.S. War Department, Adjutant General's Office in *Notes of Edwin C. Gabel* (Clerk at Philadelphia Quartermaster Depot (PQMD), from 1909-1949; H. A. Royce, *A Sketch of the Organization of the Quartermaster's Department from 1774 to 1868* (Washington, 1869), 12-16; Erna Risch, *Quartermaster Support of the Army: A History of the Corps, 1775-1939* (Washington, 1962), 110-113; Edward Steere, *The Graves Registration Service in World War II, Q.M.C. Historical Studies, No. 21* (Washington, D.C., 1951), 3.

Creating a Military Supply System

The Quartermaster's Department had a convoluted, but interesting, beginning. After the Revolutionary War, the functions of the Quartermaster's Department were essentially non-existent, and Congress abolished the entity in 1785. However, the increase in Indian hostilities in 1791 convinced President George Washington to approve a temporary appointment of a quartermaster general, held by the Secretary of War Henry Knox. The secretary of war authorized military officers to hire "contractors of provisions" to furnish supplies to troops stationed on the frontier.[2]

On May 8, 1792, Congress transferred to the Treasury Department "all purchases and contracts for supplying the Army with provisions, clothing, supplies in the Quartermaster Department, military stores, Indian goods, or all other supplies or articles for the use of the Department of War." That same year, the president appointed Gen. Anthony Wayne as Commander of the Army and shortly afterward, James O'Hara was chosen as quartermaster general before resigning just four years later. In 1795, Congress established the office of "Purveyor of Public Supplies" under the supervision of the commissioner of revenue in the U.S. Treasury Department led by Alexander Hamilton. Ultimately, on June 1, 1796—the same day Tennessee became a state—Congress established the Quartermaster's Department and authorized the first official quartermaster general, John Wilkins, Jr.[3]

Working in conjunction with the Department of the Treasury, Wilkins supported the use of military agents and contractors for the Quartermaster's Department, and, in 1800, the War Department employed agents to carry out supply duties in New York and Tennessee. Because the Quartermaster's Department was considered an essential need only during time of war, the agency had an unstable existence for a decade and a half. But in 1816, the United States Army reorganized and the Quartermaster's Department

2 Steere, *The Graves Registration Service in World War II*, 3; *Journals of the Continental Congress, Vol. XXXIV, 1788-1799*, 586.

3 *Annals of Congress, 2nd Congress, 1791-1793*, 1383-1386; Risch, *Quartermaster Support of the Army*, 82-83, 112.

became a permanent element of the Federal government under the sole authority of the secretary of war.[4]

Thomas S. Jesup, appointed quartermaster general in 1818, faithfully served in the position for the next forty-two years bringing continuity, training, and supply procedures to the department. In the decades preceding the Civil War, Jesup became instrumental in ensuring that soldiers and sailors had better weapons and improved uniforms. He improved soldiers' health through mandating rations of fruits, vegetables, fresh meats, and dairy into their diet to reduce scurvy, a disease caused by vitamin and iron deficiencies. The improved nutritional requirements forced the Quartermaster's Department to advance food preservation, such as canning vegetables, milk, and fruits, and to improve the refrigeration and transportation of fresh foods to troops serving in the field or on the water.[5]

In all previous American wars, the transportation of food and supplies by wagon train for the Army was practically unknown. By the Civil War, however, mobile operations for delivering food and supplies had advanced to the point that goods were now transported to troops in the field by regimental wagon trains and steam locomotives. Infantry in the field advanced on foot, known as light marching order. Company and regimental supply wagons followed long columns of marching troops two miles to the rear. Supply wagons hauled such things as officers' correspondence, field furniture, trunks, knapsacks, blankets, tents, water barrels, and most importantly, food.[6]

In the Civil War, when armies went into camp, rations were issued to companies by the company quartermasters. Generally, company quartermasters held the enlisted rank of sergeant and were supervised by company grade officers, either a lieutenant or a captain. Company

---

4 Secretary of War to William Irvine, June 30, 1801, RG 107, *Records of the Office of the Secretary of War*, Military Book, vol. 1, 99 (Washington, D. C. n.d.).

5 Risch, *Quartermaster Support of the Army*, 179, 184-85; Herbert R. Rifkind, *Fresh Foods for the Armed Forces: The Quartermaster Market Center System, 1941-1948* (in Two Parts) Q.M.C. Historical Studies, No. 20 (Washington, D.C., 1951), 2.

6 Rifkind, *Fresh Foods for the Armed Forces*, 2; Samuel C. Prescott, *Troop Feeding Programs: A Survey of Rationing and Subsistence in the United States Army, 1775 to 1940* (National Defense Research Committee, Office of Scientific Research and Development, Washington, D.C., 1944), online resource http://naldc.nal.usda.gov/download/CAT, vol. 1, 7-9.

quartermasters had the enormous responsibility of assuring that supplies and rations for about 100 men remained available and accessible at a moment's notice. Company supplies and rations were assigned to the quartermaster sergeants by the regimental and assistant regimental quartermasters who typically reported to the major or lieutenant colonel of the regiment. Other duties of the Quartermaster's Department included hauling fuel, such as firewood and coal by wagon train.[7]

Thousands of letters written home by Civil War soldiers described the receipt of food, clothing, or any sort of new supplies. These goods provided soldiers with comfort that any loved one could comprehend. Writing about creature comforts provided a common link to home and offered assurance to loved ones that their sons, husbands and fathers were not in need or suffering from the horrors of war. Cpl. Lorenzo Atwood of the 43rd Wisconsin Infantry, for example, while traveling to Nashville in 1864, wrote about supplies while in camp at Milwaukee, Wisconsin:

> We paraded for roll call at 6, had breakfast at 6 ½, commenced drawing our cloths at 8. I can eat my rations every time which consists of a cup of coffee, a slice of bread about the size of one half this sheet of paper and one inch thick and a small piece of beef for breakfast, and the same reversed for dinner, and for supper minus the meat, Fridays we have fish boiled instead of beef, We have enough for our health and that is good enough, we have had a few messes of beans and rice, Ed is cook now, (a good one too).[8]

The Meigs Turnaround

At the start of the Civil War, the Quartermaster's Department was effectively defunct because of questionable distributions of supplies during the leading up to the war and poor oversight by Quartermaster General Joseph E. Johnston and the Secretary of War John B. Floyd. After only ten months in the position and just days after the Civil War began, Johnston resigned to join the Confederate Army as a brigadier general.

For almost two months, and likely the most critical period of the secession crisis, the lack of a competent quartermaster general severely

7 Prescott, *Troop Feeding Programs*, 2-6.

8 Atwood, September 25, 1864.

handicapped the initial efforts of the Union forces. Lincoln informed his military leaders that as long as the rebellion continued, government troops should be well-supplied. It was Lincoln's personal responsibility to ensure the Army had the best and most up-to-date equipment needed to win the war. However, Lincoln's chief of ordnance, James W. Ripley, was opposed to practically every new product available such as breech-loading and repeating rifles, and the "coffee-mill gun," the predecessor of the modern machine gun.[9]

In early May 1861, Lincoln found a solution to the supply problems that had plagued the Army. Weighing heavily upon the recommendation of Secretary of State William Seward and Postmaster General Montgomery Blair, Lincoln appointed Montgomery Cunningham Meigs as quartermaster general, a position with the rank of brigadier general and the overall command of the Quartermaster's Department. Meigs proved to be a superb administrator who worked tirelessly to make sure Union soldiers operating in all theaters of the war received the supplies they needed for large-scale campaigns and support operations. He quickly transformed the department into a magnificent tool of war. More importantly, as a career Army officer, Meigs understood the essential nature of logistical operations.

Under Meigs' leadership, wagons, boats, and railroads distributed supplies to troops camped and fighting across the South. Meigs earned Lincoln's support and the respect of military officers and cabinet members. Secretary of State Seward, who initially recommended him for the position, recalled that, "without the services of this eminent soldier the national cause must have been lost or deeply imperiled."[10]

Quartermaster Responsibilities

Various chief quartermasters served under Meigs, who personally selected and assigned them to posts where Union forces had secured strongholds. Meigs selected three chief quartermasters to administer Federal

9 David Herbert Donald, *Lincoln* (London, 1995), 431.

10 General Montgomery Cunningham Meigs, *Scientific American*, January 30, 1892, 71; Miller, *Second Only to Grant*, 183-88; McPherson, *Ordeal by Fire*, 198; Russell Weigley, *Quartermaster General of the Union Army: A Biography of M.C. Meigs* (New York, 1959), 172, 181.

supply needs in the Western Theater. These men were: Brig. Gen. Robert Allen, who oversaw supply operations in Louisville, Kentucky; Col. James L. Donaldson, who Meigs had transferred from a small depot in Baltimore to become the chief quartermaster of the Nashville Depot; and Maj. Langdon C. Easton, a seasoned quartermaster whose experience dated back to the Mexican War and who had been handling quartermaster responsibilities for the entire western United States out of Fort Leavenworth, Kansas. Langdon, highly recommended to Meigs by Maj. Gen. William T. Sherman, received the job of chief quartermaster for the Army of the Cumberland. As a favor from Sherman, Langdon rapidly rose to major general in March 1864. In preparation for Sherman's move south against Atlanta and Grant's advance in Virginia against Richmond, supply demands on Allen, Donaldson, and Langdon were so tremendous that each had to stockpile reserve supplies. This meant ensuring that wagons and horse teams were in top condition to transfer supplies to both fronts efficiently and without delay.[11]

In the Union Army, assistant quartermasters served under chief quartermasters handling all inventory and the purchase of goods from private vendors. The assistant quartermasters (AQM) were responsible for fulfilling the supply requests at brigade, division, and even corps levels. These federally appointed staff officers either received a commission by Congress or were appointed by the president with a rank of lieutenant or captain. The assistant quartermasters managed the intricate work of administering requests from hundreds of field officers and quartermaster sergeants and oversaw the distribution of those supplies.

Regimental quartermasters (RQM) were elected by their own regiments organized from men within the same town or region. They were appointed by a governor with the rank of first lieutenant and only responsible for their regimental supply needs. During the Civil War, a common routine included assigning regimental quartermasters as acting assistant quartermasters (AAQM) because assistant quartermasters were in such short supply.[12]

---

11 Ibid, 229; Prescott, *Troop Feeding Programs*, 7-11; *OR* 4, Series 3, pt. 1, 241-43.

12 Simon Perkins, Jr.: A Brief Biography in *The Papers of Simon Perkins, Jr., Assistant Quartermaster, Nashville Depot* (Nashville, TN, TSLA, Microfilm Department, Microfilm Accession number 1527, Box 1, Folder 1), 3-4.

Eaton Depot, part of the Nashville Depot, Nashville, Tennessee, 1864. *Library of Congress*

Procedures for supplying troops were established shortly after Federal troops occupied Nashville in February 1862. Like Lincoln, Governor Andrew Johnson understood that to win the war, armed forces on the move must be maintained with a reliable supply chain of ammunition, clothing, and especially food. In the spring of 1862, only two operational supply depots—one in St. Louis, Missouri, and the other in Louisville, Kentucky—serviced military operations in the Western Theater. As the war moved south, the Quartermaster's Department selected Nashville as a prime location for consolidating supplies because of access to the Cumberland River and the railroad system intersecting the city.

At the Nashville Depot, the assistant quartermasters had responsibility for ensuring that military supplies were received and accounted for from places such as Johnsonville. At Johnsonville, Capt. Henry Howland oversaw the distribution of supplies loaded onto trains and shipped to the Nashville Depot. After the goods reached Nashville, responsibility transferred to a variety of assistant quartermasters assigned there, such as Capt. William Alonzo Wainwright. Wainwright served at the Nashville Depot from June 1864 to December 1865, and helped close the depot after the war's end.

During his tenure there, he administered thousands of supply requisitions to and from Johnsonville.[13]

After the supplies were processed at the Nashville Depot, they were distributed to outlying posts at Clarksville, Columbia, Chattanooga, Franklin, Gallatin, Murfreesboro, Pulaski, and Springfield in Tennessee, and at Bridgeport, Decatur, and Guntersville, in northern Alabama.[14]

During the Nashville Depot's existence, quartermaster offices were regularly inundated with requests from other supply depots. All supply shipments from the Nashville Depot to other Union occupied areas in Tennessee, as well as other posts outside the state, came under the responsibility of the assistant quartermasters. For instance, in November 1863, assistant quartermasters in charge of the garrison post located at Stevenson, Alabama, requested from the Nashville Depot "Clothing, Garrison Equipage and Quartermaster stores so needed for the resupply of the Post. The goods are very much needed to supply the demand."[15]

In addition to supplying clothing and equipment for a variety of infantry garrisons, Meigs, acting under the recommendation of Secretary Stanton because of pressure from Maj. Gen. William S. Rosecrans in Nashville, helped create a United States Cavalry Bureau in July 1863. Under this new bureau, purchases of horses were made by the Quartermaster's Department instead of by "bogus and bribing contractors," as Meigs reported to Rosecrans. Cavalry officers selected by the Quartermaster's Department conducted all inspections of horses and mules selected for purchase by the army.[16]

The largest cavalry depot in the Western Theater was at St. Louis, Missouri, where 12,000 horses and mules were corralled. The Nashville Depot was similar and just one of many locations where Union occupiers

13 William A. Wainwright, biographical sketch in *United States Assistant Quartermaster Records, 1861-1870* (Nashville, TN, TSLA, Microfilm Department, Microfilm Accession # 1652, THS 729,780, microfilm), 4-6; Risch, *Quartermaster Support of the Army*, 179, 184-85, 333-37.

14 *OR* 52, pt.1, 680-89.

15 W. A. Manen to Captain S. Perkins, A.Q.M., Nov 11, 1863, in *The Papers of Simon Perkins, Jr., Assistant Quartermaster, Nashville Depot*, Nashville, TSLA, accession # 1527, Box 2, Folder 16.

16 Miller, *Second Only to Grant*, 183.

Taylor Depot, Food and Rations Warehouse, Nashville Depot, United States Quartermaster's Department, Nashville, Tennessee, 1864. *Library of Congress*

established temporary corrals designed to hold up to 5,000 horses and mules. Under the same actions that established the Cavalry Bureau's corrals in Nashville, Johnsonville followed the pattern with the establishment of a six-acre horse corral built close to the northern spur of the Nashville and Northwestern Railroad. Cpl. Atwood described the corral as being "a little to the right of the store house is a parell [corral] in which there is some 1000 horses and mules. one of the boats at the wharf was loaded with horses."[17]

Every day, hundreds and eventually thousands of telegrams and written requisitions, invoices, receipts, orders, and service contracts, inundated quartermaster operations. During a major campaign, such as Sherman's 1864 advance into Georgia, it was not uncommon for a quartermaster employee to work at least twenty hours each day. Quartermaster employees usually worked inside dark wooden warehouses with little ventilation that often reached temperatures of 100 degrees in the summer months and well below freezing during the winter.

17 Ibid, 185; Atwood, October 27, 1864.

Some of the most requested supply items included tents and tarpaulins, blankets and clothing items such as jackets, blouses, overcoats, shirts, trousers, drawers, and stockings. Other items regularly distributed from the depots at Nashville and Johnsonville included boots, bootees, and slippers, and common infantry equipment such as canteens, haversacks, and knapsacks. Due to the magnitude of the Nashville Depot, Chief Quartermaster Col. James Donaldson regularly received requests from the assistant quartermasters of the other two major supply depots in St. Louis and Louisville.[18]

The Nashville Depot consisted of many buildings, the largest of which included the Taylor Depot, an immense supply storage warehouse 517 feet long by 190 feet wide used to store food and rations for the Army of the Cumberland. The Taylor Depot was located southeast of the state capitol in Nashville's train gulch, which at that time stretched around the base of Capitol Hill, where repair shops, corrals, and rail yards were located.[19]

18 *OR* 39, pt.1, 356; Ralph C. Gordon, "Nashville and the U.S. Christian Commission in the Civil War," *Tennessee Historical Quarterly* (Summer 1996), 98-111.

19 Ibid. The Taylor Depot stood where the Country Music Hall of Fame and Museum currently sits today in downtown Nashville.

Bibliography

Manuscript Sources

Central Michigan University

Ralzemond Parker Collection, Frank Drake Letters, 1864.

Duke University

Walter M. Howland Papers, David M. Rubenstein Rare Book & Manuscript Library, 1864.

National Archives

Affidavits from representatives of the states of Ohio, Tennessee, Kentucky, Illinois, and Iowa regarding the destruction of privately owned transports destroyed at Johnsonville, Tennessee, on November 4, 1864. Affidavits sworn and subscribed from January to May, 1865, at Nashville, Tennessee, U.S. Navy Records 1864-65, Courts Martial, RG 11-86, U.S. Navy Department.

Annual Reports of the Assistant Commissioner, Freedmen's Bureau of Tennessee, September 30, 1867, pp. 5-6 and October 10, 1868, p.4. *Records of the Commissioner, Records of the Bureau of Refugees, Freedmen, and Abandoned Lands*, RG 105

Letters of Johnsonville agents John Enoch and John L. Wilson to Assistant Commissioners Fisk, Lewis, Carlin, and Thompson of the Tennessee Freedmen's Bureau received from 1866-1869, *Records of the Tennessee field offices of the Bureau of Refugees, Freedmen, and Abandoned Lands*, 1865-1872, MF1911, RG 105, Reel 21.

Lieutenant Samuel W. Treat to Colonel L.B. Parsons, Johnsonville, Tennessee, November 24, 1864, Records of the Office of the Secretary of War, Military Book, Vol. 1.

William Given Press Book and Job Office Argument made by Col. William Given, 102nd O.V. in the Case of Capt. J.D. Stubbs, A.Q.M. before Court Martial in Nashville, Tennessee, 1864.

U.S. Navy Records, Acting Volunteer Lieutenant Edward M. King to AQM Henry Howland, Johnsonville, Tennessee, November 3, 1864.

U.S. Navy Deck Log from USS *Kate*, 1865-66.

U.S. Navy Records, Courts Martial, Acting Volunteer Lieutenant Edward M. King, 1865.

Vessels Bought, Sold, and Chartered by the United States, 1861-1868: Report by the Quartermaster General Relative to Vessels Bought, Sold, and Chartered Since April 1861. 40th Congress, 2nd Session, House Executive Document No. 337, 1865.

Tennessee State Library and Archives

1890 Special Census Schedules, Civil War Union Veterans & Their Widows: West Tennessee, "Benton Co. through Weakley Co.," Microfilm, RG 98.

Diary of Mrs. Louisa Brown Pearl, 1862.

Jill Knight Garrett Collection.

Roster of Negroes Impressed for work on the Northwestern Railroad, 1863, microfilm, RG 4.

Scrap Book of John F. Shannon, clipping about "Old Reynoldsburg" by J. Ben Fuqua in Jill Knight Garrett Collection, TSLA manuscripts.

Simon Perkins, Jr. Papers, Quartermaster Records, Nashville Depot, 1862-63.

William Wainwright Papers, Quartermaster Records, Nashville Depot, 1861-1870.

Wisconsin Historical Society

Lyman C. Draper Manuscript Collection.

Letter from Orderly Sergeant W. Wilkins to Colonel Amasa Cobb, 43rd Wisconsin, November 6, 1864.

Private Collections

Lorenzo D. Atwood Letters, 1864. Warren and Robin Atwood Collection.

George Eric Moore, "Memories and Experiences of George Eric Moore," self-published memoirs, 1977

Newspapers

Cincinnati Gazette [Ohio]

Daily National Intelligencer [Washington]

Daily National Journal [Washington]

Dyer County Herald [Tennessee]

Gazette [Nashville]

Indianapolis Daily Journal [Indiana]

Louisville Democrat [Kentucky]

Nashville Daily Press

Nashville Daily Union

Nashville Dispatch

Nashville Republican

Nashville Whig and Tennessee Advertiser

Nashville Union and American

National Intelligencer [Washington]

Periodicals

America's Civil War

Civil War History

Civil War Times Illustrated

Confederate Veteran

Journal of the Civil War Era

Tennessee Historical Quarterly

The River Counties Quarterly

Scientific American

Published Primary Sources

Acts of the General Assembly of Kentucky, Vol. II, 1855-56. n.p.

Acts Passed at the First Session of the Eighth General Assembly of the State of Tennessee, Begun and Held at Knoxville, on Monday the Eighteenth Day of September, One Thousand Eight Hundred and Nine. Knoxville: George Wilson, 1809.

Acts Passed at the First Session of the Eleventh General Assembly of the State of Tennessee, Begun and Held at Nashville, on Monday the Eighteenth Day of September, One Thousand Eight Hundred and Fifteen. Nashville: T.G. Bradford, Printer to the State, 1815.

Acts Passed at the First Session of the Fourteenth General Assembly of the State of Tennessee, on Monday the Eighteenth Day of September, One Thousand Eight Hundred and Twenty-One. Knoxville: Heiskell & Brown, 1821.

Acts Passed at the First Session of the Twenty-Ninth General Assembly of the State of Tennessee, For the Years 1851-2. Nashville: Bang and McKinnie, 1852.

Acts Passed at the First Session of the Thirtieth General Assembly of the State of Tennessee, For the Years 1853-4. Nashville: McKinnie & Brown, 1854.

Acts Passed at the First Session of the Thirtieth-Seventh General Assembly of the State of Tennessee, For the Year 1871. Nashville: Jones, Purvis & Brown Co., 1871.

Annals of Congress, 2nd Congress. No publisher provided, 1791-93.

Deputy State Historic Preservation Officer, "National Register Nomination, Johnsonville Historic District." Humphreys County, Tennessee, Section 7, 1990.

Forty-Second Annual Report of the Bureau of American Ethnology, To the Secretary of the Smithsonian Institution, 1924-1925. Washington: United States Government Printing Office, 1928.

General Orders No. 78, The U.S. War Department, Adjutant General's Office in NOTES of Edwin C. Gabel (Clerk at Philadelphia Quartermaster Depot from 1909-1949). No publisher provided, July 25, 1873.

Given, William. *Argument made by Col. William Given, 102nd O.V. in the Case of Capt. J.D. Stubbs, A.Q.M. before Court Martial in Nashville, Tennessee.* William Given Press Book and Job Office, Nashville, TN, 1864.

Irion, Jack B. and David V. Beard. *Underwater Archaeological Assessment of Civil War Shipwrecks in Kentucky Lake, Benton and Humphries Counties, Tennessee.* Tennessee Department of Archaeology, Department of Environment and Conservation. Nashville, TN, 1993.

James, Stephen R., Jr. *Additional Archaeological Investigations of Two Battle of Johnsonville Troop Transports Site 40HS338, Tennessee River, Humphries County, Tennessee*. Pan American Consultants, Inc. Memphis, TN, 2011.

Legislative History of the Louisville & Nashville R.R. Co. and Roads in its System. No publisher provided, 1898.

Mahan, D. H. *A Complete Treatise on Field Fortification, with the General Outlines of the Principles Regulating to the Arrangement, the Attack, and the Defence of Permanent Works*. New York: Wiley and Long, 1836.

McKee, John Miller (An Eye-Witness). *The Great Panic: Being Incidents Connected with Two Weeks of the War in Tennessee. Nashville*: Johnson and Whiting Publishers, 1862.

Muscle Shoals *Hearings, Before the Committee on Agriculture and Forestry, United States Senate, Sixty-Seventh Congress, Second Session*. Washington: Government Printing Office, 1922.

Nashville City and Business Directory for 1860-61. Nashville: L.P. Williams and Company Publishers, 1860.

Natchez Trace Parkway Survey, U.S. Department of the Interior. Washington, D.C.: U.S. Government Printing Office, 1941.

Official Records of the Union and Confederate Navies in the War of the Rebellion, 30 vols. Washington, D.C.: United States Government Printing Office, 1894-1927.

Payne, R.G. *Report to the General Assembly on the Condition of the Railroads in Tennessee*. Nashville: G.C. Torbett & Co., Printers, 1857.
———. *Report of the Committee of the City Council of Nashville, Upon the Affairs of the Nashville and Northwestern Railroad Company*, 1859.

Sistler, Byron and Barbara, eds., *1850 Census-Tennessee*, 4 vols. Nashville: Byron Sistler & Associates, 1991.
———. *1860 Census-Tennessee*, 5 vols. Nashville: Byron Sistler & Associates, 1981.
———. *1870 Census-Tennessee*, 4 vols. Nashville: Byron Sistler & Associates, 1985.
———. *1890 Civil War Veterans Census-Tennessee*. Nashville: Byron Sistler & Associates, 1978.

Smith, Samuel D., Benjamin C. Nance, and Fred M. Prouty. *A Survey of Civil War Era Military Sites in Tennessee*. Nashville: Department of Environment and Conservation, Division of Archeology, Research Series No. 14. Nashville: State of Tennessee Printing Division, 2003.

Telegraph book, 1863, Correspondence of General Alvan Gillem, Adjutant General, Department of the Cumberland, vol. 40, and *Letter Book*, vol. 41, RG 21, microfilm, TSLA, Nashville, TN.

Tennesseans in the Civil War, Vols. 1&2. Civil War Centennial Commission of Tennessee, 1964.

The Administrative History of the Nashville Depot. In "The Papers of William Alonzo Wainwright, 1832-1904, United States Assistant Quartermaster Records 1861-1870," MF 1652, Box 1, Folder 1, TSLA, Nashville, TN.

The Annual Report of the President and Directors of the Louisville and Nashville Railroad Company: Commencing on the First Monday in October 1856, and Ending October 1857. Louisville: C. Settle, Third Street, Over Madden's Bookstore, 1857.

The Official Atlas of the Civil War, Plate XIV. Washington, D.C.: United States Government Printing Office, 1894.

The War of the Rebellion: A Compilation of the Official Records of the Union and Confederate Armies, 130 vols. Washington, D.C.: U.S. Government Printing Office, 1880-1901.

The Official Records of the Union and Confederate Navies in the War of the Rebellion, 30 vols. Washington, D.C.: U.S. Government Printing Office, 1894.

U.S. Statutes at Large, 37th Congress, 2nd Session, 1862. *Vessels Bought, Sold, and Chartered by the United States, 1861-1868: Report by the Quartermaster General Relative to Vessels Bought, Sold, and Chartered Since April 1861*.40th Congress, 2nd Session, House Executive Document No. 337, 1867-68.

Yeatman, James E. *A Report on the Condition of the Freedmen of the Mississippi, Presented to the Western Sanitary Commission, December 17, 1863.* St. Louis: Western Sanitary Commission Room, 1864.

Published Secondary Sources

Abernathy, Thomas B. *From Frontier to Plantation in Tennessee: A Study in Frontier Democracy.* Chapel Hill: University of North Carolina Press, 1932.

Adams, Ephraim D. *Great Britain and the American Civil War*, 2 vols. New York: Longmans, Green and Company, 1925.

Ash, Stephen V. *Middle Tennessee Society Transformed 1860-1870.* Baton Rouge: Louisiana State University Press, 1988.

Baker, Jean H. *Affairs of Party: The Political Culture of Northern Democrats in the Mid-Nineteenth Century.* Ithaca, NY: Cornell University Press, 1983.

Basler, Roy P., Ed., *The Collected Works of Abraham Lincoln*, 9 Vols. New Brunswick, NJ: Rutgers University Press, 1953-55.

Beach, Ursula Smith. *Along the Warioto or A History of Montgomery County, Tennessee.* Nashville: McQuiddy Press, 1964.

Berlin, Ira, Barbara J. Fields, Steven F. Miller, Joseph P. Reidy, Leslie S. Rowland, eds., *Free at Last: A Documentary History of Slavery, Freedom, and the Civil War.* New York: The New Press, 1992.

———. *Generations of Captivity: A History of African-American Slaves.* Cambridge: Harvard University Press, 2003.

———. *Many Thousands Gone: The First Two Centuries of Slavery in North America.* Cambridge: Harvard University Press, 1998.

———. Joseph P. Reidy, and Leslie S. Rowland, eds. *Freedom: A Documentary History of Emancipation 1861-1867, Selected from the Holdings of the National Archives of the United States, Series II, The Black Military Experience* Cambridge: Cambridge University Press, 1982.

Bergeron, Paul H., Stephen V. Ash and Jeanette Keith. *Tennesseans and Their History.* Knoxville: The University of Tennessee Press, 1999.

Blight, David. *Frederick Douglass' Civil War: Keeping Faith in Jubilee.* Baton Rouge: Louisiana State University Press, 1989.

———. *Race and Reunion: The Civil War in American Memory.* Cambridge: Harvard University Press, 2012.

Boatner, Mark M., III. *The Civil War Dictionary.* New York: David McKay Company, Inc., 1959.

Brown, Myers E., Ed. *Nathan Bedford Forrest and the Confederate Cavalry in West Tennessee: Tennessee in the Civil War.* The Best of the Tennessee Historical Quarterly, vol. 5. Nashville: The *Tennessee Historical Society*, 2013.

Caldwell, Willie Mae. *The Genealogy of the Knott Family 1617-1989.* Published by the Author for Knott's Berry Farm, 1989.

Cimprich, John. *Slavery's End in Tennessee, 1861-1865.* Tuscaloosa: The University of Alabama Press, 1985.

Clayton, W.W., *History of Davidson County, Tennessee, With Illustrations and Biographical Sketches of its Prominent Men and Pioneers.* Philadelphia: J.W. Lewis and Company, 1880.

Cooling, Benjamin F. *Forts Henry and Donelson: Keys to the Confederate Heartland.* Knoxville: The University of Tennessee Press, 1987.

Cornish, Dudley Taylor. *The Sable Arm: Negro Troops in the Union Army, 1861-1865*. New York: Longmans, Green and Co., 1956.

Cox, Jacob D. *The Battle of Franklin, Tennessee, November 30, 1864: A Monograph*. New York: Charles Scribner's Sons, 1897.

Craig, Berry. *Kentucky Confederates: Secession, Civil War, and the Jackson Purchase*. Lexington: University Press of Kentucky, 2014.

Davison, Eddy W. and Daniel Foxx. *Nathan Bedford Forrest: In Search of the Enigma*. Gretna, LA: Pelican Publishing Company, 2007.

deGregory, Crystal A., ed. *Emancipation and the Fight for Freedom. Tennessee African Americans, 1860-1900*. Tennessee in the Civil War: The Best of the Tennessee Historical Society, vol. 6. Nashville: The Tennessee Historical Society, 2013.

Donald, David Herbert. *Lincoln*. London: Johnathan Cape Publishers, 1995.

Douglass, Fredrick. *Life and Times of Fredrick Douglass*. Hartford: Park Publishing Company, 1881.

Downs, Gregory P. *After Appomattox: Military Occupation and the Ends of War*. Cambridge: Harvard University Press, 2015.

Faust, Drew Gilpin. *This Republic of Suffering: Death in the Civil War*. Cambridge: Harvard University Press, 2007.

Finger, John, *Tennessee Frontiers: Three Regions in Transition*. Bloomington: Indiana University Press, 2001.

Fischer, Marjorie Hood and Ruth Blake Burns, eds., *Humphreys County, Tennessee Records: Tax Lists 1837-1843-Marriages 1888-1900*. Vista, CA: Ram Press, 1987.

Fitch, John. *Annals of the Army of the Cumberland: Comprising Biographies, Descriptions of Departments, Accounts of Expeditions, Skirmishes, and Battles* Philadelphia: J.B. Lippincott & Co., 1864.

Fleche, Andre. *The Revolution of 1861: The American Civil War in the Age of Nationalist Conflict*. Chapel Hill: The University of North Carolina Press, 2012.

Foster, Gaines M. *Ghosts of the Confederacy: Defeat, the Lost Cause, and the Emergence of the New South, 1865-1913*. New York: Oxford University Press, 1987.

Gaines, W. Craig. *Encyclopedia of Civil War Shipwrecks*. Baton Rouge: Louisiana State University Press, 2008.

Gallagher, Gary. *The Union War*. Cambridge, MA: Harvard University Press, 2011.

Garrett, Jill Knight. *The History of Humphreys County, Tennessee*. Columbia, TN: Self-published, 1963.

George, Henry. *History of the 3rd, 7th, 8th, and 12th Kentucky, C.S.A.*. Louisville. KY: C.T. Dearing Printing Company, 1911.

Gibson, Charles Dana and E. Kay Gibson. *The Army's Navy Series, Volume II, Assault and Logistics: Union Army Coastal and River Operations 1861-1866*. Camden, Maine: Ensign Press, 1995.

Goodspeed, Weston. *History of Tennessee: From Earliest Time to the Present: Together with an Historical and Biographical Sketch of Montgomery, Robertson, Humphreys, Stewart, Dickson, Cheatham, and Houston Counties*. Nashville, TN: The Goodspeed Publishing Company, 1886.

―――. *History of Tennessee: With Sketches of Gibson, Obion, Weakley, Dyer, and Lake Counties*. Nashville: The Goodspeed Publishing Company, 1887.

Goodstein, Anita S. *Nashville 1780-1860: From Frontier to City*. Gainesville: The University of Florida Press, 1989.

Gott, Kendal D. *Where the South Lost the War: An Analysis of the Fort Henry-Donelson Campaign, February 1862*. Mechanicsburg, PA: Stackpole Books, 2003.

Graf, Leroy P. and Ralph W. Haskins, eds. *The Papers of Andrew Johnson, vols. 1-7.* Knoxville: The University of Tennessee Press, 1979.

Guelzo, Allen C. *Lincoln's Emancipation Proclamation: The End of Slavery in America.* New York: Simon and Schuster, 2004.

Haggard, John V. *Procurement of Clothing and Textiles, 1945-1953.* QMC Historical Studies, Series II, No. 3. Washington, D.C.: U.S. Government Printing Office, 1957.

Hancock, Richard R. *Hancock's Diary: or, A History of the Second Tennessee Confederate Cavalry, with sketches of First and Seventh battalions; also, portraits and biographical sketches. Two volumes in one.* Nashville: Brandon Printing Co., 1887.

Hess, Earl J. *The Civil War in the West: Victory and Defeat from the Appalachians to the Mississippi.* Chapel Hill: The University of North Carolina Press, 2012.

Higgs, David W. *Nathan Bedford Forrest and the Battle of Johnsonville.* Nashville: The Tennessee Historical Commission, 1976.

Hines, Edward W., *Corporate History of the Louisville & Nashville Railroad Company and Roads In Its System.* Louisville: John P. Morton & Company, 1905.

Hoffman, Mark. *"My Brave Mechanics:" The First Michigan Engineers and Their Civil War.* Detroit: Wayne State University Press, 2007.

Holzer, Harold. *Emancipating Lincoln: The Proclamation in Text, Context, and Memory.* Cambridge: Harvard University Press, 2012.

————. Edna Greene Medford, and Frank J. Williams. *The Emancipation Proclamation: Three Views.* Baton Rouge: Louisiana State University Press, 2006.

Horton, James Oliver and Lois E. Horton. *Slavery and the Making of America.* New York: Oxford University Press, 2005.

Hunt, Robert. *The Good Men Who Won the War: Army of the Cumberland Veterans and Emancipation Memory.* Tuscaloosa: The University of Alabama Press, 2010.

Hunter, Robert, ed. *Sketches of War History 1861-1865, vol. 1.* Cincinnati: Robert Clarke & Co., 1888.

Johnson, Robert Underwood and Clarence Clough Buel, eds. *Battles and Leaders of the Civil War, vol. 1.* New York: The Century Co., 1887.

Jones, James B. Jr., ed. *Tennessee in the Civil War: Selected Contemporary Accounts of Military and Other Events, Month by Month.* Jefferson, NC: McFarland and Company, Inc. Publishers, 2011.

Jordan, Thomas and J. P. Pryor. *The Campaigns of Lieut.-Gen. Forrest and of Forrest's Cavalry.* New Orleans and New York: Blelock & Co., 1868.

Kolchin, Peter. *American Slavery 1619-1877.* New York: Hill and Wang, 1993.

Leonard, Elizabeth D. *Men of Color to Arms! Black Soldiers, Indian Wars, and the Quest for Equality.* New York: W.W. Norton and Company, 2010.

Lovett, Bobby L. *The African-American History of Nashville, Tennessee, 1780-1930.* Fayetteville: The University of Arkansas Press, 1999.

Maness, Lonnie E. *An Untutored Genius: The Military Career of General Nathan Bedford Forrest.* Oxford, Mississippi: The Guild Bindery Press, 1990.

Marshall, E.H. *History of Obion County.* Union City, TN: H.A. Lanzer Co., 1970.

Marszalek, John F. *Sherman: A Soldier's Passion for Order.* New York: The Free Press, 1993.

Maslowski, Peter. *Treason Must Be Made Odious: Military Occupation and Wartime Reconstruction in Nashville, Tennessee, 1862-65.* New York: KTO Press, 1978.

Mathes, James Harvey. *General Forrest.* New York: D. Appleton and Company, 1902.

McClain, Iris Hopkins. *A History of Stewart County, Tennessee.* Self-Published, 1965.

McPherson, Edward, ed. *The Political History of the United States During the Great Rebellion*, 2nd ed. Washington: Philip and Solomons, 1865.

McPherson, James M. *The Negro's Civil War: How American Negroes Felt and Acted During the War for the Union*. New York: Pantheon Books, 1965.

———. *Ordeal by Fire: The Civil War and Reconstruction*. New York: McGraw-Hill Publishing Company, 1982.

———. *Battle Cry of Freedom: The Civil War Era*. New York: Oxford University Press, 1988.

———. *For Cause and Comrades: Why Men Fought in the Civil War*. New York: Oxford University Press, 1997.

———. *Marching Toward Freedom: The Negro in the Civil War, 1861-1865*. New York: Alfred A. Knopf, 1965.

Miller, David W. *Second Only to Grant: Quartermaster General Montgomery C. Meigs*. Shippensburg: White Mane, 2001.

Mitchell, Reid. *Civil War Soldiers*. New York, NY: Viking-Penguin Group Publishers, 1988.

Morris, Eastin, Robert M. McBride and Owen Meredith, eds. *Tennessee Gazetteer 1834 and Matthew Rhea's Map of the State of Tennessee 1832*. Nashville: The Gazetteer Press, 1971.

Morton, John Watson. *The Artillery of Nathan Bedford Forrest's Cavalry*. Nashville: Publishing House of the M.E. Church, South, Smith and Lamar Agents, 1909.

Nelson, Megan Kate. *Ruin Nation: Destruction and the American Civil War*. Athens: The University of Georgia Press, 2012.

Quarles, Benjamin. *The Negro in the Civil War*. Boston: Little Brown and Company, 1953.

Rifkind, Herbert R. *Fresh Foods for the Armed Forces: The Quartermaster Market Center System, 1941-1948* (In Two Parts), Q M.C. Historical Studies, No. 20. Washington, D.C.: The U.S. Government Printing Office, 1951.

Risch, Erna. *Quartermaster Support of the Army: A History of the Corps, 1775-1939*. Washington, D.C.: U.S. Government Printing Office, 1962.

Royce, H. A. *A Sketch of the Organization of the Quartermaster's Department from 1774 to 1868*. Washington: Government Printing Office, 1869.

Schein, Richard H. ed., *Landscape and Race in the United States*. New York: Routledge, Taylor & Francis Group, 2006.

Schult, Dain L. *Nashville, Chattanooga, and St. Louis: A History of "The Dixie Line."* Lynchburg, VA: TLC Publishing Inc., 2001.

Shackel, Paul A. *Memory in Black and White: Race, Commemoration, and the Post-Bellum Landscape*. Walnut Creek, CA: Altamira Press, 2003.

Shannon, Fred Albert. *The Organization and Administration of the Union Army 1861-1865, 2 vols*. Cleveland: Arthur H. Clark Co., 1928.

Sherman, William T. *Memories of General W.T. Sherman, Vol. 1&2 Together*. New York: Charles L. Webster and Co., 1891.

Siddali, Silvana R. *From Property to Person: Slavery and the Confiscation Acts, 1861-1862*. Baton Rouge: Louisiana State University Press, 2005.

Sideman, Belle B. and Lillian Friedman, eds. *Europe Looks at the Civil War: An Anthology*. New York: Orion Publishers, 1960.

Simon, John Y., ed. *The Papers of Ulysses S. Grant, 28 vols*. Carbondale: Southern Illinois University Press, 1967-2005.

Simpson, Brooks D. and Jean V. Berlin, eds. *Sherman's Civil War: Collected Correspondence of William T. Sherman, 1860-1865*. Chapel Hill: The University of North Carolina Press, 1999.

———. *Ulysses S. Grant: Triumph Over Adversity, 1822-1865*. Boston: Houghton Mifflin Company, 2000.

Slaughter, G. H. *Stage Coaches and Railroads or The Past and the Present of Transportation Facilities From Nashville, through Tennessee, Kentucky, and Surrounding Territory*. Nashville: Hasslock and Ambrose Printers and Publishers, 1894.

Smith, John David. *Lincoln and the U.S. Colored Troops*. Carbondale: Southern Illinois University Press, 2013.

———. ed., *Black Soldiers in Blue: African American Troops in the Civil War Era*. Chapel Hill: The University of North Carolina Press, 2002.

Smith, Jonathan K.T. *The Wyly Saga*. Memphis: Padmoor Press, 1981.

———. *An Historical Survey of the Road System of Benton County, Tennessee*. Memphis, TN: Published by Author, 1976.

———. *Historic Benton: A People's History of Benton County, Tennessee*. Memphis: Richard H. Harris Printer, 1975.

Spence, Jerome D. and David L. Spence. *A History of Hickman County, Tennessee*. *Nashville*: Gospel Advocate Publishing Company, 1900.

Stearns, Frank Preston. *The Life and Public Services of George Luther Stearns*. Philadelphia: J.B. Lippencott Company, 1907.

Steere, Edward. *The Graves Registration Service in World War II, Q.M.C. Historical Studies*, No. 21.Washington, D.C.: United States Government Printing Office, 1951.

Summers, Mark Wahlgren. *The Ordeal of the Union: A New History of Reconstruction*. Chapel Hill: The University of North Carolina Press, 2014.

Trefousse, Hans L. *Andrew Johnson: A Biography*. New York: W.W. Norton and Company, 1989.

Underwood, Robert and Clarence Clough Buel, eds. *Battles and Leaders of the Civil War, vol. 1*. New York: The Century Co., 1887.

Van Horne, Thomas B. *History of the Army of the Cumberland, Its Organization, Campaigns, and Battles, vol. 2*. Wilmington, NC: Broadfoot Publishing Company, 1988.

Way, Frederick, Jr. and Joseph Rutter. *Way's Packet Directory, 1848-1994*. Athens, OH: Ohio University Press, 1994.

Weigley, Russell. *Quartermaster General of the Union Army: A Biography of M.C. Meigs*. New York: Columbia University Press, 1959.

West, Carroll Van, ed. *Tennessee Encyclopedia of History & Culture*. Nashville: Rutledge Hill Press, 1998.

———. *Tennessee in the Civil War: The Best of the Tennessee Historical Quarterly, vol.1*. Nashville: The Tennessee Historical Society, 2011.

Westwood, Howard C. *Black Troops, White Commanders, and Freedmen during the Civil War*. Carbondale: Southern Illinois University Press, 1992.

———. *The Beginnings of West Tennessee: In the Land of the Chickasaws, 1541-1841*. Johnson City, TN: The Watauga Press, 1930.

Wilson, James Harrison. *Under the Old Flag, 2 Vols*. New York: D. Appleton and Company, 1912.

Wooldridge, John, ed. *History of Nashville, Tenn*. Nashville: Publishing House of the Methodist Episcopal Church, South, 1890.

Worth, Ray S. *Tennessee Cousins: A History of Tennessee People*. Austin, TX: Published by the Author, 1950.

Wyeth, John Allen. *That Devil Forrest: Life of General Nathan Bedford Forrest*. New York: Harper & Brothers Publishers, 1959.

Young, J.P. *The Seventh Tennessee Cavalry: A History*. Dayton, Ohio: Morningside Bookshop Press, 1976.

Zeller, Bob. *The Blue and Gray in Black and White: A History of Civil War Photography*. Westport, CT: Praeger Publishers, 2005.

Articles and Essays

[Anon] "Forrest's Chief of Artillery-Morton." *Confederate Veteran* 8, no. 4 (April 1900):   171.

Baily, Anne. "The USCT in the Confederate Heartland, 1864." *In Black Soldiers in Blue: African American Troops in the Civil War Era*, edited by John David Smith. Chapel Hill: The University of North Carolina Press, 2002.

Bergeron, Paul H. "Andrew Johnson." *In The Tennessee Encyclopedia of History and Culture*, edited by Carroll Van West, 481-84. Nashville: Rutledge Hill Press, 1998.

Brooks, Addie Lou. "The Building of the Trunk Line Railroads in West Tennessee, 1852-1861." In *Tennessee Old and New, 1796-1946, vol. 2* (1973): 204-11.

Brown, Colonel Campbell H. "Forrest's Johnsonville Raid." *Civil War Times Illustrated* 3, vol. 4 (June 1965): 33-34.

Burt, Jesse C. "Sherman's Logistics and Andrew Johnson," *Tennessee Historical Quarterly* 15 (1956): 24-51.

Cimprich, John. "Military Governor Johnson and Tennessee Blacks, 1862-65." *Tennessee Historical Quarterly* 39 (1980):11-43.

Crutcher, T.E. "Witness to the Capture of the Mazeppa," *Confederate Veteran* 37, No. 11 (November 1929): 71.

Dinkins, Captain James. "Destroying Military Stores and Gunboats," *Confederate Veteran* 34, no. 5 (May 1926): 176-79.

Gamble, Bonnie. "Nashville and Chattanooga Railroad." In *The Tennessee Encyclopedia of History and Culture*, edited by Carroll Van West, 767-68. Nashville: Rutledge Hill Press, 1998.

Gardner, Theodore. "The First Kansas Battery: An Historical Sketch, With Personal Reminiscences of Army Life, 1861-63." In *Collections of the Kansas State Historical Society 1915-1918: Together with Addresses at Annual Meetings, Memorials and Miscellaneous Papers*, Vol. 14, William E. Connelley, ed., 275-80. Topeka: Kansas State Printing, 1918.

Garrett, Jill K. "Guerillas and Bushwhackers in Middle Tennessee during the Civil War." In Jill Garrett Collection, 77-79. Microfilm, Box 11, Roll 1, TSLA, Nashville, TN.

Gordon, Ralph C. "Nashville and the U.S. Christian Commission in the Civil War." *Tennessee Historical Quarterly* (Summer 1996): 98-111.

Gracey, Frank P. "Captain Gracey's Paper." In John W. Morton "Battle of Johnsonville." *Southern Historical Society Papers* 10 (1882): 78-102.

Hardesty, Donald. "Ethnographic Landscapes: Transforming Nature into Culture." In *Preserving Cultural Landscapes in America*, edited by Arnold R. Alanen and Robert Z. Melnick,169-85. Baltimore: The Johns Hopkins University Press, 2000.

Johnson, Edward A. "Railroads." In *The Tennessee Encyclopedia of History and Culture*, edited by Carroll Van West, 769-73. Nashville: Rutledge Hill Press, 1998.

Jordan, Weymouth T. "The Freedmen's Bureau in Tennessee." The *East Tennessee Historical Society's Publications* 11 (1939): 54–55.

Kajencki, Francis C. "The Man Who Beat the Devil." *Civil War Times Illustrated*, 5, vol. 37 (October 1998): 40-43.

Lovett, Bobby L. "Contraband Camps (1864-1866)." In *The Tennessee Encyclopedia of History and Culture*, edited by Carroll Van West, 203-04. Nashville: Rutledge Hill Press, 1998.

———. "Nashville's Fort Negley: A Symbol of Black's Involvement with the Union Army." In *Tennessee in the Civil War* vol. 1, edited by Carroll Van West, 123-39. Nashville: The Tennessee Historical Society, 2011.

McPherson, James M. "No More Auction Block for Me." In *Marching Toward Freedom: The Negro in the Civil War, 1861-1865*, 32-40. New York: Alfred A. Knopf, 1965.

Smith, Jonathan K.T. "Old Reynoldsburgh." Unpublished essay, date unknown.

Szcodronski, Cheri LaFlamme. "From Contraband to Freedmen: General Grant, Chaplain Eaton, and Grand Junction, Tennessee." *Tennessee Historical Quarterlyy* 72, # 2 (Summer 2013): 106-27.

Van Horne, Thomas B. "The Engineer Service in the Army of the Cumberland." In *History of the Army of the Cumberland, Its Organization, Campaigns, and Battles*, vol. 2, 439-458. Wilmington, NC: Broadfoot Publishing Company, 1988.

Westwood, Howard C. "Lincoln's Position on Black Enlistments." In *Black Troops, White Commanders, and Freedmen during the Civil War*, 1-20. Carbondale: Southern Illinois University Press, 1992.

Whitaker, Larry H. "Civil War." In *The Tennessee Encyclopedia of History and Culture*, edited by Carroll Van West, 168-71. Nashville, TN: Rutledge Hill Press, 1998.

Wigginton, Russell. "Louisville and Nashville Railroad." In *The Tennessee Encyclopedia of History and Culture*, edited by Carroll Van West, 765-66. Nashville: Rutledge Hill Press, 1998.

Wyatt, Robert G. "Johnsonville Times: Johnsonville, Held by Federals, Destroyed in Battle." In *The Nashville Banner* 1 (March 1958):1.

———. "The Johnsonville Times: TVA Dam Brings Death of Old Town, Birth of New Johnsonville." In *The Nashville Banner* 5 (March 1958): 1.

Dissertations

Ash, Stephen V. "Civil War, Black Freedom, and Social Change in the Upper South: Middle Tennessee, 1860-1870." Ph.D. Dissertation, University of Tennessee, Knoxville, 1983.

Lovett, Bobby L. "The Negro in Tennessee, 1861-1866: A Socio-Military History of the Civil War." Ph.D. Dissertation, University of Arkansas, 1978.

Moore, Wayne. "Farm Communities and Economic Growth in the Lower Tennessee Valley: Humphreys County, Tennessee, 1785-1980." Ph.D. Dissertation, U. of Rochester, NY, 1990.

Land Grant and Deed Books

Deed Books A-E, Registrar's Office of Humphreys County, Waverly, TN.

Land Grant Book, A-1 (Revolutionary) Grant #260, warrant #761, TSLA, Nashville, TN.

Online Sources

Lincoln, Abraham. "The Gettysburg Address," Nov. 19, 1863. Abraham Lincoln Online, 2005.

Maloney, Christopher, "Treaty of Fort Jackson," in *The Encyclopedia of Alabama*, Auburn University Online source, 2011.

"12th Regiment, United States Colored Troops." On-line Soldiers and Sailors Database, Regimental Histories, National Park Service.

19th Century Newspapers, online service, TSLA.

Prescott, Samuel C. *Troop Feeding Programs: A Survey of Rationing and Subsistence in the United States Army, 1775 to 1940*, Vol. 1. National Defense Research Committee, Office of Scientific Research and Development. Washington, D.C.: The U.S. Government Printing Office, 1944, Online Resource http://naldc.nal.usda.gov/download/CAT.

Tennessee Valley Authority, historical resource center for river depth levels on the Tennessee River at Johnsonville, Tennessee, online service.

Index

About the Author

Jerry T. Wooten, Ph.D., is the Park Manager for Bicentennial Capitol Mall State Park in Nashville, Tennessee. Formerly, he served as Park Manager at Johnsonville State Historic Park, as Director of State Historic Sites for the Tennessee Historical Commission, and as Park Historian at the Pamplin Historical Park and National Museum of the Civil War Soldier in Petersburg, Virginia.

Originally from Clarksville, Tennessee, Jerry is an American History and Public History graduate of Austin Peay State University (BS), Murray State University (MA), and Middle Tennessee State University (Ph.D.). He has researched, written, and presented programs about the Civil War for most of his professional life, and serves on the Tennessee Civil War Preservation Association's Board of Directors.

Jerry is a frequent speaker at Civil War roundtables, historical organizations, state and national parks, and museums.